Breakthrough Language Series

FURTHER SPANISH

Dr Sandra Truscott

Adult Education Tutor in Spanish
Co-author of Pan *Breakthrough Spanish* and author of
Companion Spanish Grammar

General editor Professor Brian Hill

Head of the Language Centre, Brighton Polytechnic

Series adviser
Janet Jenkins   International Extension College, Cambridge

Acknowledgements

I would like to thank all those who have contributed to this course: Catherine Bruzzone and Sally Wood, my editors; all the Spaniards and Latin Americans who helped with our recordings and coped with my innumerable questions, especially Margarita Mesa and her family in Oviedo; and my husband who initiated me into word processing and wrote the computer programmes for the vocabulary.

Location and studio recordings, tape production: Gerald Ramshaw, Polytechnic of Central London
Acting: Eloísa Fernández, Pepe Rivarola, Susan Comb
Music: David Stoll
Book design and illustrations: Gillian Riley
Editor: Sally Wood

We are grateful to the following for permission to reproduce copyright material:
Radio programmes
Radio Asturias Cadena Ser, Radio Nacional de España, Radiocadena Española
Radio advertisements: Danone, Deportes El Roxin, Leche la Polesa

Texts
Cambio 16 pp. 19, 20, 67, 84, 164, 195, 196 RENFE p. 52 Guía del Ocio p. 68 Telva p. 83 Antena Semanal (Sunday newspaper magazine, Madrid) pp. 99, 100 La Nueva España p. 115 Sony España S.A. p. 147 Investronica p. 163 Universidad de Murcia (Cursos de perfeccionamiento para profesores de español) p. 180 Hispalengua p. 179 IBM p. 36 Thomas Cook p. 148 Guía ilustrada de Asturias p. 132 Viaca Tours p. 131

Photographs
Gerald Ramshaw pp. 7, 8, 11, 23, 24, 27, 28, 30, 39, 71, 74, 77, 87, 90, 108, 135, 137, 138, 142, 151, 165, 167, 172, 173, 190 Spanish National Tourist Board pp. 14, 76, 86, 118, 119, 126, 134, 183, 184 Agencia Efe pp. 78, 188, 198 Sandra Truscott pp. 12, 21, 103, 158 Jean-Luc Barbanneau pp. 122, 123 William Truscott p. 55

First published by Pan Books Ltd 1987

This edition published 1988 by
THE MACMILLAN PRESS LTD
Houndmills, Basingstoke, Hampshire RG21 2XS
and London
Companies and representatives
throughout the world

ISBN 0–333–48184–4

Printed in Hong Kong

10   9   8   7   6   5   4   3
00 99 98 97 96 95 94 93 92

Contents

What this course is all about

Take your time to read through the next couple of pages, which explain the course to you. Understanding what is expected of you and how the course is built up will make learning easier.

Breakthrough Further Spanish is the result of listening to hundreds of people telling us what they want and how they learn. It's not a beginner's course – the emphasis is on 'further'. You should already be beyond the 'para mí un café solo' stage if you want to make the most of this course. It helps you to keep up your existing Spanish and puts you in situations where you can use your language for making real and useful contacts, getting to know the Spanish and their country better.

There is no specific progression, though we do advise you to start with Unit 1. The earlier units are generally easier, and vocabulary is built up gradually. Each unit has a carefully selected balance of the following:

- Interviews/eavesdropped conversations with ordinary Spanish people which carry key vocabulary/idioms and structures. They are recorded on location in Spain so you practise understanding the real language right from the start. To help you, there is a transcript in the book of each dialogue you'll hear on the cassette, plus essential vocabulary, explanatory notes and exercises directly associated with the text. Please note that you are not expected to switch on and understand immediately. Learning comes from a combination of listening – using pause and rewind buttons as many times as necessary – and studying the text.
- A list of key words and phrases follows the introductory dialogues and exercises. You can use this to check that you have mastered the most important elements before proceeding.
- Grammar is the cement of the language. It helps you to understand how Spanish works and in each unit we've included a short analysis of the items we think you'll find useful. But *Breakthrough Further Spanish* is not a grammar course. Understanding when you hear or read something and making yourself understood are more important than knowing all the troublesome intricacies, which Spaniards themselves often get wrong. Don't get bogged down here. If you find some of the points too fiddly, just move on.
- A short reading section comes next. It consists of two or more exercises based on authentic examples you might see in the streets of a Spanish town or read in Spanish brochures, papers and magazines.
- Radio comprehensions unique to this course then give you some extended listening practice. In co-operation with **Radio Nacional**, **Radiocadena** and **Cadena SER**, we have selected and edited parts of real radio programmes to give you some more genuine listening practice and to help you to extend your vocabulary further *if you wish*. You can approach these in different ways. More advanced learners might be able to listen in and complete the various listening exercises. On the other hand, you might need to go through them bit by bit, helped by the transcripts at the back of the book. It's up to you to select the approach which most suits your experience and your needs.
- A speaking section in which you can practise relating information to your own life concludes each unit. The tasks here are open-ended. That means there is no right or wrong answer, though we do give you some ideas on what to say, and on the cassette you'll find a model version spoken by our two actors, Pepe Rivarola and Eloísa Fernández.

At the end of the book is a comprehensive vocabulary (both Spanish–English and English–Spanish). This contains all the words in the course apart from the most basic ones, like **él**, **ella**, **uno**, **dos** etc. or obvious ones such as **posible**, **probable** etc. where the spelling and meaning are much the same as in English.

How to work through a unit

1 Study guide

At the beginning of each unit is a grid which shows you on what page the individual sections appear. Use this as a check-list to cross off the tasks you have completed.

2 Diálogos Dialogues

In each unit four dialogues recorded on location in Spain introduce the new language material, covering different aspects of the unit theme. You are not expected to understand each dialogue first time. Just listen, then rewind and, using your pause button, study line by line and read the vocabulary and the notes. Key phrases are marked ♦ and you should try to remember them, as you'll practise them in the exercises. When you think you've mastered a dialogue, rewind to the beginning and, without using your book, listen again right through, to see if you've really understood. Zero your tape counter at the beginning of each new cassette side and note the numbers for each dialogue in the ☐ as you go along.

3 Trabajos prácticos Exercises

There are three exercises linked to each dialogue. The first two practise listening comprehension and vocabulary reinforcement; the last one gives you an opportunity to speak. In most speaking exercises in this section, you're given a prompt in English by our presenter, Susan Comb. Stop the tape, say your part aloud in Spanish, then start the tape again and listen to the correct version which will be given by either Pepe or Eloísa. You will probably need to go over the speaking exercises a few times until you are familiar with the pattern. Before you start speaking, read the instruction to each exercise in your book.

4 Giros importantes Key phrases

This is a list of the most important words and phrases from all four dialogues which were marked ♦ in the notes. Try to learn this page by heart.

5 Gramática Grammar

As this is not a grammar course, the selections and explanations on these two pages are not exhaustive, we are just highlighting some of the key elements in the Spanish language. Skip this section if you really don't like grammar, but give it a try first. The grammar section is interspersed with short exercises, so that you can test yourself.

6 Lectura Reading

This section is based on passages taken from original Spanish brochures, newspapers or magazines. Some of it might appear quite difficult at first, but we have included some extra vocabulary to help you to understand the extracts. Make sure you've really understood the gist of each passage before doing the exercise linked with it.

7 Radio Radio

These authentic excerpts from Spanish radio are, of course, spoken at normal speed. The first time you hear them you may not understand very much at all. But this is a useful way of sharpening your listening skills. If you persevere you will find that, by the time you get to the later units, you will be able to tune in to real Spanish much more easily. Included as part of this section are a vocabulary and some listening tasks, often general questions to be answered. Working on these will help you to understand what is said.

There is also a transcript of the recordings (see p. 214). Depending on how difficult you find the excerpts, you can use the transcripts in different ways. If you do understand fairly easily, then it is probably best not to look at the transcripts until after you have done the exercises. To make it easier you could, however, read the transcripts through before listening, and/or listen and read at the same time. You will have to decide what suits you best.

8 Te toca a tí hablar Open-ended speaking exercises

The last section in each unit gives you the opportunity to speak again, but much more freely than in the exercises linked to the dialogues. You can adapt the exercise to your own situation. We'll only give you some guidelines or phrases to use with the instruction to each exercise in your book. On the cassette Pepe or Eloísa will speak a model version for you, but your version can be quite different without being wrong.

Making the most of this course

- There is a lot of material, so decide what you want most from the course and allocate your time between the sections accordingly.

- We've tried to make the course as interesting and enjoyable as possible, but language learning is not easy. So be patient, and above all don't get angry with yourself if you feel you're progressing too slowly.

- Have confidence. Real language is complex and you won't understand everything first time. Treat it as a challenge and build up your knowledge slowly, selecting what is important at each stage.

- Try to study regularly but in short periods. Thirty minutes a day is usually better than a block of three and a half hours per week.

- It helps to articulate, to speak the words out loud. This may seem strange at first, but actually using the words, to yourself or with a friend, is a good way of practising and remembering.

- Don't be afraid to write in the book and make your own notes. With most exercises which need writing or filling in, we've provided the necessary space, but if there isn't enough room, just use an extra bit of paper or, better still, have your own special course exercise book for these tasks and for extended notes.

Symbols and abbreviations

If your cassette recorder has a counter, set it to zero at the start of each unit and then write the number that marks the beginning of each dialogue in the box. This will help you to find the right place on the tape quickly when you want to rewind.

This indicates a key word or phrase in the dialogues.

This marks the speaking exercises in the dialogue section and the open-ended speaking exercises at the end of each unit.

m. masculine	*pl.* plural
f. feminine	*lit.* literally
sing. singular	*coll.* colloquial

1 Hoy por mí, mañana por tí

What you will learn

- how to describe a night out
- buying a book
- something about the Spanish game of **parchís**
. . . and about a favourite swimming place

Study guide

Diálogo 1
¿Qué te gusta hacer cuando sales de noche?

The dialogues present the new material. Work on them until you can understand them and pay special attention to the words and phrases marked ▶ in the vocabulary and notes underneath.

Gustavo   Bueno, yo prefiero ir a una taberna a oír música, a conversar con un amigo.

Claudia   A mí me gusta; a veces en las tabernas hay pista de baile, entonces me gusta tomar un sifón y bailar también.

Veronica   En verano, prefiero salir a caminar, cerca de la costa.

Andrés   Ir de bares.

Carmen   Ir de copas.

Marga   Me gusta ir a cenar fuera con los amigos, después ir a tomar una copa a un pub y luego ir a una discoteca.

salir to go out	▶ **sifón** (m.) whisky and soda
taberna (f.) bar, pub	**costa** (f.) coast
▶ **a veces** sometimes	**fuera** outside

Hoy por mí, mañana por tí. A Spanish proverb which means roughly: we'll do things my way today and your way tomorrow.

Yo prefiero I prefer. **Preferir** is a radical-changing verb, where the 'e' in the root changes to 'ie' in certain persons. More about this in the grammar section on page 18.

oír música. To hear (listen to) music. You could also say **escuchar música**.

▶ **A mí me gusta**. I personally like (lit. To me it pleases me). There's more about how to express likes and dislikes in the grammar section on page 17.

▶ **Ir de bares. Ir de copas**. These phrases mean more or less the same thing – to go bar-hopping or on a pub crawl!

We think you will know enough Spanish already to understand the rest; even if you don't understand every word, keep listening until you follow the gist. As this is the first unit, the exercises are a little easier.

Trabajos prácticos Exercises

1 Now say what *you* like to do in the evening: you can use either **prefiero** (I prefer) or **me gusta** (I like). We've done the first one for you. (Answers on page 199.)

me gusta bailar/prefiero bailar

a. I like/prefer to go dancing ....

b. to go drinking ....

c. to go out for a walk ....

d. to go out for a meal ....

e. to talk to my friends ....

f. to go and listen to music ....

g. to go to a disco ....

2 Listen to dialogue 1 again. Was it a man (**hombre**) or woman (**mujer**) who made the following remarks? (Answers on page 199.)

	hombre	mujer
a. me gusta tomar un sifón.		
b. me gusta ir a tomar una copa a un pub.		
c. prefiero ir a una taberna.		
d. a veces en las tabernas hay pista de baile.		
e. ir de bares.		
f. en verano prefiero salir a caminar.		

Now for the first speaking activity. There is one for each dialogue to help you to practise the key words and phrases. Read the introduction (paragraph 8, page 6), before you start.

3 Our actor, Pepe Rivarola, will now ask you what you like to do in the evening. Use the information here to create your replies. Stop the tape to answer in Spanish. There won't be any prompts, but you will hear the dialogue in full after you've worked through the exercise.

a. I prefer to go out to a pub.
b. I like chatting with friends and listening to music.
c. Yes, if there's a dance floor.
d. In summer I like to go to the coast and eat outside.

Diálogo 2
Me gustaría comprar una novela

Marga   Mire, me gustaría comprar una novela. ¿Cuál me recomienda?

Eduardo   Bueno, en principio yo recomendaría por ejemplo ésta de Emilio Romero, *Retratos de época*, o esta otra, *Retratos de mujeres en la corte del rey Juan Carlos*, o ésta de Gerald Brenan, *Laberinto español*.

Marga   ¿Tiene otro tipo de novela un poco más informal? ¿de evasión?

Eduardo   Sí, tenemos, por ejemplo, de Vázquez Figueroa toda esta serie que son un poco más amenas.

Marga   Qué, ¿Está teniendo mucho éxito esta serie?

Eduardo   Se está vendiendo bastante bien este verano.

Marga   ¿Es en plan dedicado más a la gente joven?

Eduardo   Sí, más de viajes, de aventuras, están ambientadas en países hispano-americanos. También el tipo de encuadernación es más rústico, ¿no?

Marga   Sí.

Eduardo   Más económico también – y si no, lo que puedo decir también es esta otra que ha sido un éxito en televisión, *El Pájaro canta hasta morir*.

Marga   ¿*El Pájaro espino*?

Eduardo   Sí.

Marga   Ah no, ya ví la película, gracias.

Eduardo   Ah bueno, entonces nada.

◗ **en principio** first of all
serie (f.) series
ameno pleasant, light

viaje (m.) journey
encuadernación (f.) binding
rústico ordinary, cheap

¿Cuál me recomienda? Which do you recommend? **Recomendar** is another radical-changing verb where the 'e' in the stem changes to 'ie' in certain persons (see page 18).

Retratos de época *Portraits of our Times.*

Retratos de mujeres en la corte del rey Juan Carlos Portraits of Women in the Court of King Juan Carlos.

toda esta serie que son un poco más amenas. Eduardo should really make the verb **ser** and **ameno** agree with **serie** but he is thinking of **novelas** which is why he uses the plural and feminine forms.

◗ **¿Está teniendo mucho éxito?** Is it very popular/successful? This is an example of a continuous tense; as is **se está vendiendo bastante bien** it's selling quite well. There is a note on this tense in the grammar section on page 17.

◗ **¿Es en plan dedicado a la gente joven?** Is it designed for young people? **en plan** loosely means an arrangement or set-up: **vamos en plan de turistas** we are going as tourists.

están ambientadas en países hispano-americanos They are set in Spanish American countries. **Ambiente** means atmosphere.

lo que puedo decir . . . Eduardo has expressed himself rather loosely here; he probably should have used the verb **recomendar** rather than **decir**.

El Pájaro canta hasta morir The bird sings until death (until it dies).

El Pájaro espino *The Thorn Birds.*

Trabajos prácticos   *Exercises*

4 Listen to dialogue 2 carefully once more and answer the following questions in English. (Answers on page 199.)

a. What four book titles did Eduardo mention?

i ....

ii ....

iii ....

iv ....

b. What two types of less serious books did he mention?

i ....

ii ....

c. Why are the Vázquez Figueroa books:

i cheaper? ....

ii more suitable for young people? ....

5 Here's a list of books which are or have been popular in Spain. See if you can work out the original English title. Use the vocabulary in the back of the book to help. (Answers on page 199.)

a. El Amante ....

b. El Nombre de la rosa ....

c. El Décimo hombre ....

d. La Joya de la corona ....

e. Los Mitos griegos ....

6 Dialogue 2 has been changed to make it a little easier to understand. Listen to it as often as you need, then take the part of the customer, asking the questions in Spanish.

Diálogo 3
Jugar al parchís

Marga	Así que los sábados por la tarde jugáis al parchís.
Araceli	Sí, señora, jugamos al parchís. A veces toda la tarde, a veces cinco horas.
Marga	¡Cinco horas!
Araceli	Y hasta más. Hemos estado hasta las cuatro de la madrugada.
Marga	Oye una cosa, pero me dijeron de que ellos solían hacer trampas.
Margarita	¡Trampas! ¡Son unos tramposos! Unos mentirosos. Dicen que sacaron una ficha y no la sacaron, que salieron con cinco; a lo mejor con cinco tienen que salir con una ficha, como tú sabes . . . pues sacan dos fichas y bueno cuentan de más . . .
Marga	Pues yo no puedo creer eso de mi padre.
Araceli	Sí, ¿no? pues puedes creerlo de tu padre y de mi marido, vamos, que como si fuera tu tío.
Marga	¿Y Paco?
Araceli	¿Paco? Tan tramposo, lo que pasa es que ése habla menos – las mata callando.

mentiroso liar	**partida** (f.) game
▶ **a lo mejor** perhaps	

parchís is a board game which is very popular in Spain. It's similar to Ludo.

Hemos estado hasta las cuatro de la madrugada. We've been (playing) until four o'clock in the morning. **La madrugada** means the small hours, very early.

▶ **suelen hacer trampas** they usually cheat. **Tramposos**, cheats.

Dicen que sacaron una ficha y no la sacaron They say they took out a counter [to start a board game] and they didn't.

que salieron con cinco that they threw a five.

como si fuera tu tío as if he were your uncle. **Fuera** is the subjunctive form of **ser**. Araceli means they are hand-in-glove in cheating at parchís.

las mata callando (lit. he kills them silently). Araceli means that he doesn't make a fuss, so no one notices what he's up to.

Trabajos prácticos   *Exercises*

7 Some of dialogue 3 is reproduced here – but without the verbs. Listen to the dialogue again and fill in the blanks. Try not to look at the script. (Answers on page 199.)

a. Así que los sábados por la tarde .... al parchís.

b. Sí, señora, ... al parchís.

c. .... hasta las cuatro de la

madrugada.

d. .... una cosa, pero me .... de

que ellos .... hacer trampas.

e. ¡ .... unos tramposos!

f. .... que .... una ficha y no la

.............................., que .... con cinco.

8 Now listen again to the second half of dialogue 3. It has been transcribed – but not very accurately. Can you spot the differences between the original and the transcribed version? Underline the variations and write in the original underneath. (Answers on page 199.)

¡Pero yo no puedo creer esto de mi madre!

Sí, ¿no? puedes creerlo de tu madre y de mi esposa, vamos, que como

si fuera tu tía.

¿Y Paquita?

Tan mentirosa, lo que pasa es que ella habla menos – las asesina

calladita.

9 Here is a dialogue similar to dialogue 3. However, it got out of order in the printing. Rearrange it so that it makes sense: then take the part of Marga when you hear the conversation on tape. (Answers on page 199.)

Araceli   Pues puedes creértelo. Son unos mentirosos.
Marga   ¿Es cierto? ¿Cómo podéis estar jugando tanto tiempo?
Marga   ¿Y cuánto tiempo jugáis?
Araceli   Sí, casi todos los sábados echamos una partida.
Marga   ¡No puedo creer eso de mi tío!
Marga   ¿Jugáis al parchís todos los sábados?
Marga   ¡Ojo! ¡mi padre no es un tramposo!
Araceli   Porque nuestros maridos son unos tramposos y nosotras queremos ganar la partida.
Araceli   Muchas horas, hemos estado jugando hasta las tres de la madrugada.
Araceli   ¡A que sí! Y Carlos también.

Diálogo 4
¿Te gusta ir a la playa?

Marga Sí, en el fin de semana, me gusta ir a la playa. Siempre voy a Verdicio, es una playa que realmente me gusta porque está dividida en tres playas. Una que es mucho más grande, otra un poquitín intermedia y otra que es mucho más pequeña. Eh, es un sitio bastante tranquilo, por eso me gusta, porque aunque haya gente, apenas se nota y tienes la posibilidad de elegir entre estar en la arena, estar en las rocas tomando el sol, o estar en un prado. El problema es que es una playa hasta cierto punto peligrosa porque tiene mucha resaca. Entonces no te puedes confiar mucho en el mar, porque te estás bañando y te arrastra, notas que el mar te lleva. Y por otra parte, no sé, parece que siempre despeja allí antes, que hay menos nubes y que el sol parece que calienta más. No sé, es un sitio un tanto peculiar.

▶ **fin de semana** (m.) weekend
playa (f.) beach
siempre always
sitio (m.) place
elegir (i) to choose
arena (f.) sand
prado (m.) meadow
resaca (f.) undercurrent
arrastrar to drag
nube (f.) cloud

otra un poquitín intermedia another (beach) a little bit in between. You can change **poco** (a bit) to **poquito** (a little bit) and even add another diminutive (**ín**) to make it that much smaller. **In** is the diminutive used in Asturias; **un momentín**, a moment; in other parts of Spain **un momentito** is more usual.

▶ **aunque haya gente**, **apenas se nota** although there are people, you hardly notice them. **Haya** is the subjunctive form of **hay**: you need the subjunctive after Marga's use of **aunque**, although (see page 81). **Se nota**, one notices.

▶ **hasta cierto punto peligrosa** dangerous up to a point.

no te puedes confiar mucho en el mar you can't really trust the sea. **Confiarse** takes the preposition **en**.

notas que el mar te lleva you realise that the sea is carrying you off.

por otra parte, no sé, parece que siempre despeja allí antes on the other hand, I don't know, it always seems to clear up earlier there.

el sol parece que calienta más the sun seems to be warmer. **Calentar** is another radical-changing verb (see page 18.)

▶ **es un sitio un tanto peculiar** it's a rather strange place.

Trabajos prácticos   *Exercises*

10 Here are some pictures which illustrate the beaches at Verdicio. Find the phrase that best describes them in Spanish, choosing from the material in dialogue 4. (Answers on page 199.)

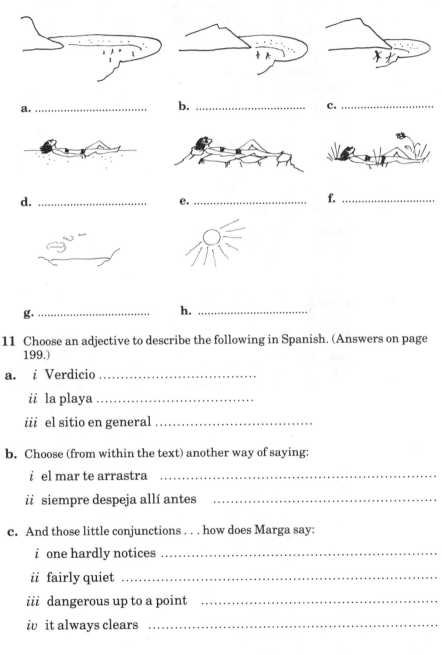

a. ....   **b.** ....   **c.** ....

d. ....   **e.** ....   **f.** ....

g. ....   **h.** ....

11 Choose an adjective to describe the following in Spanish. (Answers on page 199.)

a.   *i* Verdicio ....

     ii la playa ....

     iii el sitio en general ....

b. Choose (from within the text) another way of saying:

     i el mar te arrastra ....

     ii siempre despeja allí antes ....

c. And those little conjunctions . . . how does Marga say:

     i one hardly notices ....

     ii fairly quiet ....

     iii dangerous up to a point ....

     iv it always clears ....

12 There's a beach in Northern Spain that you always go to. On the tape, Pepe asks you why it's so special. Susan will suggest answers in English. Stop the tape to answer in Spanish, then start it again and check your reply.

UNIT 1   15

Giros importantes *Key phrases*

Here is a summary of the most important words and phrases you have met so far. You should spend some time learning them by heart; first cover up the English and see if you can translate from the Spanish, then cover up the Spanish and try to translate the English into Spanish. The vocabulary has been arranged in the order in which it appeared in the dialogues. For other, more elementary words, refer to the general vocabulary list at the back of the book.

Prefiero ir a una taberna	I prefer to go to a pub
Prefiero salir a caminar	I prefer to go out for a walk
Me gusta tomar un sifón	I like to have a whisky and soda
Ir de bares	
Ir de copas	To go out drinking, for a drink
¿Cuál me recomienda?	Which do you recommend?
¿Tiene otro tipo de novela?	Do you have any other kind of novel?
¿Es en plan dedicado a la gente joven?	Is it more appropriate for young people?
Ya ví la película	I've already seen the film
Jugar al parchís	To play parchís
Suelen hacer trampas	They usually cheat
Sacar una ficha	To take out a counter (i.e., to start a board game)
Es un sitio bastante tranquilo	It's a fairly quiet spot
Estar en la arena	To be on the sand
Estar en las rocas tomando el sol	To be sunbathing on the rocks
Estar en un prado	To be on the grass
Hasta cierto punto peligrosa	Dangerous up to a point
Por otra parte	On the other hand
Hay menos nubes	There are fewer clouds
Es un sitio un tanto peculiar	It's a rather strange place

Gramática *Grammar*

The grammar section picks up language points which have appeared in the
dialogues and helps you to learn them through examples and exercises. Refer
to the introduction on page 5 before you read on.

Gustar

Gustar is the word used in Spanish to express likes and dislikes, but it is
important to remember that it means 'to please'. So 'I like wine' is expressed
as 'wine pleases me': **me gusta el vino**. Because of this, **gustar** will always
appear in the third person, either in the singular or plural. So:

me gusta el vino (I like wine) and **me gustan los caramelos** (I like
sweets, sweets please me).

The words **a mí** preceding **me gusta** emphasize who does the liking (in this
case, I) and could be translated as 'I *personally* like'.
Here are all the possible forms:

me gusta I like	**nos gusta** we like
te gusta you like	**os gusta** you (pl.) like
le gusta you (**Vd**) like, he/she likes	**les gusta** you (**Vds**) like, they like.

Remember to use **te** with a person you address as **tú** and **le** for the polite
usted form. **Os** and **les** are the plural forms of these pronouns. (In Latin
America **os** is not used; only **les** is used.)

You can also use **gustar** with verbs: **me gusta bailar** I like dancing.
And you can use it in different tenses: **Me gustó la película** I enjoyed the
film. **No me gustaba nada** I used not to like it at all (or, I didn't like it at
all).

13 Now for a little practice. How would you say the following in Spanish?
(Answers on page 199.)

a. I like listening to music. ....

b. But he likes chatting in the pub. (Use **charlar**.) ....

c. I like going for walks. ....

d. But he likes dancing in the disco. ....

e. I like reading serious books. ....

f. But he likes reading adventure novels. ....

¡No nos llevamos muy bien!

Continuous tenses

Do you remember Marga talking about novels in dialogue 2? She asked
whether they were very successful: **¿Están teniendo mucho éxito?** And
Eduardo replied **Sí, se están vendiendo bastante bien**. Yes, they are
selling quite well. Instead of using the ordinary present tense, **tienen**
mucho éxito, and **venden bastante bien**, Marga and Eduardo want to
convey that these activities are on-going. Compare these two sentences:

Hablo alemán y francés. I speak German and French.
Estoy hablando español ahora. I am speaking Spanish now.

The first statement is a general one: the second tells us what I am doing at this moment. Spanish continuous tenses are formed in the same way as the English: with the appropriate person and tense of the verb **estar**, to be, and the present participle of the descriptive verb. Present participles are formed by adding **ando** to the stem of an **ar** verb and **iendo** to an **ir** or **er** verb. Here are some examples of the present continuous tense.

estoy comiendo I am eating   **estamos cocinando** we are cooking
estás vendiendo you are selling   **estáis escuchando** you are listening
está mirando he/she is looking   **están subiendo** they are going up

14 Can you recognise where to use a continuous present tense rather than an ordinary present tense? Translate these sentences into Spanish using the appropriate tense. (Answers on page 200.)

a. I speak Spanish fairly well. ....

b. I am working in Madrid. ....

c. I study Spanish in an evening class. ....

d. It's selling very well. ....

e. I've got this book by Vázquez Figueroa. ....

f. The sea can drag you along when you are swimming. ....

g. I'm listening to the radio. ....

Radical-changing verbs (e→ie)

These are verbs which change in the root (radical means 'of a root') or the stem when the stress falls upon it. Their endings stay the same as those of regular verbs. You will recognise these verbs in the vocabulary as the radical change is shown in brackets after the verb.

In the present indicative tense the radical change occurs in the singular and in the third person plural. The verbs which occurred in this unit are **preferir (yo prefiero)**, **recomendar (¿qué recomiendas?)** and **calentar (el sol calienta más)**. As you see, the **e** of the stem changes to **ie**. You will find the full form of these verbs on page 224.

15 Describe what is happening in each of these pictures: use the third person singular because this will do for **usted**, **él**, **ella** or a neuter (it). The verbs are given in their infinitive forms. (Answers on page 200.)

sentarse

a. ....

encender la luz

b. ....

despertarse

c. ....

nevar

d. ....

querer éste

e. ....

f. perder el monedero

....

Lectura

This section is intended to give you practice in reading Spanish. Don't expect to understand every word: just try to get the gist of the passage with the help of the vocabulary and exercises.

16 One thing you might like to do at the weekend is to go to the theatre. Here's a review of Bertolt Brecht's *Madre Coraje*. See how much you can understand, and then answer the questions below. (Answers on page 200.)

De Batalla en Batalla

Hace casi veinte años se estrenaba por fin en España la tragedia de la guerra en toda su crudeza, que Brecht había ideado a partir de una obra de Grimmelhausen, en el momento en que olfateó el aire de Europa, cargado de muerte, en 1941. Tanto el tema como los personajes estaban ya en ese poeta épico del siglo 18, pero Brecht le dio una dimensión de tragedia griega, con esa Madre Coraje que arrastra su pesada carreta por los campos de la guerra de los Treinta Años. Madre Coraje medra con las matanzas pero también éstas se van cobrando en sus hijos, que mueren, hasta que llega un día en que a la cantinera nada le queda por vender y nadie tiene nada para comprarle.

batalla (f.) battle
estrenarse to break out
guerra (f.) war
crudeza (f.) rawness
idear to envisage, think up
olfatear to sniff
cargado de heavy with
griego Greek

coraje (m.) courage
arrastrar to drag
pesado heavy
carreta (f.) cart
medrar to grow, thrive
matanza (f.) killing
cobrar to claim
cantinera (f.) barmaid/waitress

a. When was the play first shown in Spain?
- [ ] 20 years ago
- [ ] In 1941
- [ ] In the 18th century

b. What is the English title of the play?
- [ ] Courageous Mother
- [ ] Mother Courage
- [ ] One Battle to the Next

c. During which war is the play set?
- [ ] In the Second World War
- [ ] In the Spanish Civil War
- [ ] In the Thirty Years' War

d. What happens at the end of the play?
- [ ] She keeps running her bar
- [ ] She has nothing left to sell
- [ ] She drags her cart through the countryside

Here's a piece from a magazine about what you can do in the summer if you go to a youth camp.

Aula bajo el sol

Practicar el esquí sobre hierba, la equitación, el squash, la fotografía, o incluso experimentar cómo se hace una radio FM, son algunas de las actividades del campamento para gente joven, que tendrá lugar del 1 al 15 de agosto en la sierra del Cadí, en pleno Pirineo. El precio es de 16.000 pesetas e incluye, además de pensión completa, todas las actividades propias de una acampada.

Teléfonos: 442 98 75 (Manolo) 265 42 01 (Pepa)

aula (f.) classroom
esquí (m.) ski
hierba (f.) grass
incluso even
algunos some
campamento (m.) camp
gente (f.) people
joven young
tener (ie) lugar to take place
precio (m.) price
además besides
propio appropriate to
acampada (f.) camp

17 Here's a grid to fill in with the details you will need to know if you are going camping. (Answers on page 200.)

actividades	
¿cuándo?	
¿dónde?	
¿precio?	
¿incluye?	
teléfonos	

Radio

Next on the tape you will hear extracts from Spanish radio broadcasts. They are intended to give you practice in listening to spoken Spanish but you are not expected to understand more than the general drift of what is said. Finding the answers to the exercises and questions on each of the extracts will help you to focus on the key points – as will the vocabulary. Complete transcripts of all radio extracts can be found at the back of the book. Read page 5 of the introduction before proceeding.

The first item is an advertisement for bicycles: cycling is a very popular sport in Europe. The following vocabulary will help you to understand the text.

necesitar to need
rodar (here) to ride
buscar to look for
a su medida made to measure
proporcionar to give

18 Try transcribing the advertisement. Use the pause button as often as you need. (Answers on page 214.)

And now Charo introduces a piece about what we should be buying in the way of groceries for the weekend. You'll need the following vocabulary. (Transcript on page 214.)

acercarse to draw near
la compra diaria daily shopping
incrementarse to increase
campo (m.) countryside
piscina (f.) swimming pool
fácil (here) probable
invitado (m.) guest

alegría (f.) happiness
cariño (m.) love
carro de la compra (m.) shopping trolley
charcutería (f.) cold cuts
quesería (f.) cheese shop
entremeses (m.pl.) starters
queso de bola (m.) round (Dutch) cheese

19 Answer the following questions in English. (Answers on page 200.)

a. What are these all types of? **manchego, azul, cabral, asturiano**.

....

b. What do you think **centros comerciales** are? ....

c. When do our friends and relatives tend to visit us? ....

d. What departments will Charo visit? ....

e. What is she going to buy? ....

f. What day of the week is it? ....

g. Where does Charo say people will be going? ....

Our last radio extract is taken from a sports report about **fútbol juvenil**: the Spanish juvenile soccer team. They obviously haven't been doing too well in the game they played in the Soviet Union. (Transcript on page 214.)

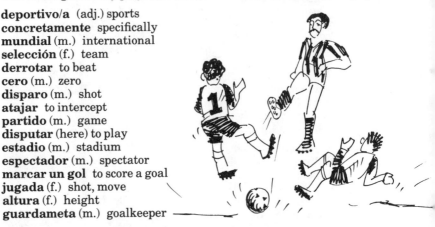

deportivo/a (adj.) sports
concretamente specifically
mundial (m.) international
selección (f.) team
derrotar to beat
cero (m.) zero
disparo (m.) shot
atajar to intercept
partido (m.) game
disputar (here) to play
estadio (m.) stadium
espectador (m.) spectator
marcar un gol to score a goal
jugada (f.) shot, move
altura (f.) height
guardameta (m.) goalkeeper

20 Can you put these sentences and phrases in the order in which they were said? (Answers on page 200.)

a. ☐ Los goles fueron marcados en el minuto cuarenta y nueve.
b. ☐ Hay que seguir con una mala noticia.
c. ☐ Un disparo a media altura.
d. ☐ Una buena noticia para el fútbol.
e. ☐ La selección de Brasil ha derrotado esta tarde a la de España.
f. ☐ Ante unos veinticinco mil espectadores.
g. ☐ En este mundial que España está jugando en Tiflis.

Te toca a tí hablar It's your turn to speak

This section aims to give you practice in relating the language you have learned so far to your own life. Don't worry too much about making mistakes – the important thing is to think how you can communicate what you want to say and then say it out loud. There are no 'correct' answers for this section, but on the tape you will find models to help you and to let you hear how other people responded. Make sure you've read page 6 in the introduction.

21 What do you like to do in the evening? Compose your answer, drawing on your previous knowledge and what you've learnt in this unit. Say your answer out loud, then listen to Eloísa's version on the tape.

2 Coser y cantar

What you will learn

- How to talk about your **daily routine**
- Something about a **personal computer**
- What **colours** can do for you
  - ... and how to sell unwanted items by phone

Study guide

		Page
	Diálogo 1 y Trabajos prácticos	24
	Diálogo 2 y Trabajos prácticos	26
	Diálogo 3 y Trabajos prácticos	28
	Diálogo 4 y Trabajos prácticos	30
	Giros importantes	32
	Gramática	33
	Lectura	35
	Radio	37
	Te toca a tí hablar	38

Diálogo 1
Es todos los días lo mismo

Marga   ¿Tú eres ama de casa, no?

Araceli   Sí, soy ama de casa.

Marga   ¿Te gusta realizar este trabajo?

Araceli   Bueno, sí me gusta. Cuando me casé ya sabía que iba a ser ama de casa.

Marga   ¿Qué ventajas o desventajas la encuentras?

Araceli   Yo ventajas, todas, porque estoy muy a gusto.

Marga   ¿Y desventajas?

Araceli   Desventajas, pues claro, estás siempre en casa. No tienes la oportunidad de salir, expansionar.

Marga   ¿Y cuál es el trabajo que menos te gusta realizar dentro de la casa?

Araceli   Bueno, el que menos me gusta es el cocinar, porque aunque como, me gusta, si me lo dan hecho, cualquier cosa. No me gusta mucho cocinar a pesar de que lo hago.

Marga   ¿Tú piensas que es un trabajo muy poco remunerado?

Araceli   Sí, creo que está muy poco remunerado porque lo haces hoy, lo haces mañana y es todos los días lo mismo . . .

> ◆ **ama de casa** (f.) housewife   **desventaja** (f.) disadvantage
> **realizar** to do   **fuera** outside
> **casarse** to get married   **dentro** inside
> **ventaja** (f.) advantage   ◆ **a pesar de** in spite of

> ◆ **Yo ventajas, todas, porque estoy muy a gusto.** It has every advantage, because it suits me very well. Araceli has omitted the verb here.
>
> **aunque como, me gusta, si me lo dan hecho, cualquier cosa.** Araceli has become a little muddled here. What she means is that she will eat anything if it's cooked for her rather than have to cook something herself!
>
> ◆ **muy poco remunerado** very unrewarding (or badly paid).
>
> ◆ **es todos los días lo mismo** every day it's the same. For more about neuters (**lo mismo**), see Unit 12.

Trabajos prácticos

1 Listen again to the conversation between Araceli and Marga in dialogue 1 and then find the equivalent in Spanish of the following English phrases. (Answers on page 200.)

a. What work do you least like doing? ....

b. Do you think it's a poorly paid job? ....

c. I already knew I was going to be a housewife. ....

....

d. Of course the disadvantages are that you are always at home. ....

....

e. What I like least is cooking. ....

2 Here are some of the things that Araceli and Marga mentioned in dialogue 1. Put them in the order in which they occurred. Try not to look at the transcript! (Answers on page 200.)

a. ☐ No me gusta mucho cocinar a pesar de que lo hago.

b. ☐ No tienes la oportunidad de salir.

c. ☐ Bueno, sí me gusta.

d. ☐ Yo, ventajas, todas.

e. ☐ Cuando me casé ya sabía que iba a ser ama de casa.

f. ☐ Es todos los días lo mismo.

3 Now you take Araceli's part in a conversation with Pepe. Answer the questions on the tape by following the suggestions made in English by Susan. Stop the tape to answer in Spanish, then start it again and check your answers against those given by Eloísa. You'll need to know **me siento un poco limitada**, I feel a bit restricted.

Diálogo 2
¿Qué tipo de maquinaria sueles reparar

Marga	¿A qué hora entras a trabajar?
Manolo	A las ocho de la mañana.
Marga	¿Y qué sueles hacer cuando llegues al taller?
Manolo	Bueno, te cambias de ropa, entras en el taller, ¿no? y haces el trabajo que tengas que realizar, o sea, trabajos de taller o trabajo de campo, depende de que haya alguna máquina averiada por fuera.
Marga	¿Y qué trabajo sueles hacer?
Manolo	En general, o sea, trabajos en general, maquinaria de obras públicas, de todo, motores, convertidores, transmisiones hidráulicas, diferenciales, frenos . . .
Marga	¿Y haces alguna diferencia entre el trabajo en el taller y el trabajo en el campo?
Manolo	Sí. Sí, porque en el taller trabajas con unas comodidades que no tienes en el campo.
Marga	¿Y qué tipo de maquinaria sueles reparar?
Manolo	Maquinaria de obras públicas, tipo excavadoras, maquinaria que anda sacando madera de los montes.

taller (m.) workshop
campo (m.) field, countryside
motor (m.) engine
convertidor (m.) transformer

diferencial (m.) differential
comodidades (f.pl.) amenities
excavadora (f.) excavator

cuando llegues al taller when you arrive at the workshop. **Llegues** is a subjunctive form used after **cuando** when it refers to a future event. If **cuando** refers to what you do regularly, the indicative is used. So: **cuando voy a España** every time I go to Spain/whenever I go to Spain, but: **cuando vaya a España en verano** . . . when I go to Spain next summer . . . For more about subjunctives, see Units 5 and 6.

haces el trabajo que tengas que hacer you do whatever work you have got to do. ◗ **Tener que** means to have to do something. (The subjunctive **tengas** is used here because it's not clear precisely what work is involved.)

depende de que haya alguna máquina averiada It depends on whether there is a machine that's broken down. **Haya** is again subjunctive, used here to express uncertainty after **depende**.

maquinaria de obras públicas road-construction machinery (lit. machinery for public works). ◗ **Obras** is often used on its own to mean roadworks.

transmisiones hidráulicas hydraulic transmission.

maquinaria que anda sacando madera de los montes machinery which collects wood from upland areas. **Monte** can mean mountain, but here it means uncultivated land covered in shrubs and trees.

Trabajos prácticos

4 Here are a few questions to make sure you fully understood dialogue 2. Answer in English. (Answers on page 200.)

a. Name three types of machinery which Manolo repairs.

i .... *ii* .... *iii* ....

b. Why is working in the workshop easier than working elsewhere?

....

c. What three things does Manolo do when he gets to work in the morning?

i ....

ii ....

iii ....

d. What sort of work does Manolo do? ....

....

5 Can you remember the words that Manolo uses for the following items? (Answers on page 200.)

a. engine ....

b. roadworks ....

c. workshop ....

d. machine ....

e. broken down ....

f. facilities ....

6 The dialogue between Marga and Manolo has been recorded on the tape in a simplified form. Listen to it carefully, memorize Manolo's rôle and then take his part in the conversation that follows.

Diálogo 3
En el centro de control

Gustavo   Por las mañanas, después de desayunar, me dirijo a mi departamento en el centro de control, en donde desarrollo experimentos de simulación, con un computador personal. Después de hacer las primeras pruebas, generalmente me voy a verme con mi supervisor, para discutir los resultados de las pruebas y, dependiendo del resultado de esta discusión, vuelvo al microcomputador y hago otras simulaciones para mirar cómo varía la conducta del modelo con distintos datos de información. Generalmente esto lo hago por las mañanas y por las tardes hago unas revisiones bibliográficas para tratar de ajustar mis trabajos teóricos a los trabajos del laboratorio.

▶ **dirigirse** to go
▶ **desarrollar** to develop, undertake

prueba (f.) trial
volver to return
ajustar to fit, adjust

después de desayunar after breakfast. There is more about the use of the infinitive after a preposition in the grammar section, on page 35.

me dirijo. Dirigirse literally means to direct oneself. It has a spelling change in some instances: **g** changes to **j** before an **o** or **a**.

donde desarrollo experimentos de simulación con un computador personal where I carry out simulation experiments with a personal computer. You will find two words for a scientific experiment – **experiencia** or **experimento**; the latter seems to be becoming more popular.

dependiendo del resultado de esta discusión depending on the result of this discussion.

para mirar como varía la conducta del modelo con distintos datos de información to see how the model reacts to different data. **Datos** (m.pl.) data, information.

hago unas revisiones bibliográficas I check on the bibliography (lit. I do some bibliographical checks). **Una revisión** can also mean a medical check-up.

para tratar de ajustar mis trabajos teóricos a los trabajos del laboratorio to try to match up my theoretical work with my work in the laboratory.

Trabajos prácticos

7 Listen again to Gustavo (dialogue 3) and then fill in the following details in Spanish. (Answers on page 200.)

a. Me dirijo a mi departamento

¿dónde? ....

¿cuándo? ....

b. Voy a verme con mi supervisor

¿por qué? ....

c. Hago otras simulaciones

¿por qué? ....

d. Hago unas revisiones bibliográficas

¿cuándo? ....

¿por qué? ....

8 Here is some of Gustavo's 'dialogue' with various synonyms substituted. Underline the words that have been changed. Try not to look at the transcript of the original: listen to the dialogue again instead. (Answers on page 200.)

Por las mañanas, después de desayunar, me voy a mi departamento en el centro de control en donde hago experiencias de simulación con un ordenador personal. Después de hacer las primeras pruebas, normalmente voy a hablar con mi supervisor, para comentar los resultados de los experimentos y, según el resultado de esta charla, regreso al microcomputador y desarrollo otras simulaciones para ver cómo varía la conducta del modelo con diferentes datos de información. Normalmente esto lo hago hasta las doce y, después de las dos, hago unos trabajos bibliográficos para intentar ajustar mis trabajos teóricos a los trabajos prácticos.

9 Now match the questions with their answers. Then listen to the tape where you will hear the questions again. Try to answer them without looking at your book. (Answers on page 201.)

a. ¿Qué haces primero por la mañana? ☐ Para ajustar la parte teórica a la parte técnica.

b. ¿Y después? ☐ Desayuno y voy a la universidad.

c. ¿Y qué haces por las tardes? ☐ Hago revisiones bibliográficas.

d. ¿Para qué? ☐ Discutimos los resultados de las pruebas.

e. ¿Qué haces con tu supervisor? ☐ Hago unos experimentos en el laboratorio.

Diálogo 4
¡El teléfono está sonando sin parar!

Marga Sí, mira, me suelo levantar sobre las ocho de la mañana y de la que subo al taller suelo pasar por RENFE, por equipajes, para pasar a recoger la mercancía que nosotros pedimos de repuestos, de carretillas o de maquinaria industrial. Suelo llegar al taller sobre las nueve y media y entonces es cuando realmente empieza el duro trabajo. Tengo que encargarme de atender al teléfono que no para de sonar, y de llevar la contabilidad y facturación al día. Se dice muy rápidamente, pero mantenerlo todo bien es bastante difícil, porque el teléfono está sonando sin parar. A última hora de la mañana, cuando vamos a comer, a la una, siempre tengo que pasar por el banco, bien a dejar xerocopias de proveedores, que nosotros tenemos que pagar, o bien llevar remesas de letras al banco para que el banco nos las descuente.

recoger to pick up
mercancía (f.) goods
repuestos (m.pl.) parts
carretilla (f.) fork-lift truck
empezar (**ie**) to begin
▶ **encargarse** to be responsible for
dejar to leave
proveedor (m.) supplier
remesa (f.) remittance
letra (f.) bill, draft

▶ **sobre las ocho de la mañana** about eight o'clock in the morning.

y de la que subo al taller and while I'm going up to the workshop. A more usual construction would be **mientras que subo al taller**.

empieza el duro trabajo the really hard work begins. Radical-changing verbs like **empezar** are dealt with in Unit 1 (see page 18).

atender al teléfono que no para de sonar to answer the telephone which never stops ringing. **Atender** is used also in retail situations: **atender a un cliente** to help a customer.

llevar la contabilidad y la facturación al día to keep the accounts up to date. ▶ **Llevar al día** to keep up to date ▶ **mantenerse al día** to keep oneself up to date.

▶ **se dice muy rápidamente, pero . . .** (lit. one says it very quickly, but . . .) it doesn't seem a lot but . . .

A última hora de la mañana Last thing in the morning.

el teléfono está sonando sin parar (lit. the telephone is ringing without stopping) the telephone never stops ringing.

▶ **bien a . . . o bien . . .** either to . . . or to.

llevar remesas de letras al banco para que el banco nos las descuente to take payments to the bank to be credited to our account.

Trabajos prácticos

10 Listen to the account of Marga's day (dialogue 4) and then complete the following sentences in Spanish without looking at the transcript. (Answers on page 201.)

a. .... sobre las ocho.

b. .... sobre las nueve y media.

c. .... de atender al teléfono.

d. ....

porque el teléfono está sonando sin parar.

e. .... siempre tengo

que pasar por el banco.

11 Number each sentence in the order in which you heard it on the tape. (Answers on page 201.)

a. ☐ Me suelo levantar a las ocho de la mañana.
b. ☐ Vamos a comer a la una.
c. ☐ Tengo que llevar la contabilidad y la facturación al día.
d. ☐ Tengo que encargarme de atender al teléfono.
e. ☐ Siempre tengo que pasar por el banco.
f. ☐ Suelo pasar por RENFE, por equipajes.

12 In this exercise we have given you a number of possible replies to the questions you will hear on tape. Only one will be right. Choose the correct response for the question on tape, say it out loud, then listen to the entire dialogue to see if you were right. (Answers on page 201.)

a. ☐ Me levanto a las siete de la mañana
b. ☐ Me levanto a las tres de la tarde
c. ☐ Voy a comer

a. ☐ Sí, normalmente voy al taller
b. ☐ No, normalmente voy al taller
c. ☐ Sí, nos quedamos en el taller

a. ☐ Suelo dormir
b. ☐ Atiendo al teléfono
c. ☐ Paso por RENFE

a. ☐ Sobre las ocho
b. ☐ A eso de las nueve
c. ☐ A la una

a. ☐ Normalmente, sí
b. ☐ Nos dirijimos al banco
c. ☐ Sí, en el banco empieza el duro trabajo

Giros importantes

Soy ama de casa	I'm a housewife
¿Qué ventajas o desventajas encuentras?	What advantages or disadvantages do you find?
Estoy muy a gusto	I'm very content
Estás siempre en casa	You're always in the house
No tienes la oportunidad de salir	You don't have the chance to get out
Es un trabajo muy poco remunerado	It's a very badly paid (unrewarding) job
Es todos los días lo mismo	Every day it's the same
¿A qué hora entras a trabajar?	What time do you start work?
Cuando llegues a . . .	When you arrive at . . .
Te cambias de ropa	You change your clothes
Entras en el taller	You go into the workshop
¿Qué trabajo sueles hacer?	What sort of work do you usually do?
Maquinaria de obras públicas	Road-construction machinery
Después de desayunar	After breakfast
Me dirijo a mi departamento	I go to my department
Un computador personal	A personal computer
Sobre las ocho de la mañana	About eight o'clock in the morning
Suelo pasar por . . .	I usually drop into . . .
Para recoger la mercancía	To pick up the goods
Suelo llegar a . . .	I usually arrive at . . .
Empieza el duro trabajo	The really hard work begins
Atender al teléfono	To answer the phone
Llevar la facturación al día	To keep the accounts up to date
Se dice muy rápidamente pero . . .	It doesn't seem a lot, but . . .
Es bastante difícil	It's quite difficult
El teléfono está sonando sin parar	The telephone never stops ringing
A última hora de la mañana	Last thing in the morning
Bien a . . . o bien . . .	Either to . . . or to . . .

Gramática

Reflexive verbs

Reflexive verbs refer back to the subject (the person doing the action): **lavarse** (to wash oneself) is the reflexive form of **lavar** (to wash). There are many more of these verbs in Spanish than there are in English but you won't have any trouble recognising which Spanish verbs are reflexive because they are always accompanied by the pronouns **me, te, se, nos** or **os**.

The reflexive is used with the definite article where in English the possessive would be used:

se lavan las manos they are washing their hands.

It is also used in the third person where in English the passive voice, or 'you', 'they' or 'one' would be used:

se habla inglés English is spoken; **se puede ir en coche** one can go by car.

To form the reflexive, take the usual parts of the verb and put the pronoun in front.

me levant **o** I get (myself) up	**nos** levant **amos** we get (ourselves) up
te levant **as** you get (yourself) up	**os** levant **áis** you get (yourselves) up
se levant **a** he/she gets (him/herself) up	**se** levant **an** they get (themselves) up.

Remember that **se levanta(n)** is also used for **Vd(s)**. And that with infinitives (**levantar**) and present participles (**levantando**), the reflexive pronoun comes after the verb. So:
me levanto I get up, but **voy a levantarme** I'm going to get up;
me lavo I wash myself, but **estoy lavándome** I'm washing myself.
(Note: an accent is placed on the second syllable where the stress now falls.)

If you tell someone to do something you must also place the pronoun after the verb: **¡levántate!** get up! (For more about commands see Unit 4).

To summarize: reflexive pronouns go in front of the verb except with infinitives, present participles and positive commands.

13 Here are 10 very common reflexive verbs:

levantarse to get up	**ducharse** to take a shower
sentarse to sit down	**bañarse** to have a bath
irse to go away	**ponerse** to put on
quitarse to take off	**acostarse** to go to bed

Describe what is happening in each of these pictures, using the pronoun suggested for you. (Answers on page 201.)

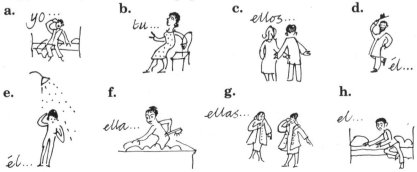

Tener que

This phrase is a very simple way of saying that you 'have to do' something. Just take the relevant form of **tener**, and add **que** and an infinitive.

Tengo que ir al banco. I've got to go to the bank.
Tienes que hacer tus experimentos. You've got to do your experiments.
Tiene que reparar esa máquina. He's got to repair that machine.

Tener que is an alternative and more colloquial form of **hay que** (it is necessary to) or **deber** (to 'ought').

14 Substitute **tener que** for **hay que** and **deber** in the following sentences. (Answers on page 201.)

a. Debo estar en el taller a las nueve. ....

b. ¡Hay que estudiar mucho más! [tú] ....

c. ¿No debes cambiarte ahora? ....

d. No hay que hacer la reparación aquí. [él] ....

e. Debe hacer las primeras pruebas. ....

Radical-changing verbs (o → ue)

Verbs ending in **ar** and **er** with an **o** in the stem change the **o** to **ue**. This occurs only in the present tense and only in persons 1, 2, 3, and 6. Two examples from this unit are **suelo** (**hacer**) I usually (do) and **vuelvo** I return. So:

soler (to be accustomed to)
suelo   solemos
sueles   soleis
suele   **suelen**

There are other types of radical-changing verbs in Units 1 and 5. But let's look a little closer at the ones in this unit. Here is a short account of a shopping expedition.

15 Underline the verbs with o → ue radical-change and give their infinitive forms. (Answers on page 201.)

¿Un día normal para mí? Bueno, yo suelo despertarme tarde cuando suena la alarma. Me cuesta mucho levantarme por la mañana porque tengo dificultades con dormirme por la noche. Enciendo la luz, bajo a desayunar: después encuentro a un amigo que me espera fuera de la casa con su coche si está lloviendo. Si hace buen tiempo, voy andando a la oficina. Trabajo hasta las seis y luego vuelvo a casa a cenar. Me siento un rato a ver la televisión: si me acuerdo, pongo mi cassette para estudiar mi lección de inglés. Salgo cuando puedo con mis compañeros de la oficina y al regresar, me acuesto sobre las doce o doce y media de la noche.

Después de and other prepositions

Any verb which follows a preposition directly must be in the infinitive. So:
después de llevar las cartas a Correos after taking the letters to the Post Office. You'll find two other examples of this usage in the short passage on page 34:
tengo dificultades con dormirme I have difficulty in falling asleep, and
pongo mi cassette para estudiar I put on (play) my cassette to study.

16 Match up the following prepositions with the appropriate infinitives to make logical sentences. (Answers on page 201.)

a. Después de   ☐ decírselo a tu padre.

b. Para   ☐ echar la siesta es una cosa muy latina.

c. Voy a   ☐ verle a él, no te lo puedo decir.

d. La costumbre de   ☐ hacer tus deberes, acuérdate de lo que dijo el profesor.

e. Sin   ☐ ir al cine, comentamos la película.

f. Antes de   ☐ llegar a ser médico, hay que estudiar mucho.

Lectura

Here's a letter written by Pablo to a friend in England recounting his daily routine and what he's been doing recently. See how much you can understand; there's a vocabulary list to help you with words you don't already know.

Estrasburgo
11 de noviembre

Querida Carmen,

¿Dónde te has metido? Hace tanto tiempo que no sé nada de tí...
Espero que estés bien y que no trabajes demasiado. ¿Qué hiciste este
verano? ¿Fuiste a Madrid? Bueno, no te hago más preguntas si me lo
cuentas todo en tu carta, ¿vale?

Como contrapartida, te cuento lo que he hecho yo (nada interesante).
Fui a Madrid unos días a finales de julio. Luego volví al norte y en
agosto hice un curso en Bruselas. Ahora estoy como becario del
gobierno y hago un estudio sobre el terrorismo (aún no lo he empezado).

A primeros de septiembre voy a Bruselas a hacer la oposición de
funcionario de la comunidad europa. Si tengo tiempo cruzaré el canal
e iré a Inglaterra. Ya te llamaré por teléfono, ¿vale?

Mi vida aquí es rutina pura. De casa al Consejo, del Consejo a la
universidad y vuelta a casa, a dormir. Los días pasan lentamente, sin
nada que merezca la pena ser recordada. Mi francés sigue siendo malo -
¡tan malo como el inglés!

Bueno, no tengo más que contarte, no hay más. Espero que me cuentas
muchas cosas; dales recuerdos a todos los amigos.

¡Cuídate! Con mucho cariño *Pablo* .

meterse (i) to put oneself
como contrapartida in exchange
becario (m.) scholarship holder
estudio (m.) study
oposición (f.) competitive examination
funcionario (m.) civil servant

cruzar to cross
canal (m.) the channel
Consejo (m.) Council
vuelta (f.) return
merecer la pena to be worthwhile
recordar (ue) to remember
cuidarse to look after oneself

17 Now look at the following statements and decide whether they are true or false, **verdad o mentira**. (Answers on page 201.)

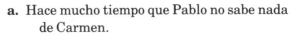

	verdad	mentira
a. Hace mucho tiempo que Pablo no sabe nada de Carmen.	☐	☐
b. Pablo hace un estudio sobre la democracia.	☐	☐
c. Pablo vive en Madrid.	☐	☐
d. Pablo tiene beca.	☐	☐
e. Pablo está contento con la vida.	☐	☐
f. Pablo habla mal el inglés.	☐	☐
g. Pablo habla mejor el francés.	☐	☐

Here is the second reading passage. Gustavo's personal computer might really have helped Marga when she was sending out all those bills.

> Ha llegado la hora de cambiar de táctica . . . con un Ordenador Personal IBM. El IBM pone un poco de orden en su mesa, modificando su forma de trabajar con la información.
>
> Imagine que un cliente llama para preguntarle sobre una factura del mes pasado. ¿Cuánto tiempo le tiene esperando al teléfono mientras revuelve todos sus papeles buscando la respuesta? Con un Ordenador Personal IBM, basta pulsar unas teclas y en cuestión de segundos, obtiene las cifras que necesita. Y lo que es más, están exactas, actualizadas y bien organizadas.

revolver (ue) to sort through   **tecla** (f.) key
bastar to be enough   **cifra** (f.) number
pulsar to push   **actualizar** to bring up to date

18 Here's an exercise in using the dictionary. Match up the list of words or phrases below with those that have the same meaning in the passage. (Answers on page 201.)

a. poner al día

....

b. números

....

c. cambiar

....

d. tocar

....

e. remover

....

f. contestación

....

g. organizar

....

Radio

The first radio extract is taken from a magazine programme and is a piece about colour. If you don't understand it all, look on page 214 for the transcript. You will need the following vocabulary.

madre previsora (f.) mother with
  foresight
cualquiera any
burlarse to scoff, make fun of
por razón de because of
piel (f.) skin
pecosa freckled
panocho golden-brown
butano (m.) butane gas
galleta (f.) biscuit

Radiocadena Española

19 Now answer the following questions in English. (Answers on page 201.)

a. Which five colours are mentioned in the text?

....

b. What colour does the modern mother dress her baby in?

....

c. What colour does the mother with foresight dress hers in?

....

d. What sort of person looks like a biscuit?

....

e. And what sort of person looks like a bottle of butane gas?

....

Our second extract is taken from a phone-in programme, for people who want to sell items over the air. You will need the following vocabulary. (Transcript on page 214.)

comodín (m.) small chest of
  drawers
comensal (m.) guest
tapizado upholstered
vitrina (f.) glass case
trinchero (m.) sideboard

armario (m.) wardrobe
cuerpo (m.) body, part
somier (m.) bed springs
colchón (m.) mattress
mueble (m.) piece of furniture

20 Here is an exercise in using numbers. How many did you catch? Fill in the gaps using figures. (Answers on page 201.)

a. What were the two telephone numbers mentioned?

i .... *ii* ....

b. And how much were the:

  i refrigerator ....

  ii sideboard and glass case ....

  iii dining table and chairs ....

  iv sewing machine ....

  v set of bedroom furniture ....

Te toca a tí hablar

21 You're leaving the country and as well as your flat, you want to sell your car and some odd bits of furniture. See if you can persuade your local radio station to help you to sell them. Remember there are no right answers, so don't feel inhibited. Then listen to how Pepe copes. Here are some small ads (**pequeños anuncios**) containing words and phrases to help you.

---

anuncios por palabras

Gijón Dos dormitorios, salón, cocina independiente, amueblados, soleados, garage, trastero opcionales.
Tel: 22 11 03.

Vendemos lámpara y cuadros en seis mil. Buen precio, semi nuevos.

Peugeot 505, aire acondicionado, garantizado.

---

22 And finally, you tell us about your daily routine, starting when you get up and ending with your evening activities. Remember that a lot of the verbs you will use will be reflexive. Then Eloísa will tell you how she spends her day as a teaching assistant in Madrid.

3 Acá y allá

What you will learn

- how to **hire a car** in Spain
- something about **travelling** by car, plane and train
- all about **traffic regulations**

. . . and what to say if things go wrong

Study guide

Diálogo 1
Quiero alquilar un coche

Marga	¡Hola buenos días!
Ismael	Buenos días, señorita, ¿qué deseaba, por favor?
Marga	Mire, es que me gustaría alquilar un coche. Voy a estar unos días aquí en Oviedo.
Ismael	Bueno ¿días cuántos, más o menos?
Marga	Como una semana. Me gustaría que fuera un coche pequeño.
Ismael	Bueno, vamos a ver, tenemos una tarifa, tenemos varias tarifas de alquiler de coches pero creo que el mejor, la mejor, la que tiene mejores condiciones es la de Europcar. Eh, tenemos un tipo de coche medio como puede ser un Ford Fiesta, un Ford Escort, un Renault nueve o un Renault once.
Marga	Bueno, yo creo que el Ford Fiesta estaría bien.
Ismael	El Ford Fiesta estaría bien. Bueno, está normalmente, la tarifa del Ford Fiesta sería por semana (si lo alquila una semana, tiene derecho a kilometraje ilimitado) y esto le costaría cinco mil trescientas ochenta y cinco pesetas por siete días de alquiler de coche.
Marga	Ah, pues muy bien, gracias.
Ismael	De nada.

europcar

▶ **alquiler de coches** (m.) car hire   **kilometraje** (m.) mileage
tarifa (f.) price

qué deseaba? can I help you? (Lit. what were you wanting?) This is the imperfect tense. The present **¿qué desea?** what do you want? is perhaps more usual. Another alternative is **¿En qué puedo servirle?** How can I help you?

me gustaría alquilar un coche I'd like to hire a car. There's more about **gustar** to like and the conditional tense on page 51. Try not to confuse the verb **alquilar** to hire with the noun **alquiler** (m.) hire.

▶ **como una semana** about a week.

Me gustaría que fuera un coche pequeño I'd like it to be a small car (lit. I would like that it were a small car). **Fuera** (from **ser** to be) is a subjunctive (see page 81): Marga uses it here because she's expressing a wish.

el mejor, la mejor the best. Ismael makes an error in gender here and then corrects himself, so don't feel too worried yourself about making mistakes.

si lo alquila una semana, tiene derecho a . . . if you hire it for the week, you have the right to . . .

Trabajos prácticos

1 To find out how much you understood of dialogue 1, here is a series of statements about the scene in the travel agency. You say whether they are **verdad** (true) or **mentira** (false). (Answers on page 201.)

	verdad	mentira
a. Marga va a estar en Oviedo unos meses	☐	☐
b. Marga pide un coche pequeño	☐	☐
c. Marga quiere comprarse un coche	☐	☐
d. La tarifa que tiene mejores condiciones es la de Hertz	☐	☐
e. Marga escoge (chooses) un Renault nueve	☐	☐
f. Alquilar el Ford Fiesta cuesta cinco mil trescientas pesetas al día	☐	☐

2 Here's part of the transcript of dialogue 1, but with the verbs missing. Try to remember them, without looking at the script, fill in the blanks and then listen to the tape again to check if you were right. (Answers on page 201.)

Marga   Hola, buenos días.

Ismael   Buenos días, señorita, ¿qué .... ?

Marga   Mire, es que .... alquilar un coche.

Voy a .... aquí unos días. Me gustaría

que .... un coche pequeño.

Ismael   Bueno, ... a ver. .... varias

tarifas, pero .... que la mejor es la de Europcar.

Marga   Bueno, yo creo que el Ford Fiesta .... bien.

Ismael   La tarifa del Ford Fiesta .... por semana. Si lo

.... una semana, ... derecho a

kilometraje ilimitado.

3 You take Marga's part in the travel agency. Answer the questions on tape by following the suggestions made in English by Susan. Stop the tape to say your answer in Spanish, then start it again and check your answers against those given by Eloísa.

Diálogo 2
Viajar en Colombia

Claudia Hay transporte por carretera, aéreo y marítimo. Por carretera es muy costoso, ya que la topografía de Colombia es muy espesa y además el diseño de las carreteras es muy anticuado, así es que el transporte por carretera es muy costoso.

Gustavo Ah, precisamente esto ha hecho desarrollar la aviación. La aviación colombiana es tal vez la más antigua en el mundo y se encuentra en operación desde hace unos cuarenta o cincuenta años. Aún cuando la aviación es bastante desarrollada, yo creo que sin embargo es importante anotar que los aeropuertos son bastante mal diseñados. Hay problemas de aeropuertos.

Claudia También existen ferrocarriles, aunque muy deficientes. Y el sistema por mar, por río, es en épocas del año, porque hay épocas del año en que el agua no es navegable, entonces no hay transporte.

aéreo air
marítimo sea
▶ **tal vez** perhaps
▶ **sin embargo** nevertheless
anotar to note
ferrocarril (m.) railway

Por carretera es muy costoso It's very expensive by road. **Caro** is the more usual word for expensive.

ya que la topografía de Colombia es muy espesa given that the terrain in Colombia is very rugged. **Ya que** is a useful expression for linking one phrase with another. An alternative is **dado que. Espeso** really means thick.

además, el diseño de las carreteras es muy anticuado besides, the layout of the roads is very out of date.

precisamente esto ha hecho desarrollar la aviación it is precisely this that has caused air transport to develop.

se encuentra en operación desde hace unos cuarenta o cincuenta años it has been in operation for about 40 or 50 years. The phrase **desde hace** is used with time expression where in English we would use 'for': I've been here for 10 months **Estoy aquí desde hace diez meses**. Note that where English uses the past tense, Spanish uses the present.

aún cuando la aviación es bastante desarrollada even though transport by air is fairly well developed.

los aeropuertos son bastante mal diseñados the airports are rather badly designed. Both **desarrollada** and **diseñados** are past participles: the **ado** ending is equivalent to the **ed** ending in English. So: **diseñado**, designed. Past participles agree with the noun they describe in gender (masculine or feminine) and number (singular or plural). Hence **desarrollada** which describes **aviación**.

También existen ferrocarriles, aunque muy deficientes. There are also railways, although very poor ones.

el sistema por mar, por río, es en épocas del año transport by sea, by river is (only possible) at certain times of the year.

Trabajos prácticos

4 Listen again to the discussion between Gustavo and Claudia in dialogue 2 and then choose the correct adjectives to complete the sentences below. (Answers on page 202.)

a. el transporte por carretera en Colombia es

.... (*costoso   barato   módico*)

b. la aviación es ....

(*subdesarrollada   desarrollada   moderna*)

c. la topografía en Colombia es ....

(*estable   espesa   extensa*)

d. los aeropuertos son mal ....

(*diseñados   construidos   planeados*)

e. hay épocas del año en que el agua no es ....

(*navegable   imposible   moderado*)

módico reasonable   **construido** built
estable stable

5 This time complete your own grid. There is space for various items of information about each subject listed. Listen to the tape and fill in the boxes. (Answers on page 202.)

a.	el transporte por carretera es costoso porque	*i*
b.	la aviación es	*i*
		ii
c.	los aeropuertos son	*i*
d.	los ferrocarriles son	*i*
e.	el sistema por mar, por río, es	*i*

6 Now for a speaking exercise. You ask a Peruvian student about his country. As in the previous exercise, follow Susan's suggestions for what to say. Again, you will hear Eloísa give the correct version. You will be using **¿cómo es?** for 'what's it like?' and **¿hay?** for 'is there/are there?'

Diálogo 3
¿Tuviste un accidente de coche?

Marga Sí, fue en noviembre y fue en el cruce de una autopista. Yo estaba esperando con, a que se pusiera el semáforo en verde, entonces en el momento en que se puso en verde, yo me puse a, a pasar, y bajaba un coche que se había pasado el semáforo en rojo. Entonces, bueno, me dio un golpe bastante fuerte, porque mi coche es pequeño y entonces no, tampoco es muy fuerte. Su coche es bastante grande, es un Peugeot 505 y tiene una defensa, una defensa realmente grande. Entonces me cogió la aleta derecha delantera y parte del morro. Y ¡bueno! creo que reaccioné bastante bien, ¿no? porque no me puse nerviosa hasta que no me bajé del coche. Yo le quité el contacto, tiré del freno de mano, apagué la radio, me quité mis gafas y salí. Y en el momento que salí, ¡me puse a temblar! Y entonces el señor me dijo: pero bueno ¿qué es que no me vió? ¿por qué no frenó? Y le dije: pues no, no le ví, si le hubiera visto, hubiera frenado. Y dice, pues, lo siento mucho y tal, y yo, ya ya ¡más lo siento yo!

cruce (m.) crossroads
autopista (f.) motorway
golpe (m.) blow
tampoco neither
defensa (f.) bumper
morro (m.) nose, front
reaccionar to react
♦ **ponerse** to become
♦ **ponerse a** to begin to
apagar to turn or switch off
frenar to brake
♦ **y tal** and so on

Yo estaba esperando con, a que se pusiera el semáforo en verde. I was waiting for the lights to turn green. Marga rethinks what she is going to say, then opts for the subjunctive (see page 81). She also uses a continuous tense, **estaba esperando**, I was waiting, instead of the ordinary imperfect, **esperaba**, I waited. Continuous tenses are dealt with on page 17.

♦ **un coche que se había pasado el semáforo en rojo** a car that had jumped the lights. (Lit. a car which had passed a traffic light on red.)

me cogió la aleta derecha delantera he caught my right front wing.

hasta que no me bajé del coche until I got out of the car.

♦ **Yo le quité el contacto** I switched off the ignition. Another use of **quitar: me quité mis gafas** I took off my glasses.

Pero bueno, ¿qué es que no me vió? What do you mean you didn't see me?

si le hubiera visto, hubiera frenado if I had seen you, I would have braked. **Hubiera** is another subjunctive (from **haber**). Marga seems to be particularly fond of this mood!

ya, ya, ¡más lo siento yo! OK, OK, I'm even sorrier than you!

Trabajos prácticos

7 Here are two lists of the parts of a car. Match the Spanish with its English equivalent. Before consulting a dictionary, have a go at working out the meanings by breaking down the words into their component parts. (Answers on page 202.)

el parabrisas ....

el limpiaparabrisas ....

la ventanilla............................

el escape ....

el techo ....

el maletero ....

el asiento delantero ....

the roof   the exhaust
the windscreen
the front seat   the window
the boot
the windscreen wipers

Now label this picture using the vocabulary you've learned in this unit plus any other words you already know.

8 Imagine you're travelling by train. Here are four types of Spanish train, each of which offers a different service. Match up the description with its symbol. (Answers on page 202.)

i 🍷   *ii* ✗   *iii* 🛏   *iv* ☕

a. Tren con servicio de restaurante (comidas, cafetería y bar). ☐
b. Tren con servicio de bar o minibar (bebidas frías y bocadillos). ☐
c. Tren con servicio de cafetería (bebidas frías y calientes, bocadillos y platos sencillos). ☐
d. Coche cama. ☐

coche cama (m.) sleeper

9 Before starting this exercise, in which you will be using the preterite tense to describe completed actions in the past, look at page 50, where you will find the full set of endings. Eloísa is now going to ask you what happened when you had that accident. She will address you as **tú** and the verb endings she uses will be **aste** for an **ar** verb and **iste** for an **ir** or **er** verb. Remember to change the endings to the first person when you reply. Susan will prompt you.

Diálogo 4
El equipaje se ha perdido

Marga ¿Sabes lo que me pasó en mi último viaje a Inglaterra? Pues que me perdieron mi equipaje. Fue una cosa un tanto extraña pero que realmente ocurrió. El problema llegó cuando llegué a Manchester y mi equipaje no aparecía por ningún sitio. Entonces, eh bueno, fui a reclamarlo naturalmente y me dijeron de que estaba en Amsterdam. Yo, es que me quedé realmente sorprendida, porque no entendía qué había ido a hacer mi equipaje a Amsterdam. Bueno, después de una serie de llamadas telefónicas, me dijeron que, al final, que estaba en Londres y entonces, que mandarían un telex para reclamarlo. Y bueno, estuve tres días sin equipaje, pero al final llegó. Y fueron tres días realmente angustiosos, porque no tenía absolutamente nada que ponerme. Y es que, estaba con la misma ropa, desde el día que había salido de casa ¡y fue algo un poco realmente asqueroso!

ocurrir to happen   **angustioso** distressing
sin without

¿Sabes lo que me pasó en mi último viaje a Inglaterra? Pues, que me perdieron mi equipaje. Do you know what happened to me on my last trip to England? Well, they lost my luggage. The extra **me** in **me perdieron mi equipaje** stresses that it was Marga's luggage they lost. Watch out for this extra pronoun elsewhere.

▶ **un tanto extraña** rather strange (**extraña** here agrees with **cosa**).

no aparecía por ningún sitio it did not appear anywhere. (Lit. it did not appear in no place.) Spanish uses two negatives where in English we would only use one. Use **ningún** or **ninguna** with a noun to mean 'no': **ninguna maleta**, no suitcase: **ningún equipaje**, no luggage. For more about negatives, see page 114.

me dijeron de que they told me. Strictly speaking, Spanish does not need the **de** in this sentence but it is a usage which is becoming quite common.

▶ **me quedé realmente sorprendida** I was really surprised (lit. I stayed really surprised). **Quedarse** means to stay or remain but is often used simply as a substitute for the verb to be.

no entendía qué había ido a hacer mi equipaje a Amsterdam. I didn't know what my luggage was doing in Amsterdam (lit. what my luggage had gone to do . . .).

después de una serie de llamadas telefónicas after a series of telephone calls.

que mandarían un telex para reclamarlo that they would send a telex to reclaim it. **Mandarían**, they would send, is an example of the conditional tense (see page 51).

▶ **no tenía absolutamente nada que ponerme** I had absolutely nothing to wear. Another double negative here, and another meaning of **ponerse**, which in this case means to wear (lit. to put on oneself).

¡fue algo un poco realmente asqueroso! it was a bit disgusting! (Lit. it was something a bit really disgusting!) Marga gets into a muddle here about how to express herself.

Trabajos prácticos

10 Now listen again to Marga's account of her lost luggage (dialogue 4) and write in the Spanish for the following phrases. (Answers on page 202.)

a. They lost my luggage ....

b. It really did happen ....

c. I arrived in Manchester but my luggage did not ....

....

d. I went to claim it ....

e. They told me it was in Amsterdam ....

f. I was really surprised ....

g. They told me they would send a telex ....

h. Finally, my luggage arrived ....

i. I had absolutely nothing to wear ....

j. It was pretty disgusting ....

11 If you send parcels by the Especial Expres service with RENFE (the Spanish railway network), there's no chance of their getting lost. The service promises seven advantages: match the advantages (on the left) with the accompanying descriptions (on the right). (Answers on page 202.)

a. Rapidez — ☐ Desde un paquete con impresos o una caja de flores.

b. Alta frecuencia — ☐ Usted mismo puede facturar sus envíos en las estaciones y despachos centrales.

c. Regularidad — ☐ Más de 100 trenes diarios, nocturnos y/o diarios.

d. Comodidad — ☐ En menos de 24 horas transporta su mercancía a la estación de destino.

e. Transporte de todo tipo de envíos — ☐ Seguridad de la mercancía y para usted y su empresa.

f. Le esperamos hasta última hora — ☐ Sus envíos salen y llegan a destino puntualmente.

g. Doble seguridad — ☐ Usted puede efectuar su envío hasta una hora antes de la salida del tren.

rapidez (f.) speed	**envío** (m.) mail
impresos (m.pl.) printed matter	**despacho** (m.) office
caja (f.) box	**mercancía** (f.) merchandise
facturar to despatch	**empresa** (f.) company

12 Pepe is now going to ask you what happened when your luggage went missing after a holiday in Spain. Most of his questions begin with ¿qué? and have a verb in the preterite (see page 50); you'll need to use this tense too.

Giros importantes

¿Qué deseaba?	What did you want?
Me gustaría alquilar un coche	I would like to hire a car
Alquiler de coche	Car hire
Tenemos un tipo de coche medio	We have a range of medium-sized cars
El Ford Fiesta estaría bien	The Ford Fiesta would suit me
La tarifa sería por semana . . .	The price per week would be . . .
Si lo alquila una semana	If you rent it for a week
Tiene derecho a kilometraje ilimitado	You are entitled to unlimited mileage
Esto le costaría por día	This would cost you per day
¿Cómo es el transporte público?	What is public transport like?
Es muy costoso/caro	It's very expensive
Ya que	Given that
Los aeropuertos son bastante mal diseñados	The airports are rather badly designed
Hay problemas de . . .	There are problems with . . .
También existen ferrocarriles	There are also railways
En épocas del año	At certain times of the year
El cruce de una autopista	The junction with a motorway
El semáforo en verde	The traffic lights on green
Me bajé del coche	I got out of the car
Yo le quité el contacto	I switched off the ignition
Tiré del freno de mano	I put on the handbrake
Apagué la radio	I switched off the radio
Me quité las gafas	I took off my glasses
Me puse a temblar	I began to tremble
Lo siento mucho	I am very sorry
Y tal	And so on
¿Sabes lo que me pasó?	Do you know what happened to me?
Fue una cosa un tanto extraña	It was rather strange
Mi equipaje no aparecía por ningún sitio	My luggage did not turn up anywhere
Fui a reclamarlo	I went to claim it
Me dijeron de que . . .	They told me that . . .
Me quedé realmente sorprendida	I was really surprised
Una serie de llamadas telefónicas	A series of telephone calls
No tenía nada que ponerme	I had nothing to wear
¡Fue un poco asqueroso!	It was pretty disgusting!

Gramática

Pronouns after prepositions

In Unit 1 we explained **me gusta**, I like: but we said very little about the phrase which preceded it – **a mí**, to me. **A mí** simply emphasizes who does the liking – in this case, me. If you were talking about your mother or your sister, you would say **a ella le gusta**, she likes. This is the equivalent of stressing the word she or I in English.

In Spanish, you need a special pronoun after prepositions like **a**, **por**, **para**, **de** – usually only if the pronoun is singular. Plural pronouns are the same as subject pronouns – **nosotros**, **vosotros** and **ellos**. The three new pronouns are:

i **mí** : a mí, de mí, para mí
ii **tí** : por tí, detrás de tí, delante de tí
iii **sí** : (meaning him/herself/themselves) **por sí, para sí** (for him/herself/themselves) but **para él** for him, **para ella** for her.

Note that the preposition **con** takes a special form: **conmigo**, with me, **contigo**, with you and **consigo** with him/herself.

13 Here are some pictures illustrating these prepositions. Fill in the correct Spanish prepositions and pronouns. (Answers on page 202.)

a. Me da el regalo

b. Le da la carta

c. Está sentado detrás

d. Está de pie delante

e. Yo tengo los niños

14 In the following dialogue between Luis and Nuria, the phrases with prepositions have been omitted: can you insert them, choosing from the list on page 50?

Luis   Marta, no mires ahora pero ¿ves a esta chica...................................

con un señor mayor?

Nuria   ¿La rubia al lado de la ventana?

Luis   Ésa. Es Magdalena, la que salía .... el año pasado.

Nuria   Ay sí, me acuerdo. Se enfadó .... porque

siempre llegabas tarde a las citas ¿no?

Luis   Sí. Se quejaba .... constantemente: decía que

no me comportaba como debía. La verdad es que ....

no me importaba demasiado que dejase de salir ....

porque ya empezaba a cansarme ....

Nuria ¡Los hombres! ¡Sois inaguantables! Todavía me acuerdo de cuando

me dejaste plantada .... del cine

Luis Marta, por favor, yo no tenía la culpa. Tú sabes el cariño que siento

....

Nuria Sí, bueno, dejemos de hablar de tonterías y miremos el menú.

.... me gustaría gambas para empezar. ¿ .... ?

Luis .... igual. Pero Marta ¿quién podría ser el tío

que está ....?

a mí   por ti   ¿Y a ti?   con ella   de ella   de mí   detrás de mí
para mí   delante de   conmigo   contigo

The preterite tense

Marga's account of her car accident contained a number of examples of a
past tense called the preterite. You will probably already know how to use it
to describe single completed actions. (The imperfect is used to describe
continuous actions in the past, see page 97.) Just to remind you, the
preterite has the following endings:

ar verbs		er and ir verbs	
reclam **é**	reclam **amos**	perd **í**	perd **imos**
reclam **aste**	reclam **asteis**	perd **iste**	perd **isteis**
reclam **ó**	reclam **aron**	perd **ió**	perd **ieron**

As always, there are some exceptions. You will find the irregular verbs in
the table at the back of the book. There are also some slight spelling
changes in this tense. For instance, verbs ending in **gar** (eg **pagar**) take a **u**
before the **e**: **pagué** (I paid), **entregué** (I gave). Verbs ending in **car**
substitute **qu** for **c**: **saqué** (I took out). These changes are intended to keep
the **g** and the **c** hard.

15 Listen again to Marga's account of her car accident and fill in the missing
words. Take care with the spelling. (Answers on page 202.)

a. Sí .... en noviembre.

b. Me .... la aleta derecha delantera.

c. Creo que .... bastante bien, ¿no?

d. No me puse nerviosa hasta que me .... del coche.

e. Yo le .... el contacto.

f. .... la radio.

g. ¿Es que no me ....?

h. Pues no, no le ....

The conditional tense

The conditional tense expresses the English 'would'.
I would like a new car: **Me gustaría un coche nuevo**.
It's easy to form. Start with the infinitive of the verb and add the following endings:

coger **ía**   coger **íamos**
coger **ías**   coger **íais**
coger **ía**   coger **ían**

16 What would you do if you had a month's paid holiday? (Answers on page 202.)

a. I would go to Colombia (**ir**).
b. I would travel to Spain (**viajar**).
c. I would hire a car for the month (**alquilar**).
d. I would sunbathe on the Costa del Sol (**tomar el sol**).
e. I would send my luggage to Amsterdam! (**enviar**).

17 Complete the following daydream by choosing from the verbs below. (Answers on page 202.)

Si yo fuera Picasso, ... un cuadro, lo

.... por millones de pesetas, me

.... un yate, ... a las Bahamas

y lo .... en grande. Pero yo soy yo – y ¡allí está el

problema!

pasaría   compraría   iría   vendería   pintaría

Lectura

This is the letter Marga wrote home after she had been stranded without her luggage. See how much you can understand.

Manchester
el 2 de agosto

¡ Hola Mama!

Espero que te encuentres bien y que en casa todo vaya sobre ruedas. Yo por el momento no me puedo quejar, aunque como ya te he dicho he perdido mi equipaje. Esta semana me han vuelto loca de tanto dar vueltas para un lado y para otro. Menos mal que por fin ha aparecido y todo se ha solucionado.

Ahora estoy intentando reclamar una indemnización de cincuenta dólares por extravío de equipaje. Si es que me pagan esta cantidad, por lo menos no lo doy todo por perdido.

Por hoy te tengo que dejar, te volveré a escribir cuando tenga más noticias.

Un beso

Marga

espero que te encuentres bien
  I hope you are well
sobre ruedas 'on wheels', fine
quejarse to complain
volverse (ue) loco to go mad
dar vueltas to rush around
menos mal it's a good thing that
aparecer to appear
intentar to try
indemnización (f.) compensation
extravío (m.) loss
por lo menos at least
no lo doy todo por perdido I
  won't consider everything lost
volver (ue) a to do something
  again
noticias (f.pl.) news
beso (m.) kiss

18 Answer the following questions about Marga's letter in English. (Answers on page 202.)

a. What has happened to Marga? ....

b. What has she been doing this week in particular? ....

c. Has the problem been resolved yet? ....

d. What is Marga trying to do? ....

e. How does she feel about it? ....

f. When will she write home again? ....

The second reading extract is taken from a leaflet issued by RENFE, the Spanish railway network, and explains the system of **días azules** (blue days), when travellers are entitled to different types of discounts (**descuentos**).

Días azules de RENFE durante enero

L	M	M	J	V	S	D
						1
2	3	**4**	**5**	**6**	7	**8**
9	10	**11**	**12**	**13**	14	**15**
16	17	**18**	**19**	**20**	21	**22**
23	24	**25**	**26**	**27**	28	**29**
30	**31**					

Venta anticipada

Se pueden adquirir billetes hasta con sesenta días de antelación en:

1 oficinas de viajes RENFE
2 estaciones autorizadas
3 despachos centrales y auxiliares
4 agencias de viajes autorizadas

Descuentos en días azules

Tarjeta familiar aplicable a:
–familias compuestas, al menos, por tres
  personas
–recorridos superiores a 100 kms en viaje
  sencillo o pagando por dicho recorrido.
–todo tipo de trenes y clases

Precios

–primera persona: precio entero por tarifa
  general.
–los restantes componentes de la familia que
  figuren en la tarjeta familiar:
● 50% de reducción sobre los precios de
  tarifa general.
● los niños entre cuatro y doce años
  abonarán la mitad de este 50%.
Requisitos: adquirir la tarjeta familiar cuyo
precio es de 100 pesetas.

venta anticipada (f.) advance sales
adquirir to acquire, buy
antelación (f.) in advance
despacho (m.) office
tarjeta (f.) card

compuesto de made up of
al menos at least
recorrido (m.) journey
abonar to pay
mitad (f.) half
cuyo whose

19 According to the pamphlet, where can you (underline the correct answer):

a. Buy tickets in advance?
   the railway station/RENFE offices/Information offices

b. Who is eligible to buy the tickets?
   families of four and more/couples/families of three and more

c. How many people have to pay full fare?   *two/three/one*

d. Who pays half the reduced rate?
   children under four/children over 12/children between four and 12

e. How much is the family rail card?
   1,000 pesetas/100 pesetas/10,000 pesetas
(Answers on page 202.)

Radio

They were changing the traffic regulations (**las normas del tráfico**) in
Oviedo when we recorded this broadcast. See how much you can
understand. (Transcript on page 215.)

dirección única descendente (f.) one-way traffic down
giro a la izquierda (m.) left turn
en funcionamiento in working order
semáforos (m.pl.) traffic lights
entronque (m.) junction
reordenación (f.) reorganisation
faltar to lack
cambio de sentido (m.)
   change of direction
regularización (f.) putting
   into working order

20 Here is a simplified map
of Oviedo. Mark the
change in traffic
regulations by placing an
arrow on the new one-way
street; a no-left-turn
signal; and traffic lights
where they should appear
on the map. (Answers on
page 203.)

In the second radio extract you will be hearing about an air disaster when a Boeing 747 crashed into the side of a mountain. You will probably have to listen to the piece several times before you understand it fully. (Transcript on page 215.)

aéreo air
emitir to broadcast
informe (m.) bulletin
precisar to make precise
datos (m.pl.) information
caja negra (f.) black box
grabación (f.) recording

despegue (m.) take-off
estruendo (m.) noise
trasero (here) back
trayectoría (f.) flight-path
aparato (m.) machine
estrellarse to crash
monte (m.) mountain

21 How much of that excerpt did you understand? Below is a series of statements: mark whether they are true (**verdad**) or false (**mentira**). (Answers on page 203.)

	verdad	mentira
a. Se saben las causas del accidente.	☐	☐
b. Han encontrado la caja negra y las grabaciones.	☐	☐
c. El estruendo ocurrió en la parte delantera del avión.	☐	☐
d. El avión se estrelló veinticinco minutos después de salir de Tokio.	☐	☐
e. Éste es el segundo informe que se ha emitido.	☐	☐

Te toca a tí hablar

 22a There are two parts to this exercise. First, describe what happened when you witnessed an accident – real or imaginary. Base your account on Marga's in dialogue 3 but do introduce new elements if you feel you can. This is your chance to use the language creatively! Then listen to Eloísa telling us her version.

 22b Now try to say how you felt at the time (shaken, numb, angry, weak etc). Call on the phrases you have learned in this unit as well as any others you know. Then Eloísa will tell you how she felt.

4 Las fiestas donde quisieras

What you will learn

- something about the **fiestas** in **Colombia**
- and those in **Teruel**
- how to decide where to go for an evening's **entertainment**
- . . . and what you can do in **Oviedo** after dark

Study guide

Diálogo 1
La fiesta del bambuco

Gustavo   Sí, mira, en Neiva se celebra la fiesta del bambuco. La fiesta del bambuco se celebra para festejar el ritmo del bambuco, que es un ritmo típico colombiano y en esta fiesta se corona a la reina del bambuco, que se escoge por atributos físicos y talento artístico, ya que se supone que debe bailar y cantar muy bien el bambuco. Además, la gente obviamente toma grandes cantidades de aguardiente en esta fiesta.

Claudia   Otra fiesta importantísima es las carnavales de Barranquilla. Esto se prepara con mucho tiempo de anticipación. La gente, las familias completas, ensayan sus danzas folklóricas durante mucho tiempo, preparan sus disfraces para las comparsas, son colores vistosísimos. La gente baila mucho en las calles, toma muchísimo aguardiente. Además, se echa mucha maizena ¿no?

Gustavo   Eh, la maizena es harina de maíz.

Claudia   Es harina blanca, es muy fina, que se la echan en la cabeza, en el pelo.

mirar to look (at)	**disfraz** (m.) disguise
festejar to celebrate	**comparsa** (f.) masquerade
ritmo (m.) rhythm	**harina** (f.) flour
coronar to crown	**maíz** (m.) maize, corn
además besides	**cabeza** (f.) head
ensayar to practise	**pelo** (m.) hair

se celebra la fiesta del bambuco the bambuco festival is celebrated. Further into the dialogue Gustavo tells us exactly what this festival is. You will notice that throughout the dialogue he and Claudia use the impersonal **se**. There is more about this on page 65.

se corona a la reina del bambuco they crown the queen of the bambuco. Note that when the direct object of a sentence is a person, the personal **a** is used after the verb. So: he sees his sister, **ve a su hermana**, but he sees the car, **ve el coche**.

se escoge por atributos físicos y talento artístico she is chosen for her physical attributes and her artistic talent.

ya que se supone que debe bailar since it's taken for granted that she can dance. **Suponerse** means to suppose.

Otra fiesta importantísima another very important festival.

Las carnavales de Barranquilla Carnival time falls in February: the most famous carnivals are probably those in the Canary Islands and Rio de Janeiro.

▶ **mucho tiempo de anticipación** a long time in advance. **Antelación** would be used in Spain rather than **anticipación**.

son colores vistosísimos they are really lively colours.

aguardiente can mean a variety of spirits – since we are in Colombia, Claudia is probably referring to rum, **aguardiente de caña**.

se echa mucha maizena, ¿no? they throw a lot of cornflour, don't they?

Trabajos prácticos

1 This first exercise is a **sopa de letras** (word scramble) – very popular in Spanish magazines. In the grid below you will find at least 12 words that occurred in the first dialogue. They appear both vertically and horizontally. Encircle them. (Answers on page 203.)

```
l  a  n  e  m  s  o  n  d  e
a  r  t  c  a  l  l  e  o  n
z  c  o  f  i  e  s  t  a  s
a  o  m  l  z  f  r  b  e  a
d  i  a  v  r  r  v  b  c  y
e  o  h  a  r  i  n  a  h  a
m  r  c  t  s  t  s  i  a  n
a  e  c  h  a  m  o  i  n  e
s  s  c  o  r  o  n  a  j  c
v  t  i  e  m  p  o  r  g  f
```

....

....

....

....

....

....

....

2 Now, can you replace all the **se**-plus-verb phrases that appeared in the dialogue with the **nosotros** form? For example, **se celebra** (one celebrates) will become **celebramos**. The only thing you have to worry about is whether the verb has an **ar**, **er**, or **ir** ending. (Answers on page 203.)

a. se corona   **b.** se escoge   **c.** se supone

....

d. se echa   **e.** se prepara

....

And now make these **nosotros** forms into verbs with **se**. (Answers on page 203.)

f. miramos   **g.** tomamos   **h.** ensayamos

....

i. bailamos   **j.** cantamos

....

3 Here is a number of short sentences that have been translated into English: try to remember the original Spanish form, say it out loud, then listen to the tape to see if you were correct. When you're satisfied with what you're saying, concentrate on how you say it – your accent and your intonation.

a. Yes, they celebrate the festival of the bambuco in Neiva.
b. It's a typical Colombian rhythm.
c. They crown the queen of the bambuco.
d. She should to sing and dance the bambuco very well.
e. Whole families practise their folk dances.
f. The colours are really lively.
g. People dance a lot in the streets.
h. They drink a lot of rum.

Diálogo 2
Fiestas en Teruel

Marga   Háblame de la fiesta de la vaquilla en Teruel.
Rafa   Pues las vaquillas son toda la fiesta ¿no? pero es el lunes de vaquilla el día más vaquillero, por decirlo así.
Marga   ¿Qué es, en el mes de julio?
Rafa   Es en la primera quincena de julio, sí.
Marga   ¿Y en qué consiste la fiesta realmente?
Rafa   Pues, mire. Fundamentalmente consiste en por la mañana, pronto, temprano, es llevar a los toros desde los corrales de la plaza de toros, a otros corrales en el centro de la ciudad. Una especie de sanfermines, pero con la característica de que aquí los llevan ensogados, los llevan con una soga de uno en uno.
Marga   Mm, o sea que no es tan peligroso.
Rafa   No es tan peligroso.
Marga   Y luego por la tarde, ¿se vuelven a soltar otra vez?
Rafa   Sí, por la tarde, los sueltan de uno en uno con una cuerda, con la vaga, se llama así, y van alternando los toros una vez que están cansados.

mes (m.) month
julio July
◆ **pronto** soon
◆ **temprano** early

◆ **tan** so
peligroso dangerous
cuerda (f.) rope
vaga (f.) rope

Háblame de la fiesta de la vaquilla en Teruel. Tell me about the festival of the young bulls in Teruel. **Háblame** is a command form: there is more about this in the grammar section on page 66.

es el lunes de vaquilla el día más vaquillero, What Rafa is saying is that the actual bull-running takes place on the Monday (the fiestas in general last for about a week).

◆ **por decirlo así** so to speak

◆ **Es en la primera quincena de julio, sí.** It's in the first fortnight of July, yes. Note that a Spanish fortnight consists of 15 days, not 14. **Quince días** is another way of saying a fortnight. **De mañana en ocho días**, a week tomorrow.

llevar a los toros desde los corrales de la plaza de toros a otros corrales . . . to take the bulls from pens in the bullring to other pens . . . Now you can see where our English word **corral** comes from! And don't forget the two opposites: **desde** from, **hasta** (or **a**) to . . .

Una especie de sanfermines a sort of San Fermín fiesta. Rafa is referring to the famous fiesta in Pamplona where the bulls run loose in the streets.

aquí los llevan ensogados here they are roped up. **Soga** is a rope; **ensogar**, to put on a rope. Two other words, **cuerda** and **vaga**, used later in the dialogue, also mean rope.

◆ **de uno en uno** one by one.

¿se vuelven a soltar otra vez? Do they let them out again? **Volver** usually means to return; here, followed by **a** and another verb, it means to do something again so it is not necessary to have **otra vez** as well. **Vuelve a decirlo**, he says it again (repeats it).

van alternando los toros, una vez que están cansados. They change the bulls around, once they are tired.

Trabajos prácticos

4 First, a crossword based on dialogue 2. **Horizontales** are clues across and **verticales**, clues down. (Answers on page 203.)

Horizontales
1 Animales
2 Es un imperativo
3 Quince días
4 Es un neutro
5 Calienta
6 Artículo
7 Las hay en todos los pueblos españoles

Verticales
1 Para——
2 Toro joven
3 Cuerda
4 Hay a eso de treinta días en cada uno
5 Hay doce en el año
6 Contrario al sí
7 Negativo
8 A él

5 Here are some synonyms for words used in the conversation between Marga and Rafa (dialogue 2). Try to identify the word in the dialogue which means the same as the words below. (Answers on page 203.)

a. concretamente ....

b. está compuesto de ....

c. sitio cerrado, destinado a los animales ....

d. zona más concurrida de una población ....

e. tipo de ....

f. particularidad ....

g. dejar en libertad ....

h. poco seguro ....

i. uno tras uno ....

6 For dialogue 2's speaking exercise, we'd like you to ask Pepe the questions that Marga asked about the festivities in Teruel. Just to remind you of what they were, they are listed below, in English. You ask the questions in Spanish, then listen to the same questions asked by Eloísa and answered by Pepe.

a. Tell me about the vaquilla festival in Teruel.
b. Is it in July?
c. And what does the fiesta consist of?
d. So it's not so dangerous?
e. And they let them loose the next day?

Diálogo 3
Te mereces eso

Charo   Vamos a salir esta noche, Eusebio ¿te apetece?

Eusebio   Bueno, pues, la verdad es que, no sé, yo estoy un poquitín cansado, pero bueno, yo creo que para complacerte a tí, sí, porque creo que te mereces eso y . . .

Charo   ¿Y adónde podríamos ir?

Eusebio   No sé, a mí me apetecería ir a una sala de fiestas, a Los Monumentos por ejemplo.

Charo   Pero podríamos ir a cenar primero también, ¿no?

Eusebio   Bueno, pues sí, vamos a cenar primero, y después nos vamos allí.

Charo   Bueno, también hay una película que está muy bien en el Royal cine. También podríamos ir a verla.

Eusebio   ¿Te apetece más ir al cine?

Charo   Las dos cosas me gustan. Tú ¿qué quieres más?

Eusebio   Bueno, anda, pues vamos al cine.

Charo   Bueno, pues muy bien, podríamos llamar a unos amigos también.

Eusebio   Bueno, pues sí.

Charo   Y después nos vamos a tomar, después de cenar, tomamos por allí algo, un irlandés . . .

Eusebio   Sí, que a mí por ejemplo un irlandés me parece muy bien ¿eh?

cansado tired
película (f.) film
cine (m.) cinema
llamar to call

▶ **¿te apetece?** do you fancy (feel like) it? The verb is **apetecer** (lit. to have an appetite for) and it works like **gustar** (see page 17). **A mí me apetece salir** I feel like going out.

▶ **para complacerte a tí** to please you.

creo que te mereces eso I think you deserve that. The verb **merecer** is frequently used in the phrase ▶ **merece la pena** it's worth it. (You also often hear **vale la pena** it's worthwhile, worth the effort.)

me apetecería ir a una sala de fiestas, a Los Monumentos, por ejemplo. I feel like going to a nightclub, to Los Monumentos, for example. Los Monumentos is a well known night spot in Oviedo.

▶ **tienes razón** you're right (lit. you have reason). If you want to say you're wrong, use either **no tienes razón** or **estás equivocado. Llevas toda la razón** means you're absolutely right.

▶ **Bueno, anda, pues . . .** Well, go on then . . . a series of 'filler' words here which are well worth learning.

tomar por allí algo, un irlandés to have a drink, an Irish coffee somewhere. **Por allí** is roughly equivalent to round about, somewhere unspecific.

Trabajos prácticos

7 Here is a multiple-choice exercise. Choose the phrase which best answers the question. (Answers on page 203.)

a. ¿Vamos a salir?
- ☐ No me apetece mucho, la verdad.
- ☐ Mañana saldremos para Córdoba.
- ☐ Salimos ayer y lo pasamos muy bien.

b. ¿Te apetece más el cine?
- ☐ A mí me encanta el teatro.
- ☐ Sí, me gustaría ver la nueva película en el cine Rex.
- ☐ ¿Por qué no vamos al centro, de compras?

c. ¿Tú qué quieres más?
- ☐ Ir a pasear y mirar escaparates.
- ☐ Quería ver a Gloria esta mañana.
- ☐ Yo quiero mucho a Maricarmen.

d. ¿Quieres cenar después?
- ☐ No, prefiero cenar antes.
- ☐ Sí, después fuimos a cenar.
- ☐ Cenaremos en el nuevo bar cerca del cine.

8 Filler words are very important in a language: they give you time to think of what to say next, and they help to 'flesh out' your basic language and make it sound more authentic. In this exercise, we've chosen some easy phrases from dialogue 3. Add some of those fillers – **no**, **verdad**, **bueno** and so on. Then listen to your tape to see what Eloísa and Pepe did with the sentences.

a. Vamos a salir. ....

b. Estoy un poquitín cansada. ....

c. Un irlandés me parece bien. ....

d. Hay una película muy buena en el cine. ....

e. ¿Adónde podríamos ir? ....

f. Las dos cosas me gustan. ....

g. Podemos llamar a unos amigos. ....

 9 In this speaking exercise, you will be asked the following questions on the tape. Work out the answers first, then stop the tape to say them out loud in Spanish. Then listen to the whole question and answer sequence.

a. ¿Quiere salir Eusebio de verdad?
b. De todas las opciones, ¿cuál es la que prefiere Eusebio?
c. ¿Cómo se llama la sala de fiestas?
d. ¿Adónde deciden ir por fin?
e. ¿Van a ir solos?
f. Y después del cine, ¿qué piensan hacer?

Diálogo 4
Oviedo de noche

Marga ¿Qué se puede hacer al atardecer en Oviedo o en la zona?

Jefe Los viajeros que nos visiten, que visiten Oviedo o la zona próxima, pueden tener la completa seguridad de que encontrarán en la ciudad una gama de diversiones muy variada. Por ejemplo, pueden escuchar música clásica en los conciertos semanales que tienen lugar en Oviedo. Pueden asistir a la temporada de ópera durante las fiestas de San Mateo. Pueden asistir a conferencias de las más variadas características. Por supuesto que existen sesiones de cinematógrafo. También las hay de teatro, aunque esporádicamente, y pueden, pues, en fin, ir a probar, a cenar la buena comida asturiana, tomar sidra, etcétera.

viajero (m.) traveller
próximo nearby
encontrar (ue) to find
ciudad (f.) city
temporada (f.) season

◗ **por supuesto** of course
esporádicamente irregularly
◗ **en fin** finally
probar (ue) to try, taste

¿Qué se puede hacer al atardecer? What can you do in the evening? **al atardecer** at nightfall (lit. on becoming evening). Use **al** plus an infinitive to mean 'on doing' something. **Al ver** on seeing, **al escuchar** on listening.

tener la completa seguridad to be completely sure.

de que encontrarán en la ciudad una gama de diversiones muy variada that they will find a very varied range of activities in the city.

conciertos semanales weekly concerts, **mensuales** monthly, **anuales** yearly.

las fiestas de San Mateo Oviedo's festival which takes place in August.

◗ **Pueden asistir a conferencias** They can attend lectures. Both **asistir** and **conferencia** are **falsos amigos**, false friends. **Asistir a** means to be present at, not to assist; **conferencia** can mean a lecture or a long-distance phone call. **Congreso** is the word for a conference.

sesiones de cinematógrafo cinema showings. Nowadays people use the shortened form **cine** for cinema. **Ir al cine**, to go to the cinema.

Las hay de teatro The tourist official is referring here to **sesiones – hay sesiones de teatro**: there are theatre performances.

la buena comida asturiana, tomar sidra. The Asturians are justly proud of their cuisine. Their regional dish is the **fabada**, a bean casserole with **morcilla** black pudding, **chorizo** hot, spiced sausage, **tocino** bacon, and **jamón** ham: all this is washed down with **sidra**, cider.

Trabajos prácticos

10 Listen carefully once again to dialogue 4 and put the following events in the order in which they occur. Try not to look at the script. (Answers on page 203.)

a. ☐ Pueden asistir a la temporada de ópera.

b. ☐ Pueden escuchar música clásica.

c. ☐ Pueden tomar sidra.

d. ☐ Pueden asistir a conferencias.

e. ☐ Existen sesiones de cinematógrafo.

f. ☐ Pueden cenar la buena comida asturiana.

11 Can you remember what the tourist official said? Look at the pictures and describe what you can do in each building. Start your sentences with **puedes** and try to vary the second verb so that all the sentences are different. (Answers on page 203.)

12 For our next speaking exercise, someone is asking you what's on in your home town. Give him the information as suggested by Susan on the tape.

Giros importantes

Se celebra la fiesta	The fiesta is celebrated
Otra fiesta importantísima	Another very important fiesta
Con mucho tiempo de anticipación (antelación)	A long time in advance
La gente baila mucho en las calles	People dance a lot in the streets
Toman muchísimo aguardiente	They drink a lot of rum
Háblame de la fiesta	Tell me about the fiesta
La primera quincena de julio	The first fortnight in July
¿En qué consiste la fiesta?	What does the fiesta consist of?
De uno en uno	One by one
No es tan peligroso	It's not so dangerous
Se vuelven a soltar	They let them loose again
Se llama así	That's what it's called
Estoy un poquitín cansado	I'm a little tired
Para complacerte a tí	To please you
Te mereces eso	You deserve that
A mí me apetece ir	I feel like going to
a una sala de fiestas	a nightclub
a un concierto	a concert
a la ópera	the opera
al cine	the cinema
al teatro	the theatre
Tienes razón	You're right
Hay una película que está muy bien en el cine	There's a very good film on at the cinema
Las dos cosas me gustan	I like both
Podríamos llamar a algunos amigos	We could ring up some friends
Un irlandés me parece bien	An Irish coffee seems a good idea to me
¿Qué se puede hacer en Oviedo?	What is there to do in Oviedo?
Una gama de diversiones muy variada	A very varied range of activities
Hay sesiones de teatro	There are theatre performances

Gramática

Se

You will already have noticed that this little word keeps cropping up in Spanish. One of its uses is as a reflexive pronoun (see Unit 2). Let's look a little more closely at the way Gustavo used it in the first dialogue in this unit. Instead of saying 'they crown' (**coronan**), 'they choose' (**escogen**), he uses **se** which is roughly equivalent to our 'one', but used much more frequently and naturally. So:

se corona one crowns, **se escoge** one chooses.

It is often used in official language and notices.

13 Here are some official notices – you supply the Spanish phrase. (Answers on page 203.)

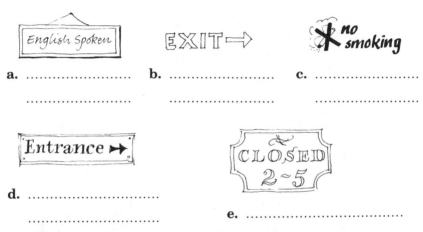

a. ....

b. ....

c. ....

....

....

....

d. ....

....

e. ....

Superlatives

In dialogue 1 Gustavo's friend Claudia used a number of words ending in **ísimo: vistosísimo** very colourful, **muchísimo** very much, **importantísima** very important. You can, of course, simply use the short word **muy** (very) if you want to emphasize a quality – **muy vistoso, muy importante**; but it is more colloquial just to add **ísimo/ísima** and **ísimos/ísimas** for the plural, to your adjective.

14 Try changing each sentence in the following exercise for one which uses an adjective with **ísimo**. (Answers on page 203.)

Imperatives

How do you tell other people to do things? There are four imperative (command) forms in Spanish (**tú**, **Vd**, **vosotros**, **Vds**), but here we'll deal only with familiar imperatives using **tú** or **vosotros**. (For the polite commands using **Vd** and **Vds**, see Unit 7.)

a. If you're speaking to one person only, form the imperative by using the third person singular of the verb. So:
Juan Gómez habla inglés Juan Gómez speaks English
becomes, in the command form:
¡Habla inglés, Juan! Speak English, Juan!

b. If you're speaking to more than one person, take the infinitive of the verb (e.g. **poner**) and substitute **d** for the **r**:
¡Poned la mesa, niños! Lay the table, children!

c. With negative familiar commands, use **no** and the relevant form of the subjunctive:
¡No hables tan alto! Don't speak so loudly!
No escribas eso! Don't write that!
You'll find the full subjunctive forms in the back of the book and there's more about the subjunctive mood in Units 5, 6 and 9.

d. Here are some irregular commands. Note that these are irregular only in the singular **tú** form.

sing	plural		sing	plural	
di	**decid**	say	**sal**	**salid**	go out
haz	**haced**	do	**sé**	**sed**	be
ve	**id**	go	**ten**	**tened**	have
pon	**poned**	put	**ven**	**venid**	come

e. One final point – the pronouns are added on to the end of positive commands, but remain in front of the verb if it is negative. So:
¡Házlo! do it, but **¡No lo hagas!** don't do it! and
Dámelo give it to me, but **¡No me lo des!** don't give it to me!

15 Match the pictures with one of the phrases below. (Answers on page 203.)

1. ¡dile 'feliz cumpleaños'!
2. ¡házlo ahora mismo!
3. ¡dámelo!
4. ¡ven aquí!
5. ¡salid de aquí, por Dios!
6. ¡pon la mesa, Jordi!

Lectura

Charo and Eusebio could have stayed at home if they had wanted to watch a film. Here's a selection of films on television for the week beginning the 16th of March:

MIERCOLES 16   El amante del amor.
21,35 TV1. 1977. 115 minutos.
Director: François Truffaut.
Intérpretes: Charles Denner, Brigitte Fossey. Un solterón se siente atraído por todas las mujeres a las que conoce. Una divertida interpretación del donjuanismo. Buena.

JUEVES 17   20.000 años en Sing-Sing.
22,05. TV2. 1932. 77 minutos.
Director: Michael Curtiz. Intérpretes: Spencer Tracy, Bette Davis. Historia del joven rebelde Tommy Connors, condenado a Sing-Sing y acusado sin culpa de un crimen. Interesante.

SABADO 19   La humanidad en peligro.
22,00. TV1. 1954. 94 minutos.
Director: Gordon Douglas.
Intérpretes: Edmund Gwen, James Witmore. Una de las primeras películas de ciencia-ficción, sobre animales monstruosos – en este caso hormigas – a causa de las explosiones nucleares. Interesante.

DOMINGO 20   El último viaje.
22,30. TV2. 1973. 81 minutos.
Director: José Antonio de la Loma.
Intérpretes: Julián Mateos, Pauline Challenor. El mundo de la droga y las aventuras de una sección especial de la Guardia Civil que trata de desarticular una banda. Mala.

solterón (m.) old bachelor
atraído attracted
donjuanismo (m.) the Don Juan syndrome
joven young

rebelde (m.) rebel
culpa (f.) guilt
hormiga (f.) ant
tratar de to attempt to
desarticular to break up

16 Now for a little detective work. Here's a description of the film that Eusebio and Charo decide to watch. Which one is it? (Answer on page 203.)

Dura más de una hora.
Empieza tarde.
No es muy vieja.
La ven el fin de semana.
No es demasiado buena.
Es una película española.

So where are Eusebio and Charo going to eat? The **Guía del ocio** (leisure guide) has a comprehensive section on restaurants. Have a look at the publicity for several local restaurants.

Apolo (Villaviciosa) teléfono 823252.

Cocina tradicional asturiana, aunque siempre preocupados por introducir innovaciones. Los más selectos mariscos y pescados, procedentes de los puertos vecinos de Lastres y Tazones.

El Náutico (Colombres) 422265.

Restaurante típico con cocina marinera, productos de las capturas que el dueño realiza diariamente. Todo tipo de pescados, destacando su besugo, salmonete y rape. Parrillada. Aprox. 1,500 pesetas.

El Cafetín (Cangas de Onís) 835294.

Situado en el mismo muelle. Su cocina se especializa en toda clase de pescados. Especialidades: fabada, lechazo de Castilla. Bodas, banquetes y comidas de empresa. Encargos.

Luisito (Ribadesella) 785622.

Cierra jueves. Especialidades: caza y truchas en temporada. Todos los días menú con tres variantes, 400 pesetas. Bolera, frontón y columpios. Conviene reservar mesa.

---

marisco (m.) shellfish
puerto (m.) port
vecino neighbouring
marinero marine
realizar to make
diariamente daily
destacar to stand out, be
  distinguished
besugo (m.) bream
salmonete (m.) red mullet
rape (m.) monk fish

parrillada (f.) grill
muelle (m.) quayside
lechazo (m.) suckling pig
boda (f.) wedding
encargo (m.) order
caza (f.) game
trucha (f.) trout
bolera (f.) bowling alley
frontón (m.) pelota court
columpio (m.) swing
conviene it's advisable to

17 a. Which restaurant would you not go to on a Thursday? ....

b. Which restaurant serves really fresh fish?..

c. Which restaurant likes to vary its menu from time to time? ....

d. Which restaurant is really convenient for the port?............................

e. Where would you go for a wedding reception? ....

f. Which restaurant caters for children?..

g. Where would you take a businessman out to lunch? ....

h. Which restaurant specialises in mullet?..

(Answers on page 204.)

Radio

Our first extract should help Charo and Eusebio to select a film. It's a 'what's on' piece about the local cinema. You'll need the following vocabulary items. (Transcript on page 216.)

sala aclimatizada (f.) air-conditioned theatre
divertido amusing
emocionante exciting
acercarse to approach
éxito (m.) success

estreno (m.) first showing
conductor (m.) driver
mayores de dieciocho años those over 18 years old
amar to love
vida (f.) life

18 You may need to listen to the first radio extract several times before you can fill in the following grid with information about which film is on where, at what time, and with what rating. (Answers on page 204.)

	Brooklyn Uno	Brooklyn Dos	Clarín Uno	Clarín Dos
película				
hora 1				
hora 2				
hora 3				
autorizada				

Our second radio extract is a piece about another popular pastime in Spain, bingo. For this item, you'll need the following vocabulary. (Transcript on page 216.)

rico (m.) rich
parado (m.) out of work
aburrido bored
cartoncito (m.) small bingo card
tachar to cross out
cartón (m.) bingo card
tirar to throw
piedra (f.) stone
propósito (m.) aim
ocio (m.) leisure
tras after

tarjeta (f.) card
pantalla (f.) screen
acabar to end
rechazar to reject
mirada (f.) look
gafe (m.) idiot
bolígrafo (m.) Biro, pen
parar to stop
calvo bald
bigote (m.) moustache
oficinista (m./f.) office worker

19 That was quite a difficult piece, so to help you to get more of a grip on it, we've transcribed a section below with the verbs missing. All you have to do is to catch those verbs and insert them in the spaces. (Answers on page 204.)

Ricos y menos ricos, parados y mujeres aburridas, pensionistas y

representantes de comercios, políticos y gente de espectáculo, todos,

absolutamente todos le .... al cartoncito. Él

que .... libre de no haber ....

.... algún cartón en su vida, que ....

la primera piedra. Mi propósito .... que hoy

.... a pasar nuestra tarde de ocio en este

templo de vicio. Tras .... sacado nuestra

tarjeta, ... una mesa en que ....

.... jugadores. En frente una pantalla de

vídeo .... casi siempre las mismas escenas de

una película que no .... nunca. La vendedora,

tras haber .... los cartones, por riguroso

turno, a nuestros compañeros de mesa, nos

.... cuantos ....

Te toca a tí hablar

 20 Finally, it's your turn to speak. Can you describe a night out? It could be at the cinema, theatre or even a bingo session! To help you to think of what to say, remember the following question words:

¿cómo? how? **¿quién?** who? **¿cuándo?** when? **¿cuánto?** how much/how many?, **¿qué?** what?

Trying to answer these questions will give you some 'pegs' to hang your description on. Then listen to Eloísa's version of her night out at the cinema.

 21 You are host to delegates of a foreign trade organisation. Describe what your town or area has to offer in the way of tourist attractions for the delegates in their spare time. To help you to marshal your arguments, concentrate on the following headings: theatre/cinema/concerts/restaurants/nightclubs/drinking establishments. Then listen to Pepe's account of Cáceres and decide which of you would have won the contract.

5 Beberás y vivirás

What you will learn
- how to describe good food – and bad
- how to make a **paella**
- the pros and cons of supermarket shopping
- . . . and all about the dining clubs in the **Basque country**

Study guide

Diálogo 1
¿Puedes describir la peor comida de tu vida?

Gustavo   Sí, en un restaurante mejicano. La comida era de una apariencia muy atractiva pero imposible de saborear porque era muy picante.

Marga   Fue en un restaurante en Oviedo y un camarero que me estaba sirviendo la sopa me la tiró por encima.

Andrés   En un restaurante me pusieron una paella que estaba muy fría y muy grasienta.

Carmen   Una vez me pusieron un gazpacho malísimo, que estaba muy fuerte, sabía mucho a vinagre.

Rafa   Bueno, que yo recuerde, la comida peor que comí fue una vez en Inglaterra, donde pedí tortilla de patatas y lo que comí era todo lo más diferente de una tortilla de patatas.

Eduardo   Sí, pues mira, fuimos a comer en la zona de Luarca, a un restaurante y el pescado estaba atrasado, no se podía comer y aparte de todo, nos lo cobraron caro y no lo quisieron cambiar.

Ricardo   Cebollas rellenas.

saborear to taste	**grasiento** greasy
pescado (m.) fish	▶ **atrasado** 'off' or 'bad'

La comida era de una apariencia muy atractiva the food looked very nice.

▶ **picante** means hot in the sense of spicy. **Caliente** means hot in temperature.

un camarero que me estaba sirviendo la sopa a waiter who was serving me the soup. **Sirviendo** is from **servir**, another type of radical-changing verb (see page 81).

me la tiró por encima he spilled it over me (lit. he threw it over me).

▶ **me pusieron una paella** they served me a paella. Notice the way Andrés uses **poner** instead of **servir** (as does Carmen).

un gazpacho a cold soup, a speciality of Andalucía.

▶ **sabía mucho a vinagre** it tasted strongly of vinegar. **Saber a** means to taste of. **Sabe a ajo** it tastes of garlic.

▶ **que yo recuerde** as far as I remember. **Recuerde** is a subjunctive form of **recordar**. **Que yo sepa** as far as I know.

pedí tortilla de patatas I asked for a Spanish omelette (lit. a potato omelette). **Pedir** is another radical-changing verb like **servir**.

todo lo más diferente de quite different from.

▶ **aparte de todo, nos lo cobraron caro** apart from everything else they charged a lot for it. **Cobrar** to charge.

no lo quisieron cambiar they wouldn't change it. Used as a negative in the preterite tense, **querer** (to want) means 'to refuse': **no quiso venir** he refused to come.

Trabajos prácticos

1 What was wrong with each dish? Listen to the dialogue again and complete the grid. (Answers on page 204.)

pescado	
comida mejicana	
sopa	
paella	
gazpacho	

sabía a vinagre   fuerte   muy picante   se la tiró encima   fría y grasienta

se lo cobraron caro   atrasado

2 In this exercise, the verbs from the dialogue have been replaced by other verbs in the preterite. Match the original sentences with the ones that have been substituted. (Answers on page 204.)

a. Me la echó encima. ....

b. Nos costó caro. ....

c. No lo cambiaron. ....

d. Me sirvieron un gazpacho que sabía a vinagre. ....

e. Estuvimos en un restaurante. ....

f. La comida peor que probé. ....

g. Salimos a comer en la zona de Luarca. ....

3 Who said what? Marga has been out and about in Oviedo doing a survey on bad restaurant meals. Listen to the tape and see if you can attribute the following remarks to the right people. (Answers on page 204.)

a. Cuando fuimos a Cangas nos sirvieron una sopa casi fría y además ¡con una mosca muerta!

b. Yo estuve en Méjico hace unos años y comí un pollo relleno con una salsa asquerosa.

c. Fue en Alemania – no me gusta la comida alemana por ser demasiado grasienta.

d. No he tenido malas experiencias. ¡La verdad es que a mí me gusta todo!

e. Cuando estuve en Inglaterra, me sirvieron una paella que parecía sopa . . .

When you've completed the exercise, rewind your tape and repeat each sentence out loud.

Diálogo 2
Paella valenciana

Paqui Para hacer una paella, necesitas aceite, ajo, pimiento, cebolla, calamares, gambas, pollo, azafrán, arroz, sal y pimienta. Primero calientas el aceite, y fríes el ajo en el aceite hasta que se dore. Luego se añade el pollo con el pimiento etcétera y una vez que, pasados diez minutos, se añade el resto, como es los calamares o las gambas: se mezcla todo otra vez y luego se añade el arroz. Se añade el arroz y el azafrán, se mezcla bien y se le añade el agua, por taza de arroz dos de agua y nada más. Se decora con gambas etcétera, con limón, con huevo cocido y está listo para servir.

necesitar to need
aceite (m.) oil
ajo (m.) garlic
cebolla (f.) onion
calamares (m.pl.) squid
gamba (f.) prawn
azafrán (m.) saffron
arroz (m.) rice
añadirse to add
taza (f.) cup
decorar to decorate
limón (m.) lemon

Para hacer una paella to make a paella. Paella is the regional dish of Valencia made, as Paqui says, with rice and either fish or meat. In a classic paella you should not mix fish and meat, but chicken is always an acceptable addition.

▶ **pimiento/pimienta.** Be careful with this pair. **Pimiento** means red or green pepper. **Pimienta** means pepper (to go with salt): **sal y pimienta** salt and pepper.

Primero calientas el aceite y fríes el ajo First you warm the oil and fry the garlic. Both these verbs (**calentar** and **freír**) are of the radical-changing type (see pages 18 and 81.)

hasta que se dore until it goes brown: **dorarse** to turn golden. **Dore** is a subjunctive. More about this on page 81.

una vez que, pasados diez minutos after 10 minutes. Paqui changes her mind about what to say. She starts with 'once it's (cooked)', then decides to give a time limit instead. It's very common to do this when you're talking naturally: don't feel inhibited if your own Spanish is not absolutely correct.

se mezcla todo otra vez you mix it all together again.

se le añade el agua you add the water to it (**le**, to it).

huevo cocido boiled egg, **huevos revueltos** scrambled eggs, **huevo frito** fried egg.

Trabajos prácticos

4 Here are some illustrations of the ingredients which Paqui mentioned in her recipe. Write down everything that went into that paella. (Answers on page 204.)

a. ....   f. ....

b. ....   g. ....

c. ....   h. ....

d. ....   i. ....

e. ....   j. ....

5 How did Paqui give the following instructions? (Answers on page 204.)

a. First you heat the oil ....

b. Then you fry the garlic ....

c. Then you add the chicken ....

d. You mix it all up again ....

e. Two cups of water for each cup of rice ....

f. You decorate it with prawns ....

6 Here is another recipe for a different type of paella. Listen to it as often as you need and then put the following instructions in the order in which you heard them. (Answers on page 204.)

You will need the following vocabulary items:
picado chopped up
sazonar to season

a. ☐ Se adorna el arroz con pimientos.
b. ☐ Se prepara un arroz blanco.
c. ☐ Se fríe la cebolla picada.
d. ☐ Se pone un pimiento picado.
e. ☐ Se sazona con sal.
f. ☐ Se pone el pescado con su salsa.
g. ☐ Se añade el tomate.

Then try to reconstruct the recipe, out loud. Rewind your tape and listen again to check if you were right.

Diálogo 3
¿Prefieres el supermercado o la tienda de esquina?

Claudia   Generalmente en mi pueblo se compra en una plaza de mercado, que es mejor, para mejor escoger ¿no?

Verónica   Prefiero el supermercado, porque uno queda libre, compra todo lo que necesita de una sola vez.

Marga   En un supermercado, porque la gente va a lo suyo y no te molesta.

Andrés   Prefiero en un supermercado porque puedo encontrar todas las cosas sin ir de un sitio para otro.

Carmen   En un supermercado, porque no me gusta tener que guardar la cola y esperar a que me atiendan.

Rafael   Prefiero en un supermercado por la variedad de cosas que puedo comprar.

Paqui   Depende; si es en el pueblo, prefiero la tienda porque conozco a la gente.

Ventura   Prefiero el supermercado porque hay más cantidad en diferentes artículos.

Araceli   Si voy con prisa me gusta la tienda pequeña pero si voy con tiempo me gusta el supermercado.

esquina (f.) corner
escoger to choose
molestar to bother
encontrar (ue) to find
conocer to know, be
    acquainted with
cantidad (f.) quantity

una plaza de mercado a market square, place.

▸ **uno queda libre** one is free. Here Verónica uses **uno** instead of **se**, and she also uses **quedar** (to stay) rather than **estar**.

▸ **de una sola vez** at one go.

▸ **la gente va a lo suyo y no te molesta** people mind their own business and don't bother you.

sin ir de un sitio para otro without going from one place to another. Notice that after a preposition (here: **sin** without) the verb that follows is an infinitive.

▸ **no me gusta tener que guardar la cola** I don't like having to queue. **Cola** can mean a queue or a tail.

esperar a que me atiendan wait to be served. This is a similar construction to the one on page 74, **hasta que se dore**, and we will talk about them both in the grammar section.

por la variedad de cosas because of the variety of things. **Por** is often used to mean because of, on account of.

▸ **Si voy con prisa** if I'm in a hurry, **si voy con tiempo** if I've got time.

Trabajos prácticos

7 Here's a grid about who likes to shop where. Tick the boxes to show at which type of outlet our interviewees prefer to shop. (Answers on page 204.)

	tienda	supermercado	plaza de mercado
Araceli			
Paqui			
Claudia			
Verónica			
Rafael			
Andrés			
Marga			
Carmen			
Ventura			

8 Here's another grid referring to the reasons for their choices. Write in as many reasons as you can (in English) for their preferences for the shop or the supermarket, or both. (Answers on page 204.)

tienda	supermercado

9 Now Pepe asks you why you prefer the supermarket to the corner shop. Answer the questions on tape by following the suggestions made by Susan. Stop the tape to answer in Spanish, then start it again and check your answers against those given by Eloísa.

Diálogo 4
Una forma de defenderse de las mujeres

Andrés En el País Vasco la gastronomía es una de las aficiones más importantes. Los jóvenes y los hombres vascos tienen sus sedes gastronómicas, las sociedades gastronómicas. Todos ellos, o la mayoría, pertenecen a una de las sociedades.

Carmen ¿Y qué es una sociedad gastronómica?

Andrés Es un local que los hombres alquilan y tienen sus ritos para entrar. Solamente pueden entrar hombres.

Carmen ¿Ah sí? ¿Y eso por qué es?

Andrés Pienso que esto es una derivación, una forma de protegerse. La sociedad vasca es una sociedad, es un matriarcado. Y una forma de defenderse de las mujeres es . . .

Carmen ¿Una forma de defenderse de las mujeres? ¡Eso sí que tiene gracia! ¡Vamos, hombre! ¡Ahora resulta que las mujeres estamos aquí reprimiendo a los hombres!

Andrés No, ¡no me esperaba esto!

▶ **afición** (f.) interest, hobby   **local** (m.) place
sede (f.) seat, base   **rito** (m.) ceremony
pertenecer to belong   **alquilar** to hire, rent
sociedad (f.) society   **defenderse** to defend oneself

el País Vasco the Basque Country. This area's people and language are unique and have little in common with the rest of Spain. Hence Andrés' pride in his region's traditions and customs.

sus sedes gastronómicas places where Basque men meet to cook regional dishes and eat them together – dining clubs.

Pienso que esto es [una derivación,] una forma de protegerse I believe this is [a legacy,] a way of defending oneself. Andrés means that in a matriarchy, or society dominated by women as he believes the Basque Country to be, men need a place to relax without the presence of women.

▶ **¡Eso sí que tiene gracia!** That really is a joke! **tener gracia** to be funny.

▶ **¡Vamos, hombre!** Heavens, man! Two 'filler' words expressing surprise.

¡Ahora resulta que las mujeres estamos aquí reprimiendo a los hombres! And now it turns out that we women are repressing the men! Carmen includes herself in the women, so uses the **nosotros** form.

¡no me esperaba esto! I wasn't expecting that! **Esperar** can mean to expect as well as to hope and to wait. Andrés adds the **me** here for emphasis; he was completely taken aback by Carmen's outburst!

Trabajos prácticos

10 This exercise is to test your wits – and to find out how many of those new words you've learned. Match up the definitions with the new words you met in the passage. (Answers on page 204.)

a. actividades en relación con el comer bien ....

b. contener o detener el progreso de algo ....

c. defenderse ....

d. formar parte de ....

e. ceremonias ....

f. sistema social basado en la importancia de la línea materna ....

g. sitio ....

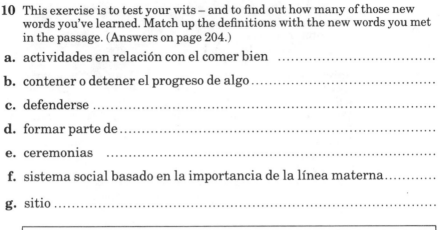

reprimir   local   protegerse   matriarcado   gastronomía

pertenecer   ritos

11 Listen to dialogue 4 again and complete the following sentences and phrases. Do not look at the script. (Answers on page 204.)

a. Una forma de defenderse ....

b. Las mujeres estamos aquí reprimiendo ....

c. ¿Qué es una ....

d. ¡Eso sí que ....

e. La gastronomía es una de ....

f. Es un local que ....

g. Solamente pueden ....

 12 For this speaking exercise, you want to know all about those dining clubs that are exclusive to men. Follow Susan's prompts on the tape. Then listen to Eloísa's version and Pepe's answers.

Giros importantes

La comida era picante — The food was spicy
Me pusieron una paella que — They gave me a paella that was
  estaba fría —   cold
      grasienta —   greasy
      fuerte —   strong
Sabía a vinagre — It tasted of vinegar
Que yo recuerde — As far as I remember
Que yo sepa — As far as I know
Pedí tortilla de patatas — I asked for (ordered) a Spanish
    omelette

Nos lo cobraron caro — They charged us a lot for it
No lo quisieron cambiar — They wouldn't change it

Para hacer una paella necesitas — To make paella, you need
  pimientos —   peppers
  cebolla —   onion
  calamares —   squid
  azafrán —   saffron
  arroz —   rice
  sal y pimienta —   salt and pepper
Se calienta el aceite — You heat the oil
Se fríe el ajo — You fry the garlic
Se añade el pollo — You add the chicken
Se mezcla todo — You mix it all up
Se decora con gambas — You garnish it with prawns
    limón —   lemon
    huevo cocido —   boiled egg

Una plaza de mercado — A market square, place
Uno queda libre — One is free
De una sola vez — At one go
La gente va a lo suyo — People mind their own business
Sin ir de un sitio para otro — Without going from one place to
    another

No me gusta tener que guardar — I don't like having to queue
  la cola
Esperar a que me atiendan — To wait to be served
Si voy con prisa — If I'm in a hurry
Si voy con tiempo — If I have plenty of time

¿Eso por qué es? — Why's that?
¡Eso sí que tiene gracia! — That really is a joke!
¡Vamos hombre! — Heavens man!
¡No me esperaba esto! — I didn't expect that!

Gramática

Radical-changing verbs (e → i)

Pedir to ask, is a radical-changing verb of the e → i type. The **e** in the stem (or root) changes to an **i** when the word stress falls upon it. In the present tense this occurs in all three singular persons and in the third person plural. So:

pido	I ask	**pedimos**	we ask
pides	you ask	**pedís**	you (pl.) ask
pide	he/she asks, you (**Vd**) ask	**piden**	they ask, you (**Vds**) ask

In the preterite (past) tense, the radical change occurs in the third persons singular and plural. So:

pedí	I asked	**pedimos**	we asked
pediste	you asked	**pedisteís**	you (pl.) asked
pidió	he/she/you (**Vd**) asked	**pidieron**	they asked, you (**Vds**) asked

In the present participle the **e** also changes to an **i** (**pidiendo**, asking) as well as in the singular and plural formal commands (¡**pida!** and ¡**pidan!** ask!). The other two verbs in this unit which change in this way are **freír** to fry and **servir** to serve. The other types of radical-changing verbs are dealt with in Units 1 and 2.

13 Here are some pictures and phrases to describe them. Can you match them up? (Answers on page 205.)

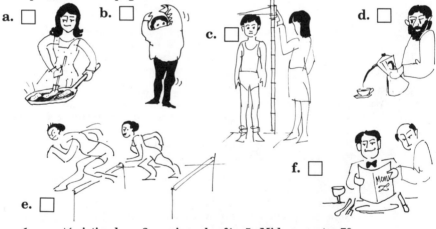

1. se está vistiendo
2. pide el menú
3. se sirve el café
4. fríe salchichas
5. Mide un metro 70
6. compite en el cien metros vallas

Now give the infinitive form of all the radical-changing verbs that were used.

The subjunctive

In formal grammar, verbs are divided up into three 'moods': the indicative (the normal form of the verb), the imperative (the command form) and the subjunctive. You may have wondered what this was when pointed out to you in the text. Used primarily to express uncertainty ('may', 'might'), the subjunctive involves a change of ending for the verb so that where you have expected an **e**, an **a** ending has occurred – or vice versa. Instead of the full range of tenses, the subjunctive has only four: the present, imperfect, perfect and pluperfect. Let's concentrate on the present for the moment.

To form the present subjunctive, take the first person singular of the present tense: **hablo** I speak, **escribo** I write. Remove the **o** and add the following endings:

– **ar** verbs

hablar to speak

habl **e**	habl **emos**
habl **es**	habl **éis**
habl **e**	habl **en**

– **er** and – **ir** verbs share the same endings:

escribir to write

escrib **a**	escrib **amos**
escrib **as**	escrib **áis**
escrib **an**	escrib **an**

An additional point is that if the verb is irregular in the first person of the present indicative (e.g. **salgo, tengo**), it will be irregular in the present subjunctive:
salga I leave; **tenga** I have.

As always, there is a number of irregular subjunctives – look these up in the verb table at the back of the book.

When to use the subjunctive

The subjunctive is used primarily to express uncertainty, and to describe cause and effect. These uses are covered in Units 6 and 9. In this unit, the subjunctive is used to express action in the future:
hasta que se dore until it browns, and
esperar a que me atiendan to wait for them to serve me.

It helps to memorize the verbs and phrases that usually introduce a subjunctive (here: **esperar a que** and **hasta que**). The subjunctive is always used after **para que:**
¡**te doy dinero para que compres comida y no bebida!** I'm giving you money to buy (so that you may buy) food and not drink!

The subjunctive is also used for negative commands (see Unit 4), both the familiar **tú** form (**no abras la ventana**, don't open the window) and the polite **Vd** form (**no abra la ventana**), as well as for polite positive commands: **abra la ventana**, open the window. (The familiar positive command would be **abre la ventana**.)

14 Here are some sentences divided into two parts. Match up the pairs and try to work out why the subjunctive is used. Note down the phrases which introduce a subjunctive. (Answers on page 205.)

a. No te vayas   no iré a la playa – tengo demasiado que
    ☐ hacer

b. Cuando vayas a casa   ☐ hasta que llegue yo

c. Tu padre trabaja   ☐ no volveré a verte

d. Mientras que viva   ☐ arregla tu habitación

e. Aunque haga sol   ☐ para que comamos todos

f. Antes de que te pongas   di a tu madre que no volveré hasta las
a estudiar   ☐ siete

Lectura

To prepare you for the soft fruit season, here's a short article about **albaricoques**, apricots.

Los albaricoques están en su punto, su piel está llena de vitaminas y los niños se los toman sin sentir. Es el momento de hacer una cura de salud con esta fruta, seca por fuera y jugosa por dentro, que, aunque se cosecha de mayo a noviembre, está álgido en los primeros meses del verano. Tiene más contenido en vitamina A que ninguna otra fruta y, a pesar del sabor dulce que ofrece la pulpa, su contenido en azúcares es muy bajo, solamente el seis por ciento. Tiene un valor alimenticio mucho más bajo que el melocotón, al que se parece en la forma exterior. Un modo distinto de servirlo es sin el hueso, cortado en cuartos: rociarlo de azúcar y del zumo de medio limón y espolvorearlo de hojas de menta fresca. Guardar en la nevera unas dos horas y servirlo con nata montada o, para los que cuidan la línea, con yogurt desnatado. Como producto de belleza, da buenísimos resultados. Si se deja sobre la cara durante media hora, quedará una piel suave y aterciopelada con color de albaricoque, ¡seguramente!

en su punto at their peak
piel (f.) skin
salud (f.) health
jugoso juicy
álgido most prolific
a pesar de in spite of
sabor (m.) taste
dulce sweet
azúcar (m.) sugar
melocotón (m.) peach

hueso (m.) stone
rociar to sprinkle
zumo (m.) juice
espolvorear to dust
hoja (f.) leaf
menta (f.) mint
nevera (f.) refrigerator
nata montada (f.) whipped cream
belleza (f.) beauty
aterciopelado velvety

15 Here is a quiz based on that article. (Answers on page 205.)

a. Can you give two expressions in Spanish for 'at its peak'? ....
....

b. If **piel** means the outer part of the apricot, what is the word for the inner part? ....

c. What is the opposite of **por dentro**? ....

d. What is the opposite of **jugoso**? ....

e. If **nata** means cream, what does **desnatado** mean? ....

f. How do you say 'The children take them without noticing'? ....
....

g. How do you say 'to take a health cure'? ....

The next reading extract is a review from *Cambio 16* of a restaurant in Barcelona called Florián. Read it through and decide whether you would like to eat there!

¿DÓNDE COMEMOS?

Florián, Bertrán i Serra, 20. Barcelona.
Cierre, domingos y festivos.

Rosa Grau, poco a poco, ha subido hasta la cima del elenco de cocineras españolas haciéndose con un estilo propio, con acento italianizante, lo cual es muy de agradecer en un país en el que todo el mundo se dedica a imitar a los franceses.

La casa ofrece, en temporada, dos atractivas especialidades: las setas y los guisos de toro. Son, asimismo, sumamente apreciables las diversas ensaladas, aliñadas a menudo con vinagres de Modena o con los mejores de Jerez, y aceites vírgenes de oliva de insuperable calidad.

Ahora, el Florián ofrece erizos de mar recién llegados de la Costa Brava, espléndida apertura a la que puede seguir el foiegras a vino añejo o el soberbio carré de lechal.

Tan atento a la calidad como su esposa, Javier cuida de que la bodega esté a la altura de la cocina, y lo consigue.

cima (f.) summit
elenco (m.) list, cast
hacerse con to appropriate
agradecer to thank
seta (f.) mushroom
guiso (m.) stew
asimismo likewise
sumamente highly
aliñado dressed
a menudo frequently
erizo de mar (m.) sea urchin
apertura (f.) (here) entrée
añejo old, mellow
soberbio proud, magnificent
carré de lechal (m.) quarter of suckling pig
atento attentive
ciudar de que to make sure that
bodega (f.) cellar
altura (f.) (here) standard
conseguir (i) to manage

16 Here is part of a brochure that Casa Florián has produced. Fill in the details. (Answers on page 205.)

CASA FLORIÁN

Bertrán i ....

Cierre ....

Dueños .... y ....

Especialidades .... y ....

Ensaladas aliñadas con vinagres de ....

y de .... con aceites ....

MENÚ DEL DÍA

Entremeses ....

Carnes ....

....

Radio

First of all, a very short advertisement for **cuajada**
– a sort of junket. You will probably recognise
that it's made by Danone!

The word for honey is **miel**. (Transcript on page 216.)

17 What three ways do they suggest you serve the **cuajada**?
Answer in English. (Answers on page 205.)

Menú Real

Entradas

Gambas al ajillo
Sopa vichyssoise
Sopa de avellanas
Aguacates rellenos
Tortilla mallorquina
Mousse de verduras/pescado
Salmón ahumado
Caldereta de pescado

Pescados

Truchas con jamón
Langosta fría a la parisienne
Salmón Bella Vista
Parrillada de pescado con salsa romesco
Zarzuela de mariscos
Lubina Bellaeaso
Cigalas al vapor
Besugo al ajo

Carnes

Solomillo Wellington
Silla de ternera
Cordero asado a la manchega
Tierna de cerdo ahumado
Perdices estofadas

Postres

Fruta
Queso
Helado de almendra
Fillós

18 This longer extract is part of an alternative news programme which included a piece about the banquet served to the Spanish royal family on the eve of their departure from Mallorca. (Transcript on page 216.) The menu on page 85 reproduces some of the items that are mentioned. Tick those that appeared on the royal table. Here is some vocabulary to help you. (Answers on page 205.)

hacerse una idea to have an idea
cena (f.) dinner
despedirse (i) to say goodbye
entrada (f.) hors d'oeuvres
aguacate (m.) avocado

variadísimo very varied
repostería (f.) pastries
sitio (m.) place
de moda in fashion
temporada (f.) season
tener ganas de to want to

Te toca a tí hablar

19 Where do you like to shop if you've got the choice? Give as many reasons as you can for going to a supermarket. You'll then hear Eloísa talking about why she prefers **la tienda pequeña**.

6 Una vez al año no hace daño

What you will learn

- how to talk about **illness**
- how to develop a healthy lifestyle
- what to say to the **chemist**
- ... and some **simple remedies** for holiday health problems

Study guide

Diálogo 1
Tengo la tensión muy alta

Paqui ¿Sabes que tengo un problema terrible con la tensión? Tengo la tensión muy alta. Hace ocho meses que me enteré. Fui al médico, porque me encontraba muy cansada, me encontraba agotada y me dolía mucho la cabeza: entonces fui al médico y me dijo que tenía la tensión alta. Entonces me recomendó que tenía que ponerme a tratamiento, ¿no? Me dio unas pastillas y yo que no quería tomármelas pero me recomendó, porque si no quería acabar con un derrame cerebral, me dijo que tenía que seguir el tratamiento. Estoy bien ahora, mucho mejor, sí, y aparte del tratamiento es recomendable también, me recomendó, que no tomase mucha sal, que no bebiese y que descansase mucho.

médico (m.) doctor
agotado worn out
dolerse (ue) to hurt

pastilla (f.) pill
aparte de apart from

Tengo la tensión muy alta I have very high blood pressure.

▶ **Hace ocho meses que me enteré** I found out eight months ago. **Hace** is used to express the English 'ago': **hace dos años** two years ago, **hace una semana** a week ago. **Enterarse** is frequently used for 'to find out': **me voy a enterar** I'm going to find out.

me encontraba muy cansada I felt very tired. **Encontrar** means to find, and **encontrarse** (to find oneself) can be used instead of **estar**. The tense Paqui uses here is the imperfect. More about this on page 97.

▶ **Me dolía la cabeza** my head ached (lit. the head ached to me); **me duele la garganta** I have a sore throat; **me duele el estómago** I've got a stomach ache.

tenía que ponerme a tratamiento I had to follow a course of treatment.

y yo que no quería tomármelas and I didn't want to take them. Adding the **que** to this phrase makes it more emphatic. And did you notice that **tomármelas** is only **tomar** with **me** and **las** added on to the end? The **me** merely adds emphasis.

Si no quería acabar con un derrame cerebral If I didn't want to end up with a stroke.

también me recomendó que no tomase mucha sal, que no bebiese y que descansase mucho he also recommended that I shouldn't have much salt, that I shouldn't drink and that I should rest a lot. All three of these verbs are in the imperfect subjunctive. This tense is explained on page 98.

Trabajos prácticos

1 Find the answers to the clues below; the central column spells a key word in
dialogue 1. (Answers on page 205.)

a. son para la tensión alta   _ _ _ ☐ _ _ _ _ _

b. parte del cuerpo   _ _ _ ☐ _ _

c. el médico me ....   _ _ _ _ _ _ ☐ _ _

d. .... y pimienta   _ _ _ ☐ _ _

e. me dijo que no ....   _ _ _ ☐ _ _ _

f. me .... unas pastillas   _ _ ☐

g. agotada   _ _ ☐ _ _ _ _

2 Spot the verb. In this exercise, a number of verbs have been changed, either
into another tense, or into another verb with the same meaning. Without
looking at your transcript, underline where the differences occur. It would
be a good idea to listen to dialogue 1 again. (Answers on page 205.)

¿Sabes que tenía un problema terrible con la tensión? Sufro de
tensión muy alta. Hace ocho meses que me lo dijeron. Ví al médico
porque me sentía muy cansada, me sentía agotada y me dolía la
cabeza. Fui al médico y me informó de que tenía la tensión alta ¿no?
Salí con unas pastillas y yo no me decidía a tomármelas pero él
insistió si no quería terminar con un derrame cerebral, repitió que
había que seguir con el tratamiento. Me encuentro bien ahora,
mucho mejor sí, y aparte del tratamiento es recomendable, me aconsejó
que no comiese mucha sal, que no bebiese y que durmiera mucho.

3 For this speaking exercise answer Pepe's questions about your health in
Spanish. Look at the sketches in numerical order and they will suggest
what you have to say. Then listen to Eloísa's replies.

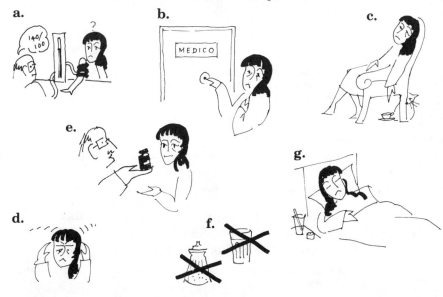

a.   **b.**   **c.**

e.

g.

d.   **f.**

Diálogo 2
¡Estás guapísima!

Marga ¡Estás guapísima! ¿Qué haces para mantenerte así?

Carmen ¡Huy, bueno! Pues, no sé, la verdad es que no hago mucho. Pero sí que soy bastante cuidadosa con el tipo de comida que tomo y eso. Por ejemplo, procuro tomar bastantes frutas y verduras frescas y ensaladas, y cosas así, y no tomar mucha grasa, porque no, creo que no son muy buenas para la piel y eso sobre todo. Y además también me gusta hacer un poco de ejercicio de vez en cuando, por ejemplo, eh, una vez a la semana voy por las tardes a clase de yoga.

Marga ¿Y practicas algún deporte más?

Carmen No, la verdad es que no tengo mucho tiempo para practicar más deporte. A veces juego al squash, pero no con mucha frecuencia.

verduras (f.pl.) green vegetables	◆ **sobre todo** above all
grasa (f.) fat	**deporte** (m.) sport
piel (f.) skin	**jugar (ue)** to play
	casi almost

◆ **¡Estás guapísima!** You look really lovely! **Guapo** means beautiful, but don't get too carried away if people call you **guapísima** (if you're female). **Eres guapísima** means you are naturally beautiful; **estás guapísima** means you have made an effort!

¿Qué haces para mantenerte así? What do you do to keep yourself like that?

¡Huy bueno! More fillers. **Huy** is a sound, equivalent here to heavens.

◆ **y eso** and so on. Carmen speaks in a very colloquial way here: notice how she says **sobre todo, así, eh, ¿por qué no?** All these phrases are used here as **paja**, straw, or fillers.

un poco de ejercicio a little exercise.

◆ **de vez en cuando** from time to time.

voy a clase de yoga I go to a yoga class. **Dar clases** means to teach. **Doy clases de yoga** I teach yoga, but **doy yoga** can mean I learn yoga.

◆ **¿Y practicas algún deporte más?** And do you do any other sport? Spanish uses the more complicated word **practicar** to express a relatively simple idea: another example of this is **quedas eliminado** you're out (eliminated) in a children's game.

◆ **A veces** sometimes. You can also use **algunas veces**.

no con mucha frecuencia not very frequently. Note **siempre** always, **nunca** never.

Trabajos prácticos

4 Listen to the extract again and then fill in the grid, in Spanish, about what Carmen does and doesn't do to keep healthy. (Answers on page 205.)

lo que sí hace Carmen	lo que no hace Carmen

5 See how much of that dialogue you can remember by filling in the blanks in each of the following sentences. Try not to look at the transcript! (Answers on page 205.)

a. ¿Qué haces para .... así?

. Soy bastante .... con el tipo de comida que tomo.

c. ¿Y .... algún deporte más?

d. .... tomar bastantes frutas.

e. me gusta hacer un poco de .... de vez en cuando.

f. .... juego a squash.

6 You meet a friend in the street. Ask her, in Spanish, why she's looking so well. Susan will prompt you in English.

Diálogo 3
Una picadura de mosquito

Señora	Buenas tardes.
Ricardo	Buenas tardes. Dígame, ¿qué deseaba?
Señora	¿Me podría dar algo para esta picadura que me . . . de un mosquito?
Ricardo	¿Cuándo la picaron?
Señora	Esta mañana.
Ricardo	Esta mañana. ¿Tiene inflamación, no?
Señora	Sí, un poquito.
Ricardo	¿Picores?
Señora	También.
Ricardo	Le podemos dar unas pastillas o una pomada o ambas cosas.
Señora	Bueno, pues, lo que usted vea que sea mejor.
Ricardo	Bueno, yo le aconsejaría las pastillas, incluso la pomada, dos o tres días para que le quitase los picores momentáneamente.
Señora	De acuerdo.
Ricardo	¿Anda bien del estómago?
Señora	Bueno, regular.
Ricardo	Es que puede tomar las pastillas con infusión de manzanilla: tres pastillas al día. La manzanilla ya sabe que le va muy bien para el estómago.
Señora	Sí.
Ricardo	¿Algo más deseaba?
Señora	Bueno, ¿y para el dolor de cabeza, qué me recomienda?
Ricardo	¿Qué? ¿Lleva muchos días con él?
Señora	Pues, de dos a tres días.
Ricardo	¿Fiebre tiene?
Señora	Pues no.
Ricardo	No tiene fiebre.
Señora	No.
Ricardo	¿Digestiones? ¿Cómo las hace? ¿bien?
Señora	Bueno, hay veces que bien, otras veces regular.
Ricardo	Bueno, puede seguir con la manzanilla, a ver si le pasa con eso que es un problema de mala digestión.
Señora	De acuerdo.

picadura (f.) bite
picar to bite, itch
picores (m.pl.) itching
pomada (f.) cream, lotion
ambos both

▶ **incluso** even, including
manzanilla (f.) camomile tea
fiebre (f.) fever
regular not very well

▶ **Dígame** Tell me. This is a polite command so the subjunctive is used (see page 113).

lo que usted vea que sea mejor whatever you think is best. Two present subjunctives here – **vea** and **sea**. This is because it's all very uncertain: the customer does not know what is best. Contrast with **esta pomada es mejor** this cream is better – a definite fact.

yo le aconsejaría las pastillas . . . para que le quitase los picores momentáneamente. I would recommend the tablets . . . to take away the irritation for the time being. **Quitase** is an imperfect subjunctive; remember to use the subjunctive after **para que** (in order to, so that).

Trabajos prácticos

7 Does the customer in dialogue 3 have the symptoms that the chemist inquires about? Tick the appropriate column. (Answers on page 205.)

	sí	no	algunas veces
¿Dolor de cabeza?			
¿Inflamación?			
¿Dolor de estómago?			
¿Fiebre?			
¿Malas digestiones?			
¿Picores?			

8 Here is the treatment recommended. Look at each sketch and answer the questions as if you were the chemist. (Answers on page 205.)

a.

¿Qué son? ....

¿Para qué son? ....

¿Cuántas veces al día? ....

b.

¿Qué es? ....

¿Para qué es? ....

¿Cuántos días? ....

c.

¿Qué es? ....

¿Para qué es? ....

9 Now you are the client. You are in a chemist's shop because you have a bad headache and would like some advice on how to treat it. On the tape Susan will tell you how to approach the chemist.

◆ **¿Anda bien del estómago?** How is your stomach? (lit. does the stomach go well?).

¿Digestiones? ¿Cómo las hace? ¿bien? How is your digestion?

La manzanilla, ya sabe que le va muy bien para el estómago. You must know that camomile tea is very good for the stomach.

◆ **¿Lleva muchos días con él?** Have you had it long? (Lit. do you carry many days with it?). This use of **llevar** is very colloquial.

◆ **De acuerdo** Agreed, very well.

Diálogo 4
Una hepatitis bastante gorda

Sandra Estuviste muy enferma el año anterior ¿verdad?

Marga Sí, tuve una hepatitis bastante gorda, que me tuvo dos meses en cama. Y bueno, los síntomas eran un tanto similares a una gripe. Me sentía terriblemente cansada, con dolor de huesos, y apenas podía comer porque me producían náuseas el olor de la comida y el olor del tabaco. Entonces me fuí al médico y me mandó hacer unos análisis. Y bueno, yo quería no pensar que no existiera la probabilidad de tener hepatitis pero los analísis, uah, dieron resultado positivo y fue terrible. Eh, además tenía la cara completamente amarilla, todo el cuerpo, y el glóbulo ocular también estaba amarillo. Y sentía unos picores horribles, estuve como un mes rascándome y, más que nada, no es que sea una enfermedad grave ¿no?: tienes que tener mucho cuidado de no coger frío y de no tomar alimentos muy fuertes, porque puede repercutir en problemas mayores.

gripe (f.) flu	**amarillo** yellow
hueso (m.) bone	**cara** (f.) face
apenas hardly	**cuerpo** (m.) body

tuve una hepatitis bastante gorda I had a fairly serious attack of hepatitis. **Gordo** means fat if applied to people and big, important or serious if applied to things. **El premio gordo** the big prize.

♦ **me tuvo dos meses en cama** it kept me in bed for two months.

♦ **me producían náuseas el olor de la comida y el olor del tabaco** the smell of food and cigarettes made me feel sick. **Oler** means to smell: it's a very irregular, radical-changing verb most commonly used in the present: **huele a cebolla** it smells of onions.

♦ **me mandó hacer unos análisis** he sent me for some tests.

yo quería no pensar que no existiera la probabilidad de tener hepatitis I didn't want to think that I might have hepatitis (the subjunctive is used here because the outcome was uncertain). Marga has got into a muddle with her negatives. She should have said: **yo no quería pensar que existiera . . .**

el glóbulo ocular también estaba amarillo my eyeball was also yellow. Notice how Marga uses **el** and not **mi** to refer to parts of the body – **la cara, el cuerpo**.

estuve como un mes rascándome I spent about a month scratching myself. **Rascándome** is the present continuous tense (see page 17) and here it follows a verb in the preterite tense (**estuve**).

♦ **y más que nada, no es que sea una enfermedad grave** and after all (lit. more than anything) it's not that it's a serious illness. The subjunctive is used here because Marga has used a negative phrase, **no es que . . .**

tienes que tener mucho cuidado de no coger frío you must be very careful not to catch cold.

puede repercutir en problemas mayores it could lead to worse problems.

Trabajos prácticos

10 Here we have a typical sufferer from hepatitis! Can you fill in the symptoms, according to Marga's description in dialogue 4? (Answers on page 206.)

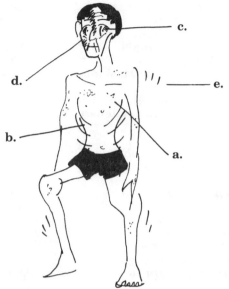

11 Answer the following questions in English on Marga's description of her illness. (Answers on page 206.)

a. If you've contracted hepatitis, what two things should you avoid?

i ....

ii ....

b. What two things made Marga feel sick?

i ....

ii ....

c. How long was Marga in bed? ....

d. What happened when Marga went to the doctor?

....

e. What did Marga not want to think about?

....

12 Here is the final speaking exercise in this section. You've just met a friend you haven't seen for a long time. She tells you she's been seriously ill. You ask her what happened. Follow Susan's prompts.

Giros importantes

Tengo un problema terrible con . . .

I've got a terrible problem with . . .

Hace ocho meses que me enteré

I found out eight months ago

Me encontraba agotada
         cansada

I felt worn out
    tired

Me dolía la cabeza
    la garganta

My head ached
My throat was sore

Fuí al médico

I went to the doctor

Tenía que seguir el tratamiento

I had to follow the treatment

¡Estás guapísima!

You look really lovely!

¿Qué haces para mantenerte así?

What do you do to keep yourself like that?

¡Huy bueno!

Well!

La verdad es que no hago mucho

The truth is I don't do much

Soy bastante ciudadosa con . . .

I am quite careful about . . .

Y eso

And so on

Un poco de ejercicio

A little exercise

de vez en cuando

from time to time

a veces

sometimes

no con much
    frecuencia

not very frequently

Voy a clases de yoga

I go to yoga classes

¿Practicas algún deporte?

Do you do any sports?

Dígame

Tell me

¿Me podría dar algo para . . .
    el dolor de cabeza?
    esta picadura de mosquito?

Could you give me anything for . . .
    a headache?
    this mosquito bite?

¿Tiene inflamación?
    picores?

Do you have any inflammation?
    itching?

Yo le aconsejaría pastillas
    pomada

I would recommend tablets
    cream

¿Anda bien del estómago?

Is your stomach all right?

Tres pastillas al día

Three tablets a day

¿Cómo hace las digestiones?

How is your digestion?

Tuve una hepatitis bastante gorda

I had a fairly serious bout of hepatitis

Me tuvo dos meses en cama

It kept me in bed for two months

Apenas podía comer (beber)

I could hardly eat (drink)

Me producía náuseas el olor de la comida (del tabaco)

The smell of food (cigarettes) made me feel sick

Me mandó hacer unos análisis

He sent me for some tests

Los análisis dieron resultado
    positivo
    negativo

The tests were
    positive
    negative

Más que nada

More than anything

Tienes que tener mucho ciudado de no coger frío

You've got to be very careful not to catch cold

Gramática

Imperfect tense

This tense is used in the following instances:

a. For habitual or repeated actions: **Nadaba todos los días** I used to swim every day.

b. For description in the past: **Nevaba y llovía constantemente** It snowed and rained constantly.

c. For events in the past that don't have a definite beginning or end: **Vivíamos en una casa grande en el campo** We lived (were living) in a large house in the country.

How to form the imperfect

There are two sets of endings – one set for **ar** verbs (**cantar**) and another for **er** and **ir** verbs (**vender**). Just add these to the verb stem.

cant **aba** I sang, I was singing

cant **abas** you sang, you were singing

cant **aba** s/he, you (**Vd.**) sang, were singing

cant **ábamos** we sang, we were singing

cant **ábais** you sang, you were singing

cant **aban** they, you (**Vds.**) sang, were singing

vend **ía** I sold, I was selling

vend **ías** you sold, you were selling

vend **ía** s/he, you (**Vd.**) sold, were selling

vend **íamos** we sold, we were selling

vend **íais** you sold, you were selling

vend **ían** they, you (**Vds.**) were selling

There are only three irregular verbs in the imperfect:
era (from **ser**) I was
iba (from **ir**) I went
veía (from **ver**) I saw

The preterite is the tense used for events or actions that are completely over and where there is a time limit. So:
Vivimos dos años en una casa grande en el campo We lived for two years in a large house in the country.

Now for some practice. What were you doing when you met an old friend?
¿Qué hacías cuando encontraste a un viejo amigo?

13 Insert the correct part of the verb below the picture. (Answers on page 206.)

a. tomar una copa en un café

b. ir a la oficina

c. recoger un coche

....

d. estar sentado en el autobús

e. estudiar en la biblioteca

....

....

f. bailar con José

....

g. vivir en París

....

....

Imperfect subjunctive

The imperfect subjunctive is formed by taking the ending **-ron** from the third person plural of the preterite and adding either of the two sets of endings below. This rule applies to all verbs, both regular and irregular.

Hablar to speak (third person plural preterite: **habla/ron**)

habla **ra**	hablá **ramos**	habla **se**	hablá **semos**
habla **ras**	habla **rais**	habla **ses**	habla **seis**
habla **ra**	habla **ran**	habla **se**	habla **sen**

The two versions are interchangeable and mean exactly the same, so be on the look-out for them. You don't need to learn them yet, but you should be able to recognise them.

The imperfect subjunctive is used in all the circumstances outlined for the present subjunctive in Unit 5, the only difference being that it follows a verb in the past tense. So:

Quiero que vengas temprano a clase I want you to come to class early. (present) but:
Quería que vinieras temprano a clase I wanted you to come to class early. (past).

14 Look carefully through this extract from a novel about a frail young man and underline any verb you think is in the subjunctive. Then try to work out why the subjunctive has been used in each case. Refer to Unit 5 if necessary. (Answers on page 206.)

Fue un adolescente frágil. Los médicos aconsejaron que no hiciera estudios, que no se cansara, y que si se casaba, que no tuviera hijos. Así que la familia se trasladó al sur de España para que el clima fuese mejor. Allí conoció a muchas señoritas sin que ninguna despertara en él mucho interés. No tardó en darse cuenta de que si quería conocer a una persona que valiera la pena, tendría que ir a otro sitio que fuera más popular. Así que fue finalmente a Madrid donde encontró a Maricarmen, mujer que le hubiera hecho feliz si no hubiese estado casada . . . .

Lectura

Here's a short article about what to do if you have an insect bite. It seems to recommend a very similar procedure to the chemist's: **una crema antialérgica y antiinflamatoria**: *a cream to prevent allergies and inflammation.*

> Las picaduras de insectos están al orden del día. Pero nunca recurra a los preparados caseros como el barro, aceites o vinagre. La solución es más sencilla.
>
> Se coge una pinza de depilar las cejas y con ella se quita el aguijón. Luego, se lava con agua y jabón, y por último, se pasa por la herida una crema antialérgica y antiinflamatoria. Si, al segundo día se observa que se ha formado un bultito amarillento, esto indica que la herida se ha infectado. Consulte, entonces, a su médico.
>
> El resto de las pequeñas picaduras se tratan con talco. Pero es mejor evitar la picadura con lociones repelentes.

recurrir to have recourse to
preparado (m.) preparation
casero household
barro (m.) mud
sencillo simple
pinza (f.) tweezers
depilar to pluck
ceja (f.) eyebrow

aguijón (m.) sting
herida (f.) wound
bulto (m.) lump
amarillento yellowish
evitar to avoid
loción repelente (f.) insect
    repellent

15 Here is a short exercise to test whether you really understood that advice: just tick the correct answer. (Answers on page 206.)

a. Which of these is not a household remedy?
- ☐ crema
- ☐ vinagre
- ☐ barro

b. What should you wash the bite with?
- ☐ aceite
- ☐ pomada
- ☐ agua y jabón

c. What should you use to take out the sting?
- ☐ talco
- ☐ pinza
- ☐ loción repelente

d. When should you become worried about infection?
- ☐ el primer día
- ☐ el segundo día
- ☐ el tercer día

Do you remember that the doctor said that Paqui should not drink any alcohol because of her blood pressure? The following article gives the same advice – alcohol can be dangerous in the summer. Read on to find out why.

No hay peor época para beber alcohol que el verano y la explicación es muy sencilla. Hay más sed, se bebe más, se pierde por transpiración el agua y así se concentra más el alcohol. De esa forma, la borrachera está asegurada.

Además el riñón trabaja más y retiene tóxicos con mayor facilidad. Una de las dolencias típicas de esta estación son los cálculos de riñón y sus consabidos ataques o cólicos. Para evitar estas molestias, nada mejor que el agua de cebada.

Se hierve, durante un largo rato, cebada de grano ligeramente tostado. Se machaca y se deja en maceración veinticuatro horas. Se añade azúcar de caña y, al servirla, zumo de limón.

época (f.) time
sed (f.) thirst
transpiración (f.) sweating
borrachera (f.) drunkenness
riñón (m.) kidney
retener to retain
dolencia (f.) pain
estación (f.) season

cálculos de riñón (m.pl.) kidney stones
consabido well known
molestia (f.) upset, annoyance
evitar to avoid
cebada (f.) barley
hervir (ie) to boil
machacar to grind
caña (f.) cane

16 Tick those things which, according to the article, occur frequently in the summer. (Answers on page 206.)

☐ you eat more   ☐ you drink more
☐ you sweat more   ☐ you are hungrier
☐ you are thirstier   ☐ you swim more
☐ you are more likely to get drunk
☐ you are more likely to get fat
☐ you are more likely to suffer from kidney problems

17 So what's the answer? A drink that's popular in England too: tick off the ingredients. (Answers on page 206.)

☐ maíz   ☐ zumo de naranja
☐ cebada perlada   ☐ azúcar de caña
☐ zumo de limón   ☐ cebada de grano
☐ granos de trigo   ☐ azúcar de remolacha

Radio

Our first radio extract is an advertisement – for one of those healthy, low-fat milks. Listen and see how much you understand. You'll need the following vocabulary. (Transcript on page 217.)

sentar (here) to suit
desnatado skimmed
alimentar to nourish

engordar to fatten
proteína (f.) protein
grasa (f.) fat

18 Listen to that advertisement once more and fill in the missing words. (Answers on page 206.)

En verano, ¡qué bien .... leche ....

.... La Polesa! ¡Leche ....

La Polesa! Te .... y no te ....

.... Leche .... La Polesa, con todas

las .... pero sin ....

¡La Polesa! La leche de ....

Radio Asturias Cadena SER has a programme that features a doctor who believes in natural herbs and remedies. A lot of listeners seem to agree with him, judging from the amount of interest and number of phone calls. (Transcript on page 217.) To complete exercise 19 you will need the following vocabulary.

edad (f.) age
mantener (ie) to maintain
pretender to try
por lo tanto therefore
deber de must
verduras (f.pl.) green vegetables

contraindicado contra-indicated
alimento (m.) food
frito fried
cerdo (m.) pig, pork
recurrir to have recourse to
crudo raw

19 Fill in the diet sheet for the old lady. What foods is she allowed, and what must she avoid? (Answers on page 206.)

María Eugenia Martínez ....Edad ....

Problema principal ....

No se puede .... sino .... el organismo.

Dieta a base de .... y ....

Alimentos indicados ....

....

....

Alimentos contraindicados ....

....

....

....

Te toca a tí hablar

20 Describe your diet. Do you try to eat healthy foods or do you just eat what you like? Then listen to Pepe telling you what sort of things he eats – and what he tries to avoid.

7 El día de la raza

What you will learn

- something about Spanish **proverbs**
- an introduction to the game of **pelota**
- some differences between European and Latin American Spanish
- ... and the significance of certain Latin **gestures**!

Study guide

Diálogo 1
Refranes españoles

Marga ¿Hay algún refrán español que sueles utilizar a menudo? y ¿qué significa?

Eduardo Díme con quien andas y te diré quien eres: con lo cual demostramos que, o sea, seleccionamos las compañías según nuestros gustos.

Jorge Bueno, te puedo decir uno que es que cuando las barbas de tu vecino veas pelar, pon las tuyas a remojar – que cuando veas que algo le pasa a tu compañero, procura no hacer lo mismo para que no te pase.

Pilar Pues sí, tengo uno asturiano que dice, la mujer y la sardina, cuanto más pequeña más sabrosina: que la sardina, cuanto más pequeña más rica es.

Araceli Bueno, pues, la mujer y la sartén en la cocina están bien – pues que como la sartén es para la cocina, la mujer, una vez que está casada, ¡en la cocina y a hacer sus cosas!

Ismael Hay un refrán asturiano que dice: hasta el cuarenta de mayo, no te quites el sayo.

Manolo En trece y martes, ni te cases ni te embarques, porque te puede salir mal.

refrán (m.) proverb
utilizar to use
♦ **a menudo** often
demostrar (ue) to show
seleccionar to choose
♦ **según** according to
gusto (m.) taste

compañero (m.) friend
rico (m.) rich, delicious
sartén (f.) frying pan
cocina (f.) kitchen
casado married
sayo (m.) tunic

Díme con quien andas y te diré quien eres Tell me you who your friends are and I'll tell you who you are (lit. tell me with whom you walk and I will tell you who you are). For more about familiar commands, see page 66. (Polite commands are dealt with on page 113.)

cuando las barbas de tu vecino veas pelar, pon las tuyas a remojar when you see your neighbour's beard falling out, put yours in to soak!

procura no hacer lo mismo para que no te pase try not to do the same so that it doesn't happen to you.

tengo uno asturiano I have an Asturian one (a proverb).

♦ **cuanto más pequeña más sabrosina** the smaller, the tastier (**ino** is the Asturian diminutive form; the root word is **sabroso**, tasty).

hasta el cuarenta de mayo, no te quites el sayo don't cast a clout till May is out (lit. until the 40th of May, don't take off your tunic). Ismael's interpretation of this is that the 40th of May should be the 10th of June, by which time summer has begun and Asturians can take off their overcoats!

en trece y martes, ni te cases ni te embarques on the 13th and on a Tuesday, don't get married, nor set sail. (13 is an unlucky number and Tuesday is traditionally an unlucky day in Spain.)

Trabajos prácticos

1 Here are some Spanish proverbs with their English equivalents – but they are not in the right order. See if you can match them. (Answers on page 206.)

a. Caer de la sartén al fuego   ☐ Better late than never

b. El hombre propone, pero Dios dispone   ☐ All that glisters is not gold

c. No se ganó Zamora en una hora   ☐ To fall out of the frying pan into the fire

d. Más vale pájaro en mano que ciento volando   ☐ Man proposes, God disposes

e. No todo lo blanco es harina   ☐ A bird in the hand is worth two in the bush

f. Más vale tarde que nunca   ☐ Rome was not built in a day

2 Complete the following Spanish proverb: – – – – – – – – – **tiene su pareja** by filling in the answers below. The first letter of each answer will spell out the two words you are looking for. Most of the clues come from the dialogue you've just listened to. And one more pointer – the second word rhymes with **pareja**. (Answers on page 206.)

a. Amigo ☐...................................

b. Provincia en el norte de España ☐...................................

c. Te ☐................................... quien eres.

d. Díme con quien ☐...................................

e. En la c-cina. ☐...................................

f. Persona que vive cerca de tí ☐...................................

g. No te cases, ni te ☐...................................

h. Décima letra del alfabeto ☐...................................

i. ¿Hay ☐................................... refrán español?

3 You know that Spaniards are very fond of quoting proverbs. Ask Pepe what some of them mean. Susan will prompt you in English.

Diálogo 2
¿Tú eres un bebé?

Marga	Si es que el otro día, iba en el coche y me pasó una cosa curiosa.
Gustavo	¿En el coche? y ¿es que tú eres un bebé, Marga?
Marga	¿Por?
Gustavo	Porque nosotros usamos la palabra 'coche' para, para el cochecito del bebé.
Marga	¡Ah no! Pues nosotros, en España, usamos la palabra 'coche' bien para el coche del niño o para los coches que utilizamos nosotros para conducir.
Gustavo	Quieres decir el carro entonces.
Marga	¿El carro?
Claudia	Es que las diferencias de vocabulario entre España y Latinoamérica son hartas, ¿no?
Marga	Bueno, sí, eso parece, pero nosotros en cambio, utilizamos la palabra carro, para no sé, el utensilio que utiliza el campesino, el agricultor, para sus trabajos. Y es un tanto extraño oír carro en lugar de coche.
Gustavo	Sí, nosotros tenemos también una diferencia muy importante y es que no usamos el vosotros, que vosotros sí lo usáis.
Todos	Ja, ja, ja, ja . . .

curioso odd, strange	**utensilio** (m.) implement
palabra (f.) word	**campesino** (m.) peasant
conducir to drive	**agricultor** (m.) farmer
▶ **en cambio** on the other hand	▶ **en lugar de** instead of

es que el otro día iba . . . the other day I was going . . . **Es que** is not really necessary here, but it introduces and emphasizes a topic.

un bebé the word **bebé** is always masculine, whether it's a girl or boy.

¿Por? is a shorthand way of saying **¿'por qué?'**.

cochecito (m.) is a pram; **sillita** (f.) a pushchair: a good example of how diminutives are used in Spanish where in English we use a completely different word.

bien para . . . o para . . . either for . . . or for . . . **Bien para tí o para tu hermano** Either for you or for your brother.

▶ **Quieres decir** You mean (lit. you want to say): **¿qué quiere decir esto?** and **¿qué significa esto?** what does this mean?

Las diferencias . . . son hartas, ¿no? the differences are many, aren't they? This is a good example of the differences between Castilian and Latin American Spanish. In Spain, it's more usual to say, **hay muchas diferencias**: **harto** is usually used for full (of food): **estoy harto** I am full, or **estoy harta de tus impertinencias,** I've had enough of your impertinence.

Y es un tanto extraño oír carro en lugar de coche And it's a bit strange to hear **carro** instead of **coche**.

no usamos el vosotros we don't use the **vosotros** form. The plural of **tú** doesn't exist in Latin America: you must use **ustedes** instead, even when talking to children and friends.

Trabajos prácticos

4 Who is speaking in these examples, a Spaniard or a Latin American?
(Answers on page 206.)

	Spaniard	Latin American
a. Ustedes tienen que obedecer a su mamá ¿no es cierto?	☐	☐
b. Estuve en el carro cuando me di cuenta de que no había echado la carta de mi marido . . .	☐	☐
c. Son hartas las diferencias entre España y Colombia, ¿verdad?	☐	☐
d. Tenía a Marta en el cochecito porque hacía un tiempo estupendo y le encanta estar fuera.	☐	☐
e. Es muy difícil ir de compras, cargada con bolsas y con la niña y la sillita también.	☐	☐

5 Can you guess the 'odd man out' in these groups of three? (Answers on page 206.)

vosotros ☐   campesino ☐
ustedes ☐   ciudadano ☐
nosotros ☐   agricultor ☐

cochecito ☐   extraño ☐
carro ☐   importante ☐
sillita ☐   curioso ☐

usar ☐
oír ☐
utilizar ☐

6 You will now hear a number of questions on tape based on dialogue 2. Pick out the answers printed here that best fit the questions. Remember to say them out loud! (Answers on page 206.)

a. La diferencia más importante es que en América no existe el 'vosotros'. Cuando hablan a los niños, tienen que tratarles de 'ustedes'. Es curioso, ¿no?

b. Un carro es un utensilio del campesino, que usa para el trabajo del campo.

c. Sí, hay muchas, sobre todo con respecto a vocabulario.

d. En España usamos las palabras 'cochecito de bebé' y en América se usa 'coche' solamente.

e. Sí, es cierto. En España se conduce un coche y no un carro.

Diálogo 3
Una especie de tenis contra el frontón

Marga Oye, Rafa, me han dicho que juegas pelota. ¿En qué consiste este juego?

Rafa Juego a pelota, a pala, sí, algunas veces.

Marga Pero ¿De qué se trata? ¿Un juego individual, o es un juego entre equipos?

Rafa Sí, bueno, normalmente nadie juega solo a pala. Como mínimo jugamos dos, pero lo más extendido es jugar dos contra dos, dos equipos.

Marga ¿Y qué necesitas para jugar a pala?

Rafa Pues, necesitamos un frontón, necesitamos la pala, y necesitamos la pelota.

Marga ¿Y qué es: a base de puntos o . . . ?

Rafa Sí, el tanteo es muy similar en todos los juegos de pala, normalmente a veintiún puntos y entonces, bueno, pues, es una especie de tenis contra el frontón.

Marga ¿Y hay varios tipos de pala, o solamente existe una modalidad?

Rafa No, existen más. No es la cesta punta, son con unas palas de madera y allí existen dos variedades, pala corta y pala larga.

juego (m.) game
pala (f.) bat
entre between
equipo (m.) team
▶ **nadie** nobody
necesitar to need
pelota (f.) ball
punto (m.) point
tanteo (m.) scoring
especie (f.) sort
contra against

modalidad (f.) variety
madera (f.) wood
corto short
largo long

la cesta punta

Oye, Rafa, me han dicho que juegas pelota Hey, Rafa, they tell me you play pelota. **Oye** (listen!) is the familiar command from **oír**, to hear. More about commands on pages 66 and 113.

Juego a pelota, a pala, sí, algunas veces Pelota is the national game in the Basque country (it's known as jai'alai in the United States). It can be played with a sort of basket hooked on to the arm (**cesta punta**) or with a bat (**pala**). **Pelota** actually means ball.

▶ **¿de qué se trata?** what's it all about? A good phrase if you want to ask about the plot of a film or a novel, for instance.

▶ **Como mínimo jugamos dos** at least two of us play. Notice that Rafa includes himself, which is why he uses the **nosotros** form.

▶ **lo más extendido** the usual thing, the most common. **Lo** is the neuter form if you are talking about a thing in general.

necesitamos un frontón we need a court. A **frontón** consists of two high walls which form an angle. Children often play against the church walls and you may see the sign **prohibido jugar a pelota** on buildings that look suitable for pelota.

pala corta y pala larga Within the type of pelota played with a bat, there are two other kinds – one played with a short-handled bat (**pala corta**) and the other with a longer handle (**pala larga**).

Trabajos prácticos

7 Here are the Spanish words for a few more sports: **ciclismo** (cycling); **fútbol** (football); **baloncesto** (basketball); **natación** (swimming). Look at the following items and name the sports for which they are required. (Answers on page 206.)

a. un frontón; una pelota; una pala ....

b. una raqueta; una pista; una pelota ....

c. una bicicleta; una carretera; frenos ....

d. unas botas; un balón; un portero ....

e. un bañador; el agua; una piscina ....

8 Several sports personalities are talking about who they are and what they do. Can you guess who they are? (Answers on page 206.)

a. Juego al golf: soy campeón del mundo y he ganado torneos en todo el mundo. Soy español, del norte de España, de Cantabria.

b. Soy inglesa, de una familia muy distinguida. Lo que más me gustan son los caballos y he participado en los juegos olímpicos varias veces.

c. Soy boxeador, 'el mejor del mundo'. Soy negro: me he cambiado de nombre.

d. Soy tenista. He estado casada con otro, que es inglés, pero yo soy americana. He ganado gran cantidad de torneos por todo el mundo.

e. Yo también soy tenista pero de Suecia. Me retiré hace unos años después de una carrera brillante.

la pala corta

9 On tape you will hear a slightly modified version of dialogue 3. Take Marga's part and ask Pepe all about the traditional game of pelota.

Diálogo 4
¿Puedes describir un gesto típicamente latino?

Carmen   Hum, sí, cuando se hace así, que es poniendo la mano hacia arriba, y haciendo movimientos intermitentes, de unir y separar los dedos, los cuatro dedos juntos contra el dedo gordo. Eso significa que hay mucha gente, que un sitio está lleno de gente.

Andrés   Mover la mano de arriba para abajo, golpeando los dedos. Esto significa gran cantidad de algo, mucho, demasiado.

Marga   Sí, por ejemplo, para decir que una cosa te gusta mucho, sueles acercar la mano con los dedos unidos hacia la boca, sueltas un beso y en el momento que das un beso, alejas la mano.

Daniel   Hay varios gestos, uno de ellos es poner la mano unos treinta centímetros sobre la cabeza. El significado de esto es decir me tienen hasta acá arriba, en la coronilla.

Verónica   Por ejemplo, para preguntar a alguna persona que está en una feria, vendiendo algo, cuánto cuesta, uno coloca tres dedos juntos y los roza, uno con otro, diciendo ¿cuánto vale?

unir to bring together	**acercar** to bring close
dedo (m.) finger	**alejar** to take away
junto together	**gesto** (m.) gesture
▶ **dedo gordo** thumb	**significado** (m.) meaning
golpear to knock, snap	**feria** (f.) fair, market
algo something	**colocar** to place
demasiado too much	**rozar** to rub

cuando se hace así when you do this (**así** like this).

▶ **Hacia arriba** upwards, **hacia abajo** downwards. **Hacia** means towards.

de unir y separar los dedos bringing together and separating the fingers. A verb following the preposition **de** will be in the infinitive.

▶ **de arriba para abajo** up and down, **de un lado para otro** from one place (side) to another.

gran cantidad de algo a large quantity of something. **Grande** is shortened to **gran** if placed before a singular noun, either masculine or feminine. (**Gran** placed in front of the noun often means great in the sense of distinguished: **un gran señor**, a great gentleman.) Otherwise, **grande** remains unchanged, whether qualifying a masculine or feminine noun: **una cantidad grande de gente** a large number of people.

sueltas un beso you blow a kiss. The verb **soltar** to let go is a radical-changing one.

das un beso you give a kiss. You can also use **besar** (to kiss).

alejar and **acercar** are opposites: by breaking words down into their component parts you can often guess the meanings quite accurately. **Lejos** far; **cerca** near.

▶ **¿cuánto cuesta? ¿cuánto vale?** How much does it cost? How much is it worth? These are more or less interchangeable.

Trabajos prácticos

10 Here are some pictures to illustrate a few of those gestures you've just heard about in dialogue 4. What do they mean? For good measure, a couple of new ones have been thrown in. One means **está perfecto** (it's perfect), the other **¡tiene una cara!** (what a cheek!). Identify the appropriate gestures, explaining what they mean in Spanish. (Answers on page 207.)

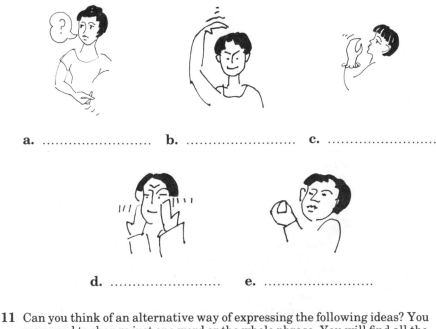

a. .... **b.** .... **c.** ....

d. .... **e.** ....

11 Can you think of an alternative way of expressing the following ideas? You may need to change just one word or the whole phrase. You will find all the alternatives in dialogue 4. (Answers on page 207.)

a. Sueltas un beso. ....

b. Me tienen hasta la coronilla. ....

c. El sitio está lleno de gente. ....

d. Los dedos juntos. ....

e. ¿Cuánto cuesta? ....

f. Mucho de algo. ....

 12 Now we'd like you to ask Pepe about that body language you see so much of in Spain and Latin America. What does it all mean? Susan will prompt you in English.

Giros importantes

¿Qué significa?	What does it mean?
O sea	That's to say
Cuánto más pequeña, más sabrosina	The smaller, the tastier
Hay un refrán que dice ...	There is a proverb that says ...
Es que el otro día	The fact is, the other day
Nosotros usamos la palabra 'coche' para ...	We use the word 'coche' for ...
Bien para ... o para ...	Either for ... or for ...
Quieres decir	You mean (to say)
En cambio	On the other hand
Es un tanto extraño oír ...	It's a bit strange to hear ...
Oye, me han dicho que ...	Hey, I hear that ...
Juego a pelota	I play pelota
¿De qué se trata?	What's it all about?
Como mínimo	At least
Como máximo	At most
Lo más extendido	The usual thing
¿Hay varios tipos de pala?	Are there several kinds of bat?
Cuando se hace así	When you do this
Hacia arriba	Upwards
Hacia abajo	Downwards
De arriba para abajo	Up and down
Dar un beso	To give a kiss
Me tienen hasta la coronilla	I've had it up to here
¿Cuánto cuesta?	How much does it cost?
¿Cuánto vale?	

Gramática

Formal (or polite) commands

Familiar commands with **tú** and **vosotros** are dealt with in Unit 4. In this unit we introduce polite commands with **usted** and **ustedes**. You'll need to use these forms of the verb in shops (**déme un kilo de tomates**, give me a kilo of tomatoes) or in restaurants (**traiga la cuenta**, bring the bill). You will also need to understand them in receiving directions (**suba esta calle**, go up this street, **cruce la plaza**, cross the square) and when reading official notices.

Polite commands are formed in the same way as the present subjunctive: take the first person singular of the present tense.
Remove the **o** and add an **e** if the verb ends in **ar** (**hable**);
     add an **a** if the verb ends in **ir** or **er** (**coma; escriba**).
If you're addressing more than one person, add a final **-n** (**hablen, coman, escriban**).

If you're telling people not to do something, use **no** in front of the verb (**no hablen**, don't speak).

If the command is positive and has pronouns attached, these come after the verb (**hábleme**, speak to me; **démelo**, give it to me).

If the command is negative, the pronouns stay in front of the verb (**no me hable**, don't speak to me; **no me lo dé**, don't give it to me).

13 The following notice appeared at a camp site. Work out what it means. (Answers on page 207.)

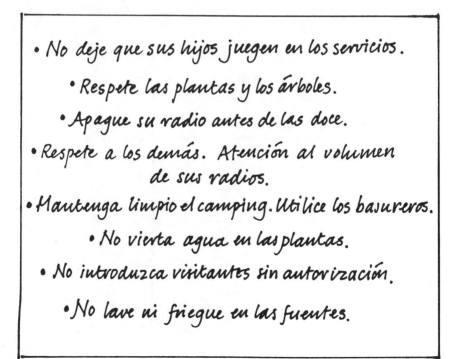

- No deje que sus hijos juegen en los servicios.
- Respete las plantas y los árboles.
- Apague su radio antes de las doce.
- Respete a los demás. Atención al volumen de sus radios.
- Mantenga limpio el camping. Utilice los basureros.
- No vierta agua en las plantas.
- No introduzca visitantes sin autorización.
- No lave ni friegue en las fuentes.

Negatives

In dialogue 4 Rafa said: **nadie juega solo a pala**, nobody plays **pala** by themselves. Let's look at some more uses of the negative.

- A simple negative is formed by placing **no** in front of the verb: **no están aquí** they aren't here.
  In most cases, you still keep the **no** before the verb if you are using another negative word such as **nunca** (never) or **nadie** (nobody):
  No voy nunca a esa tienda I never go to that shop.
  But you can drop the **no** and replace it in front of the verb with **nunca**, **nadie** etc if you want to emphasize the negative aspect:
  nunca voy a esa tienda I *never* go to that shop.

- **Ni ... ni** neither ... nor
  No me gusta ni este vestido ni el otro I like neither this dress nor the other one (or: I don't like [either] this dress or the other one).
  In English, we frequently drop the 'either', but it would be incorrect to drop the first **ni** in Spanish.

- **Ninguno** drops its final **o** if it immediately precedes a masculine noun:
  Ningún chico llegó con retraso Not a single boy arrived late. Again, this is for emphasis. Otherwise, you would say:
  No llegó con retraso ninguno No one arrived late.

14 Now for some practice. Answer these questions by using the negatives you've just learned. (Answers on page 207.)

a. ¿Vas a veces al cine? (Use **nunca**) ....

b. ¿Alguien me llamó? ....

c. ¿Estás listo para salir? ....

d. ¿Viste a tu padre o a tu hermana? (Use **ni . . . ni**) ....

e. ¿Cual de las blusas quieres? (Use **ninguna**) ....

f. ¿Tienes algo en la mano, hijo? ....

Here are three proverbs. Can you work out what they mean? (Answers on page 207.)

g. Nada creas hasta que lo veas.

....

h. Nadie sabe lo que vale el agua hasta que falte.

....

i. Ninguno nace enseñado.

....

Lectura

Now for another sport – **la vela** (sailing). It's very popular in Spain, especially in the North. This newspaper article is about a race held off the coast of Asturias.

VELA
Ganó el 'Siete Villas'

Luanco

La embarcación 'Siete Villas' ganó ayer la tercera etapa de la 1 Regata cruceros 'Principado de Asturias', Ribadesella-Luanco. La etapa, con un recorrido de 32 millas, fue dura debido a las tormentas que hubo a media tarde y que las padecieron la gran mayoría de las embarcaciones.

El first-class 10 'La Luna' de Juan Luis Tuero que entró a tres minutos del primer clasificado, hizo una reclamación al comité de protestas por la utilización de motor por parte del 'Siete Villas' desde la llamada de atención hasta la línea de salida en Ribadesella. Si esta reclamación se considera, la primera plaza sería para 'La Luna'.

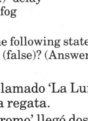

El 'Asturcromo' de José Díaz llegó con casi dos horas de retraso sobre el 'Siete Villas'. Esta embarcación tuvo muchos problemas debido a la niebla y al temporal, le rompieron los sables de las velas y en Candás no encontró la baliza y tuvo que dar la vuelta.

El resto de las embarcaciones llegaron al puerto de Luanco con un retraso de más de cuatro horas. La etapa fue dura desde el inicio, con una encalmada de más de dos horas y después se levantó un nordeste flojo y al final de la etapa, padecieron una gran tormenta en la que hubo descargas eléctricas que afectaron las comunicaciones de algunas embarcaciones y obligó a retirarse a más de diez veleros.

embarcación (f.) boat	**temporal** (f.) storm
ganar to win	**romper** to break
crucero (m.) cruiser	**sable** (m.) mast
recorrido (m.) circuit	**vela** (f.) sail
debido a owing to	**baliza** (f.) buoy
tormenta (f.) storm	**dar la vuelta** to turn round
padecer to suffer	**inicio** (m.) beginning
reclamación (f.) complaint	**nordeste** (m.) northeast wind
llamada (f.) call	**flojo** light
retraso (m.) delay	**descarga** (f.) discharge
niebla (f.) fog	**velero** (m.) yacht

15 Which of the following statements about that sailing race are **verdad** (true) or **mentira** (false)? (Answers on page 207.)

<table>
<tr><td></td><td></td><td>verdad</td><td>mentira</td></tr>
<tr><td>a.</td><td>El velero llamado 'La Luna' ganó la tercera etapa de la regata.</td><td>☐</td><td>☐</td></tr>
<tr><td>b.</td><td>El 'Asturcromo' llegó dos horas más tarde que el 'Siete Villas'.</td><td>☐</td><td>☐</td></tr>
<tr><td>c.</td><td>El tiempo era ideal para una regata.</td><td>☐</td><td>☐</td></tr>
<tr><td>d.</td><td>'La Luna' protestó contra la acción del 'Siete Villas'.</td><td>☐</td><td>☐</td></tr>
<tr><td>e.</td><td>El recorrido de la regata era de unas 32 millas.</td><td>☐</td><td>☐</td></tr>
<tr><td>f.</td><td>Se levantó un nordeste.</td><td>☐</td><td>☐</td></tr>
</table>

The next reading passage is about bulls and fiestas in Zamora.

El juego con el toro sigue siendo la base principal en muchas fiestas veraniegas. En Fermoselle (Zamora) del 19 al 27, se celebran sus renombradas ferias de San Agustín con encierros, novilladas, bailes populares y meriendas toreras, en las que nunca faltan los riquísimos asados a la parrilla. En Toro, en la misma provincia, a partir del día 18 son también las ferias y fiestas de San Agustín en las que habrá encierros, corridas, un gracioso y original desfile de carrozas y una fuente del vino para mojar los gaznates, manando a todas horas, el vino de la tierra.

El mismo día 18, se inician los festejos de la Semana Grande en Bilbao en la que habrá de todo: verbenas, jazz, cine, teatro, partidos de pelota, juegos infantiles, gigantes y cabezudos, vaquillas en el Casco Viejo y corridas en Vista Alegre, todo ello aderezado con fuegos artificiales y con el triquitraque de los toros de cohetes.

veraniego summer
renombrado famous
feria (f.) fair, market
encierro (m.) penning (of bulls)
novillada (f.) fight with young bulls
merienda (f.) picnic, snack
parrilla (f.) grill
gracioso graceful, funny
desfile (m.) procession
carroza (f.) wagon
fuente (f.) fountain
mojar el gaznate to whet your whistle

manar to flow
festejos (m.pl.) festivities
verbena (f.) open-air dance
gigante (m.) giant
cabezudo (m.) carnival figure with big head
aderezado embellished
fuegos artificiales (m.pl.) fireworks
triquitraque (m.) crack, swish
toro de cohete (m.) firework

16 Now look at this poster and fill in the blanks. (Answers on page 207.)

EL DIA ....

EN ....

VERBENAS, JAZZ, CINE
GIGANTES Y

....

CORRIDAS EN ....

JUEGOS ....

FUEGOS ....

TOROS DE ....

¡VENGAN TODOS A

PASARLO BIEN!

Radio

El décimoquinto certamen del queso de Cabrales (the 15th Cabrales cheese competition) is the subject of our radio extract. Can you find out what happened in Arenas de Cabrales? (Transcript on page 218.)

repartir to distribute
gratuitamente free, without charge
el pregón (m.) announcement
correr a cargo to be the
   responsibility of

seguidamente afterwards
rendir (i) homenaje to honour
pastora (f.) shepherdess
contar (ue) con to have, to count on

17 Answer the following questions in English. (Answers on page 207.)

a. What was distributed in Arenas de Cabrales?

....

b. And how many?

....

c. What was Eduardo Méndez Riestra's job?

....

d. What is Domitila Campillo Martínez's chief claim to fame?

....

e. Where is she from?

....

f. Where do the people come from who attend the competition?

....

Te toca a tí hablar

 18 Are you proud of the way you speak? Do you like a Scottish or an Irish brogue or a Welsh lilt? Say what you can about the different accents and vocabulary of the British Isles; then Pepe will tell you how different the Spanish spoken in the Canary islands sounds from mainland Spanish.

Bailes regionales, Oviedo

8 Día de mucho, víspera de poco

What you will learn

- how to talk about your **holidays**
- something about **winter sports**
- how to book a day excursion

... and what's worth visiting in **Asturias**

Picos de Europa

Study guide

Diálogo 1
¿Estuvistéis de vacaciones?

Ventura	¿Estuvistéis de vacaciones el año pasado?
Araceli	Sí, estuve unos días en el mes de julio.
Ventura	¿Y adónde habéis estado?
Araceli	Fuimos a Bilbao, pasamos por Zaragoza y llegamos a Barcelona.
Ventura	¿Llevaste a tus hijos contigo?
Araceli	No, fuimos mi marido y yo y un matrimonio, amigos nuestros.
Ventura	Y en Barcelona ¿cómo os ha parecido la ciudad?
Araceli	Bueno, me ha parecido muy grande y muy ruidosa, pero bueno, me gustó, es algo distinto a lo que estoy habituada aquí.
Ventura	Y el clima ¿os ha parecido estupendo?
Araceli	A mí sí, porque me gusta el calor y reconozco que hacía mucho calor, muy sofocante pero a mí me gusta el calor.
Ventura	¿Y allí tenéis algunos amigos?
Araceli	Sí, tenemos dos amigos y una noche fuimos a cenar con uno de ellos.
Ventura	¿Y cuántos días habéis estado allí en Barcelona?
Araceli	Dos, porque tuvimos que venir por urgencias.
Ventura	¿Y marchasteis con pena de Barcelona?
Araceli	Yo sí, yo hubiera quedado por el clima precisamente.

▶ **matrimonio** (m.) married couple
ruidoso noisy

clima (m.) climate
estupendo marvellous

▶ **¿Estuvisteis de vacaciones el año pasado?** Did you go on holiday last year? Notice that Ventura does not use the verb **ir** to go, but **estar** to be.
¿En qué hotel estuviste? Which hotel did you stay in?

unos días a few days.

adonde is used here rather than **donde** because it includes the idea of movement towards a place.

▶ **¿Llevaste a tus hijos contigo?** Did you take your children with you?

¿Cómo os ha parecido la ciudad? What did you think of the city? Spanish likes to use an impersonal construction here. (Lit. how did the city appear to you?).

es algo distinto a lo que estoy habituada aquí: it's a bit different from what I'm used to here (lit. different from that which . . .).

reconozco que hacía mucho calor, muy sofocante. I admit that it was very hot, really suffocating.

Dos, porque tuvimos que venir por urgencias. Two, because we had to come back because of an emergency.

▶ **¿Y marchasteis con pena de Barcelona?** And were you sorry to leave Barcelona? (lit. did you go away with sorrow from Barcelona?).

yo hubiera quedado por el clima precisamente I would have stayed simply because of the weather.

Trabajos prácticos

1 This is a question and answer dialogue, so listen to the extract once more and then answer Ventura's (modified) questions. Remember to use the same tense as he uses, and to answer in the **yo** form. (Answers on page 207.)

a. ¿Estuviste de vacaciones el año pasado? ....

b. ¿Adónde fuiste? ....

c. ¿Con quién fuiste? ....

d. ¿Cómo te ha parecido la ciudad de Barcelona? ....

e. ¿Cómo te ha parecido el clima de Cataluña? ....

f. ¿Tienes amigos en Barcelona? ....

g. ¿Cuántos días has estado en Barcelona? ....

h. ¿Marchaste con pena de Barcelona? ....

2 And now you ask the questions. Imagine you're on a beach on the Costa del Sol and you strike up a conversation with a fellow sunbather. We'll give the questions in English for you to translate, and the replies in Spanish. Remember you're only talking to one person so the verb endings will be singular. (Answers on page 207.)

a. Did you go on holiday last year? ....

Sí, estuve en Marbella durante el mes de agosto.

b. And did you take your children with you? ....

Sí, estuvimos toda la familia, cuatro hijos, mi marido y yo.

c. And what did you think of Marbella? ....

Me ha parecido preciosa, me encanta la gente elegante.

d. And the climate? ....

El clima es estupendo, hace mucho calor y a mí me encanta el sol . . .

e. Do you have any friends there? ....

No, es la primera vez que hemos estado pero conocimos a un matrimonio y pasamos mucho tiempo con ellos.

f. How many days were you there? ....

Quince días solamente, me hubiera quedado pero ¡se nos terminó el dinero!

3 Now practise that question and answer routine orally, by replying to Pepe's questions on the tape and following Susan's prompts.

Diálogo 2
La gente es fantástica

Rio de Janeiro

Ismael   Los agentes de viajes tenemos una gran facilidad para efectuar
viajes transatlánticos alrededor del mundo, y entre ellos yo he
conocido, pues, Brasil, Argentina, Rio de Janeiro, Santo Domingo
hace poco . . . Entonces, considero que dentro de estos países
sudamericanos que acabo de conocer en un plazo de un año,
considero que el más bonito para mí, a mi entender, como paisaje y
como amabilidad de la gente, y como encantadores que son,
considero que es Rio de Janeiro. Rio de Janeiro es una ciudad
preciosa, tiene unos encantos naturales fenomenales y aparte de eso,
la gente, como he dicho antes, es fantástica. Es una gente muy
agradable, y luego para el español, tiene un funcionamiento de vida
bastante económico para nosotros que considero que es interesante
hacer unas vacaciones allí.

dentro within	**amabilidad** (f.) friendliness
plazo (m.) period	**encantador** charming
paisaje (m.) countryside	**precioso** beautiful

**Los agentes de viajes tenemos una gran facilidad para efectuar
viajes transatlánticos** We travel agents can very easily undertake
transatlantic journeys. Notice that Ismael counts himself in as one of the
travel agents so he uses the **nosotros** form.

alrededor del mundo around the world.

▶ **yo he conocido . . .** I've been to . . . Although **conocer** means to know, in
this context it means that Ismael has visited these countries.

▶ **los países sudamericanos que acabo de conocer** the South American
countries I've just been to (become acquainted with). **Acabar de** means 'to
have just done' something. More about this on page 130. Rio de Janeiro and
Santo Domingo are not, of course, countries but the capitals of Brazil and
the Dominican Republic respectively.

▶ **a mi entender** in my opinion.

unos encantos naturales fenomenales some wonderful natural charms.

un funcionamiento de vida bastante económico a fairly economic way
of living. The more normal way of expressing this would be **un costo de
vida bastante económico**, a fairly economical cost of living.

▶ **considero que es interesante hacer unas vacaciones allí.** I think it's
worthwhile going on holiday there. **Interesante** means interesting too, but
in the context of prices, it means something is good value.

Trabajos prácticos

4 A lot of places in South, Central and North America were named by Spanish settlers in the 16th and 17th centuries. Match the names and their English equivalents in this exercise. (Answers on page 207.)

Colorado	the angels
Nevada	big river
Rio Tinto	snowy
Florida	red
Los Angeles	red river
Las Vegas	silver river
Rio de la Plata	holy faith
Rio Grande	the plains
Santa Fe	flowery

5 Ismael really knows how to sell a product! Look at all those adjectives which describe how marvellous the people and places are in Latin America. In the following exercise try to remember how Ismael described Brazil, without looking at the transcript. (Answers on page 207.)

a. Rio de Janeiro es una ciudad ....

b. Tiene unos encantos naturales ....

c. La gente es ....

d. Rio de Janeiro es el más .... para mí.

e. La gente es ....

f. El funcionamiento de vida es bastante ....

g. Considero que es .... hacer unas vacaciones allí.

6 By now, you're really keen to go to Latin America for your holidays. Ask your local travel agent whether he or she would recommend it. Susan will prompt you in English.

A street market in Salvador

Diálogo 3
Los deportes de nieve

Marga ¿Se puede practicar deportes de invierno en Asturias?

Sr Monge Por supuesto que sí. En Asturias se puede practicar una gama muy variada y completa de deportes. Por ejemplo, la temporada de pesca del salmón en nuestros ríos asturianos, y si se refiere usted concretamente a los deportes blancos, tenemos dos estaciones de invierno, una en San Isidro y otra en Pajares, donde se puede practicar el esquí y todos los deportes de nieve. Y para los aficionados a la montaña, tenemos uno de los colosos más difíciles de escalar de toda España, que es el famoso Naranjo de Bulnes, con una pared vertical de seiscientos metros que se ha convertido en uno de los grandes mitos de los montañeros no sólo de España, sino de todo el mundo.

gama (f.) range	**pared** (f.) wall
temporada (f.) season	**convertirse (i)** to become
pesca (f.) fishing	**mito** (m.) myth
río (m.) river	**montañero** (m.) mountaineer
esquí (m.) skiing	

¿Se puede practicar deportes de invierno? Can you practise winter sports?

▶ **Por supuesto que sí** Of course. **Por supuesto que no** Of course not.

si se refiere usted concretamente a los deportes blancos if you are referring specifically to winter sports (lit. white sports. The use of **blancos** is rather unusual; **deportes de nieve**, snow sports, is more usual). Use **me refiero a** for I mean – **me refiero a Ana**, I mean Ana.

tenemos dos estaciones de invierno we have two winter resorts. As well as meaning resort, **estación** can also mean a train or bus station and a season of the year. Apart from **invierno**, winter, the other **estaciones** are: **primavera**, spring, **verano**, summer and **otoño**, autumn.

▶ **para los aficionados a la montaña** for those who like mountains. An **aficionado** is a fan or enthusiast: **un aficionado a los toros**, a bull-fighting enthusiast. Don't forget the preposition **a** that follows.

uno de los colosos más difíciles de escalar one of the most difficult colossi to climb. Señor Monge is referring to the size of Mount Naranjo. There is more about how to form comparatives (eg *more* difficult) and superlatives (eg *most* difficult) on page 129.

▶ **no sólo de España sino de todo el mundo** not only in Spain but worldwide. Note how to form not only . . . but also . . . expressions: **No sólo por tren sino en coche** Not only by train but also by car. Also note: **No en tren sino en coche** Not by train but by car.

Trabajos prácticos

7 Fill in the grid with the relevant sports. The word for mountaineering is **alpinismo**. (Answers on page 208.)

¿qué deporte?	
ríos asturianos	
San Isidro	
Pajares	
Naranjo de Bulnes	

8 Using the picture clues as a guide, provide as much information as you can about the winter sports facilities. (Answers on page 208.)

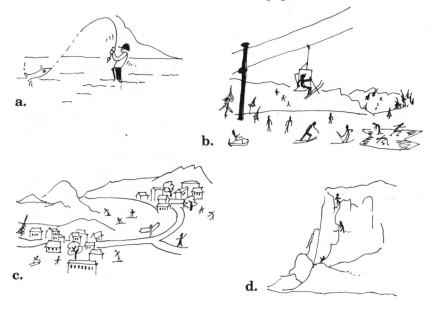

a.

b.

c.

d.

9 Now that you know something about winter sports in Asturias, perhaps you could tell Eloísa, who's from Madrid, about what you can do in the Picos de Europa if you really enjoy the outdoor life. Susan will prompt you.

Diálogo 4
Una excursión para conocer Asturias

Ismael   Buenos días, señorita, ¿qué deseaba?

Marga   Buenos días. Mire, estoy interesada en hacer una excursión para conocer un poco más Asturias y quería que me informara algo sobre ello.

Ismael   Fenomenal. Tenemos unas excursiones programadas durante los meses de julio y agosto: travesía del Cares, Picos de Europa y, por supuesto, el más importante y el más interesante, Covadonga y Lagos. Esta excursión de Covadonga y Lagos es una excursión que sale en el auto Pullman por la mañana a las nueve de la mañana, y regresa como alrededor de las diecinueve treinta o veinte horas. Lleva incluido el almuerzo y en ella se visita parte de la basílica de Covadonga que es verdaderamente excepcional y el maravilloso paisaje que se contempla desde allí. Se visita también a la vuelta, las cuevas de Tito Bustillo en Ribadesella, además de visitar también en Villaviciosa la fábrica de sidra del Gaitero y bueno, es muy completa, es una excursion preciosa, es una excursión que cualquier visitante que venga aquí a Asturias debe de conocer, porque es la más importante de toda la gama de las excursiones que hay programadas.

Covadonga

alrededor   around, about
paisaje (m.)   countryside
vuelta (f.)   return
cueva (f.)   cave
además   besides

hacer una excursión para conocer un poco más Asturias   to go on an excursion to get to know Asturias a bit better.

quería que me informara algo sobre ello   I'd like you to tell me something about it. The subjunctive (**informara**) is used here after **quería**, because it always follows verbs that involve wishing or wanting.

unas excursiones programadas   some scheduled excursions.

travesías de Cares   the river Cares passes through a narrow gorge called a **desfiladero**. It forms part of the Picos de Europa chain of mountains.

Covadonga   is a famous Spanish shrine to the Virgin Mary (known in Asturias as **la Santina**). It marks the spot where the Christians defeated the Muslims in the 8th century, so starting the Reconquest.

The **Lagos** are the famous lakes of Enol and Ercina.

Lleva incluido el almuerzo   Lunch is included (**llevar**, to carry, is meaningless here).

Las cuevas de Tito Bustillo en Ribadesella   Ribadesella is famous for an international kayak race held in August: the caves, like many in this area, have palaeolithic wall paintings.

la fábrica de sidra del Gaitero   cider, rather than wine, is drunk in this part of Spain. The **gaitero** (bagpipe player) is often seen at fiestas in Galicia.

Trabajos prácticos

10 There were a lot of details to take in about that day out in Covadonga. Place the following events in the order in which they were mentioned in dialogue 4. (Answers on page 208.)

a. ☐ Las cuevas de Tito Bustillo
b. ☐ Se sale a las nueve
c. ☐ La fábrica de sidra
d. ☐ La basílica de Covadonga
e. ☐ Se regresa a las veinte horas
f. ☐ Lleva incluido el almuerzo
g. ☐ El paisaje que se contempla desde allí

11 Here are a few questions on dialogue 4. Answer them out loud in Spanish. Try to give full sentences. (Answers on page 208.)

a. ¿Cuántas excursiones mencionó Ismael?
b. ¿Qué fabrica el Gaitero?
c. ¿Cuándo se visita las cuevas en Ribadesella?
d. ¿Se visita toda la basílica de Covadonga?
e. ¿Hay que pagar extra por el almuerzo?
f. ¿Cuál es la excursión más importante, según Ismael?

12 Tell Eloísa about your visit to Covadonga and the lakes. Below you will find picture clues to help you.

a.

incluido

b.

c.

d.

Tito Bustillo

e.

f.

g.

Giros importantes

¿Estuvisteis de vacaciones el año pasado?	Did you (pl.) go on holiday last year?
Unos días	A few days
¿Adónde habéis estado?	Where did you go?
¿Llevaste a tus hijos contigo?	Did you (sing.) take your children with you?
¿Cómo os ha parecido la ciudad?	What did you (pl.) think of the city?
Reconozco que hacía mucho calor	I admit that it was very hot
¿Marchasteis con pena de Barcelona?	Were you (pl.) sorry to leave Barcelona?
Me hubiera quedado por el clima	I would have stayed simply because of the climate
Al otro lado del mundo	To the other side of the world
He conocido Brasil	I've been to Brazil
Acabo de conocer	I've just visited (got to know)
En un plazo de un año	In the space of a year
A mi entender	In my opinion
Aparte de eso	Apart from that
Considero que es interesante hacer unas vacaciones allí	I think it's good value to go on holiday there
¿Se puede practicar deportes de invierno en Asturias?	Can you practise winter sports in Asturias?
Por supuesto que sí	Of course
Por supuesto que no	Of course not
Me refiero a la temporada de pesca	I'm talking about the fishing season
Tenemos dos estaciones de invierno	We have two winter sports resorts
Para los aficionados a montaña	For those who enjoy mountaineering
Se ha convertido en uno de los grandes mitos	It has become one of the great myths
Uno de los colosos más difíciles de escalar	One of the most difficult colossi to climb
No sólo de España sino de todo el mundo	Not only of Spain but of the entire world
Hacer una excursión	To go on an excursion
Sale por la mañana a las nueve de la mañana	It leaves in the morning at nine o'clock
Regresa alrededor de las diecinueve horas	It returns at about seven o'clock in the evening
Lleva incluido el almuerzo	It includes lunch
Se visita la basílica	You visit the basilica
A la vuelta	On the way back

Gramática

Comparatives and superlatives

In this unit we have been listening to people expressing enthusiasm about something – their job, their holidays, or their native region. Enthusiasm is often expressed by means of comparatives and superlatives. If you simply want to say that one thing is nicer, prettier, dearer, than another, use **más ...que...**

Covadonga es más bonita que Panes Covadonga is prettier than Panes.
Las cuevas de Altamira son más impresionantes que las de Tito Bustillo The caves of Altamira are more impressive than the Tito Bustillo caves.

If you want to go one further and use the superlative (nicest, prettiest, dearest) then you must use the article (**el, la, lo**) as well.

Esta estación de invierno es la más elegante de España This winter resort is the most sophisticated (one) in Spain.

El esquí es el más difícil de todos los deportes de invierno Skiing is the most difficult of all the winter sports.

If you've already used the article, you don't need to use it a second time:
el deporte más difícil de todos the most difficult sport of all.

Notice, too, how in Spanish you say:
la más elegante de España the most elegant in Spain:
la más simpática de la familia the nicest of the family.

Remember to make the adjective and article agree with the noun:
el avión más rápido del mundo the fastest plane in the world
la montaña más alta de Asturias the highest mountain in Asturias

13 Now for some practice. The pictures show two nouns which you must join together with a superlative formed from the adjective supplied. The first one has been done for you. (Answers on page 208.)

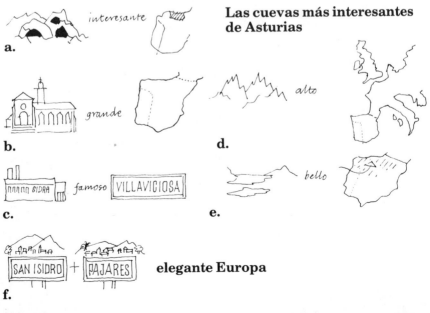

interesante **Las cuevas más interesantes de Asturias**

a.

grande / *alto*

b. / d.

famoso VILLAVICIOSA / *bello*

c. / e.

SAN ISIDRO + PAJARES **elegante Europa**

f.

Acabar de

The verb **acabar**, in the present tense, followed by **de**, which we met in the first dialogue, means 'to have just' done something:
I have just bought myself a new coat **Acabo de comprarme un nuevo abrigo**.
It is also often used in the imperfect (I had just)
I had just come out of the hairdresser's when I remembered that . . .
Acababa de salir de la peluquería, cuando me acordé de que . . .

14 Match the English phrases to the Spanish. (Answers on page 208.)

a. We had just arrived at the station when the train left.

....

b. We've only just arrived!

....

c. They had only just left the house, when the telephone rang.

....

d. They've just missed the train.

....

e. He's not here. He's just gone out.

....

f. I've just opened this parcel.

....

Acabo de abrir este paquete.

Acabábamos de llegar a la estación cuando salió el tren.

¡Si acabamos de llegar!

Acaban de perder el tren.

Acababan de salir de la casa cuando sonó el teléfono.

No está. Acaba de salir.

Lectura

Here is a description of the excursion that Ismael was describing to Marga in dialogue 4.

Excursión

Desfiladero del Cares

duración de la excursión: día completo
duración de la travesía: 6 horas
grado de dificultad: uno
fechas de salida: Mayo 12, 26: Junio 9, 23: Julio 7, 21:
Agosto 4, 15: Setiembre 1 y 8

A la llegada del autocar al pueblo de Posada de Valdeón, situado en la provincia de León, se inicia la travesía, caminando por carretera hasta el pueblo de Caín, habiendo dejado atrás Corona, con su famosa ermita. A la llegada a Caín, tiempo libre para descansar y efectuar el almuerzo. Después de finalizado el mismo se prosigue la travesía por una senda labrada en la roca que se introduce en la parte más estrecha de la garganta. Pasaremos por Culiembro, donde hace muchos años existía todavía una aldea, para llegar a las colinas tras una corta subida y descender ya a Puente Poncebos, desde donde iniciaremos el regreso en autocar a los puntos de origen.

---

travesía (f.) crossing
fecha (f.) date
iniciar to begin
caminar to walk
atrás behind
ermita (f.) hermitage
finalizar to end

proseguir (i) to continue
senda (f.) path
labrar to work
estrecho narrow
garganta (f.) gorge
aldea (f.) village
colina (f.) hill

15 Test your comprehension of that short reading passage by choosing the correct response. (Answers on page 208.)

a. En Culiembro existía
☐ un pueblo
☐ una ermita
☐ una aldea

b. Regresaremos a casa desde
☐ Caín
☐ Corona
☐ Puente Poncebos

c. Posada de Valdeón está en
☐ Asturias
☐ León
☐ Cares

d. La senda está labrada en
☐ la roca
☐ la tierra
☐ el río

e. En Caín
☐ caminamos
☐ descansamos
☐ subimos

Our second reading extract is about that 'Colossus' of the Picos de Europa, the Naranjo de Bulnes.

La montaña asturiana es invitación al paseo, a la marcha o a la escalada. Los Picos de Europa son conocidos por todo montañero. Coronar el Naranjo de Bulnes es la ambición de todo escalador; sobre todo si se realiza la escalada en invierno y por la cara oeste, abriéndose paso por las planchas de hielo que lo recubren. Para los simples 'montañeros' se yerguen las múltiples cumbres que llaman a ser conquistadas como Peña Santa y Tesorero. Situados para descansar o pasar la noche se encuentran numerosos refugios: pero si las fuerzas no alcanzan para subir a las cumbres, ahí está la garganta de Cares, maravilla de la naturaleza y que promete un inolvidable paseo entre las abruptas paredes de las calizas sobre los verdes intensos de las aguas.

paseo (m.) stroll
marcha (f.) walk
escalada (f.) climb
escalador (m.) climber
cara (f.) face
abrir paso to open a way
plancha (f.) flat surface

hielo (m.) ice
erguirse to rise
cumbre (f.) peak
alcanzar to reach
garganta (f.) gorge
inolvidable unforgettable
caliza (f.) limestone

16 A few questions now – in English, because that text was rather difficult. (Answers on page 208.)

a. What three things can you do in the mountains in Asturias?

i .... *ii* .... *iii* ....

b. Which three factors make conquering the Naranjo de Bulnes even more difficult?

i .... *ii* .... *iii* ....

c. Find out what the names of the two lesser peaks mean.

i .... *ii* ....

d. What are the **refugios** used for?

i .... *ii* ....

e. What else can you do if you're not up to mountaineering on this scale?

....

f. What are the two great contrasts in the Cares gorge?

i .... *ii* ....

Radio

The radio extract is a humorous piece about a **ticketero** – a young lad who spends his day on the beach trying to sell tickets for the evening disco. You will need the following vocabulary and phrases. (Transcript on page 218.)

zoológico veraniego (m.) summer zoo
vendedor playero ambulante (m.) travelling beach salesman
fulanazo (m.) old 'so and so'
patearse to kick
arena (f.) sand
incauto unwary
santa voluntad (f.) holy will
le importa un pimiento/ rábano he couldn't care two hoots

por las narices willy-nilly
sandía (f.) water melon
ley (f.) law
molesto/pesado annoying (person)
tener los garbanzos duros to be a bad case
encargado in charge of
chaval (m.) lad
puñalada (f.) knife wound
cornada (f.) horn wound
hambre (f.) hunger

17 Once you've listened to that radio extract, try to fill in the missing words in this transcript. (Answers on page 208.)

A nuestro .... veraniego, tenemos ....

al ticketero. Ya verán como lo .... Según como se quiera

.... el ticketero es también una especie de ....

playero ...., aunque no consienta la condición de

autónomo de aquél del que ayer les hablaba. Este ....

es eso sí, pero es que también se .... la arena en

.... de incautos. El .... de que usted quiera o no

quiera, según su .... santa voluntad, ...

el tiempo en una discoteca, a él le importa más bien un ....

Te toca a tí hablar

 18 You're in Oviedo and you'd like to go on one of the excursions you've seen in the brochure. Describe what you would like to see and do. You'll need to use the conditional tense here (see Unit 3). If you run out of material, think about those question words, **¿quién? ¿cómo? ¿cuándo? ¿qué?** and **¿por qué?** Eloísa will then suggest an excursion for you.

La Basilica,
Covadonga

9 Trabajar para la vejez, discreción es

What you will learn

- all about the daily routine of a **pharmacist** and a **travel agent**
- and of a young man who works in a **record shop**
- how to open an account in a Spanish **bank**
- . . . and how to start looking for a **job**

Study guide

Diálogo 1
Un día en la farmacia

Ricardo   Un día de trabajo en la farmacia: pues comienzo a las neuve y media, a esa hora pues normalmente empiezas a atender al público. Corriges un pedido que te viene por la mañana, lo colocas, revisas algún albarán si tienes tiempo, si el público te deja, haces alguna fórmula magistral si te viene, y esto pues todo: claro, combinándolo con el público que te llega, que tienes que atender, hasta la una y media. A la una y media cerramos, damos un pedido al almacén: que ese pedido nos sirven a las cuatro, a la hora de apertura por la tarde, y entonces ya nos vamos a comer a la una y media. Pues luego, cuando llegamos a las cuatro, cuatro y diez, nos viene el pedido que habíamos hecho por la mañana. Volvemos otra vez a revisarlo, para reponer las faltas, y seguimos atendiendo al público: revisando los pedidos, las facturas, y ésta es la vida que concluye a las siete y media de la tarde.

albarán (m.) duplicate list of purchases
dejar to leave, allow

apertura (f.) opening
factura (f.) bill

empiezas a atender al público you begin to serve the public. Ricardo uses the **tú** form to mean you in general.

corriges un pedido you correct an order. Ricardo really means that he checks it for errors.

lo colocas you place it.

revisas algún albarán you check a duplicate list of purchases. Here, **algún** implies 'some list or other'.

♦ **el público que te llega, que tienes que atender** the customers who arrive and need attending to.

haces alguna fórmula magistral you fill in some official prescription. The usual word for prescription is **receta**.

damos un pedido al almacén we send an order to the dispensary. **Almacén** (m.) usually means a store or warehouse. **Grandes almacenes** (m.pl.) department store.

nos viene el pedido que habíamos hecho por la mañana the order that we sent out in the morning arrives.

♦ **Volvemos otra vez a revisarlo** we check it again. **Volver a** means 'to do something again' (Ricardo has actually said this twice). **¿Vuelves a salir?** Are you going out again?

reponer las faltas to correct the mistakes. **Corregir** is the more common word for to correct.

♦ **seguimos atendiendo al público** we carry on serving the public. **Seguir** means 'to continue' and is followed by a present participle.

ésta es la vida que concluye a las siete y media de la tarde this is the life that ends at half past seven in the evening.

Trabajos prácticos

1 Ricardo, the chemist, gave a breakdown of his day. Complete the grid below, noting (in Spanish) what Ricardo does and when, using the first person. Give as much information as you can. (Answers on page 208.)

a las nueve y media	
por la mañana	
a la una y media	
a las cuatro	
a las siete y media	

2 Can you remember the order in which Ricardo worked? Here is a list of what he did during the day: number each activity in the order in which it occurred. To check the sequence, listen to dialogue 1 again on the tape. (Answers on page 208.)

a. ☐ Volvemos otra vez a revisarlo.

b. ☐ Nos vamos a comer a la una y media.

c. ☐ Haces alguna fórmula magistral.

d. ☐ Corriges un pedido que te viene por la mañana.

e. ☐ Ésta es la vida que concluye a las siete y media de la tarde.

f. ☐ Damos un pedido al almacén.

3 Now you are the interviewer. Sr Pérez is a pharmacist in a large town in the north of Spain. Ask him about his daily routine. You'll be practising the question words **¿cómo?** (how) **¿cuántos?** (how many) **¿qué?** (what) and **¿cuándo?** (when). Susan will prompt you.

Diálogo 2
Soy agente de viajes

Ismael Soy agente de viajes – tengo una agencia de viajes en Oviedo y
anteriormente he trabajado con Viajes Melia unos quince años,
quince, dieciseis años. Actualmente tengo esta agencia de viajes; he
decidido instalarme por cuenta propia porque considero que todas
las personas con cierto ánimo de superación deben de intentar
conseguir, pues buscarse su trabajo y su vida trabajando para uno
mismo. La experiencia después de cinco años me demuestra que
efectivamente estaba en lo acertado. Concretamente, estoy muy
satisfecho de la labor que estoy realizando en esta agencia de viajes
y actualmente, después de cinco años, pues la clientela cada vez es
mucho mejor, cada vez es mayor, las ventas van mucho mejor y lo
que en principio era un temor tremendo hacer este cambio
importante, pues actualmente me siento muy satisfecho y muy feliz
de haber dado este paso importante.

▶ **actualmente** now, at the moment
intentar to try
▶ **conseguir (i)** to obtain, achieve
demostrar (ue) to show

concretamente specifically
venta (f.) sale
temor (m.) fear
cambio (m.) change

Soy agente de viajes I am a travel agent (**agencia de viajes**, travel agency)

Viajes Melia Melia Travel, one of the biggest travel agencies in Spain.

▶ **he decidido instalarme por cuenta propia** I have decided to set myself
up on my own account (working for myself).

con cierto ánimo de superación with a certain drive to get ahead.

buscarse su trabajo y su vida to search for your own work and life. The
extra **se** on the end of **buscar** suggests personal involvement – you look for
your own benefit.

efectivamente estaba en lo acertado I was certainly right.

estoy muy satisfecho de la labor que estoy realizando I am very
satisfied with the work I'm doing.

▶ **cada vez es mayor** it's getting bigger and bigger. Ismael is referring to his
clientele (**la clientela**).

**me siento muy satisfecho y muy feliz de haber dado este paso
importante** I feel very satisfied and happy to have taken this important
step.

Trabajos prácticos

4 Ismael is very pleased at the way his business is progressing: he uses a lot of adjectives to describe how he feels about the development of his travel agency. Complete the sentences below with the words Ismael used in dialogue 2. Try not to look back at the transcript. (Answers on page 209.)

a. Me siento muy .... y ....

b. Todas las personas con ....

c. La clientela cada vez es mucho .... cada vez es

....

d. En principio era un temor ....:...

e. Este cambio ....

5 Can you remember more of the phrases that Ismael used? Match up the English version with its Spanish equivalent in the box below. (Answers on page 209.)

I decided to set up on my own

....

I was right ....

At the moment I feel very satisfied

....

The work I'm doing

....

The number of clients is growing

....

Actualmente me siento muy satisfecho

Estaba en lo acertado

He decidido instalarme por cuenta propia

La clientela cada vez es mayor

La labor que estoy realizando

6 You've just left a job you've been in for 15 years to set up on your own. Tell Pepe how you feel now you've made this great step forward in your career. Susan will prompt you.

Diálogo 3
¿Cuántos sois en la empresa?

Marga	Oye, ¿cuánto tiempo llevas trabajando aquí?
Joven	Tres años.
Marga	¿Y cuántos sois en la empresa?
Joven	En la empresa aquí en esta sucursal somos seis ahora mismo.
Marga	¿Y qué? ¿tiene otra sucursal?
Joven	Tenemos en Gijón y Avilés.
Marga	¿Y cuántos soléis tener allí más o menos? ¿seis también?
Joven	Pues no, vamos, en Gijón son sobre unas veinte personas y en Avilés otras cinco o seis aproximadamente.
Marga	Mm . . . ¿y qué horario tenéis?
Joven	Pues el horario es de diez a una y cuarto y de cuatro a ocho.
Marga	Es un poco pesado ¿no?
Joven	Bastante.
Marga	Y de vacaciones, ¿cómo andáis?
Joven	Treinta días o cuarenta, depende de la antigüedad de cada uno en la empresa.
Marga	¿Y os suelen pagar el sueldo a final de mes?
Joven	El último día que se trabaje de mes.
Marga	Ya, y por ejemplo, ¿soléis hacer puentes festivos?
Joven	No, puentes nunca se hacen.
Marga	¿Nunca?
Joven	Nunca.
Marga	O sea que ¿trabajáis los sábados por la tarde?
Joven	Sábado por la tarde, o sábado por la mañana, depende de cómo te toque

empresa (f.) business
sucursal (f.) branch
horario (m.) timetable

♦ **pesado** tiresome, heavy
sueldo (m.) salary

♦ **¿cuánto tiempo llevas trabajando aquí?** how long have you been working here? Notice how Marga uses the verb **llevar** (lit. to carry) with the present participle. **¿Cuánto tiempo llevas estudiando español?** How long have you been studying Spanish?

♦ **en Gijón son sobre unas veinte personas** in Gijón there are about 20 people. You could say **una veintena de personas** to express the same idea.

Y de vacaciones ¿cómo andáis? And what is your holiday allowance? (Lit. And of holidays, how do you walk?) This is very colloquial.

depende de la antigüedad de cada uno en la empresa it depends how long you've been with the firm (lit. it depends on the seniority of each one in the firm).

el último día que se trabaje de mes the last working day in the month. Notice the subjunctive **trabaje**: it's used here because of the imprecise date. For more about this, see page 145.

♦ **¿soléis hacer puentes festivos?** do you normally 'bridge the gap' between holidays? The **puente** (bridge) is the period between one day off and the next, when Spaniards don't bother to go to work.

♦ **depende de cómo te toque** It depends on whether it's your turn. This subjunctive (**te toque**) is like the last one: the young man is uncertain about when he's going to have to work. **Te toca a tí**, It's your turn.

Trabajos prácticos

7 The young man in the video shop was full of information about his conditions of employment. See if you can remember the exact details in dialogue 3 by ticking the appropriate box. (Answers on page 209.)

a. Trabaja en la tienda desde hace
- ☐ dos años
- ☐ cinco años
- ☐ tres años

b. ¿Cuántos hay en la sucursal en Gijón?
- ☐ una veintena
- ☐ una treintena
- ☐ una cuarentena

c. ¿Cuántos días de vacaciones tiene?
- ☐ veinte
- ☐ treinta
- ☐ cincuenta

d. ¿Hacen puentes festivos?
- ☐ sí
- ☐ no

e. ¿Cuántas sucursales hay?
- ☐ una
- ☐ dos
- ☐ tres

8 Now you take the part of the young man – only this time, your conditions of employment aren't quite the same. Write your answers to the questions in the spaces provided, according to the suggestions outlined for you. (Answers on page 209.)

a. *¿Desde cuántos años trabajas en esta empresa?*

....

b. *¿Y cuántos sois en esta sucursal?*

....

c. *¿La empresa tiene más sucursales?*

....

d. *Y de vacaciones ¿qué tienes al año?*

....

....

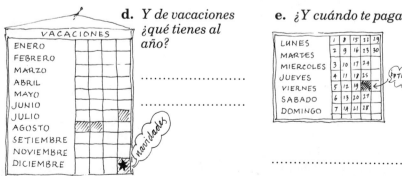

e. *¿Y cuándo te pagan?*

....

9 Now try some of those questions orally. You've just changed your job and a friend rings you to ask how your first day went. Susan will prompt you.

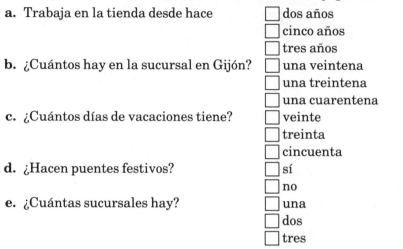

Diálogo 4
Quiero abrir una cuenta corriente

Sandra	Mire usted, soy inglesa y quiero abrir una cuenta corriente aquí en España. ¿Me puede decir lo que hay que hacer?
Gerente	Sí, si usted está residiendo en España, solamente con tener la tarjeta de residencia es suficiente.
Sandra	¿Y necesito una cierta cantidad para abrir la cuenta?
Gerente	No, en principio no hay ninguna cantidad estipulada.
Sandra	¿Y me puede facilitar un talonario?
Gerente	Sí, lo que es la cuenta corriente, porque hay dos casos, puede ser libreta de ahorros o cuenta corriente.
Sandra	¿Y cuál es la diferencia?
Gerente	La diferencia está en que la cuenta corriente tiene más, perdón, la libreta de ahorros tiene más interés que la cuenta corriente.
Sandra	Sí.
Gerente	La libreta de ahorros se mueve por otro sistema que la cuenta corriente que usa el talonario.
Sandra	Bueno, y si yo quiero sacar dinero de España para Inglaterra, ¿qué puedo hacer? ¿es legal?
Gerente	De su cuenta corriente, siempre puede retirar el saldo que tenga, bien en pesetas, que es la moneda nacional, o en divisas.
Sandra	Muy bien. ¿Lo puedo hacer ahora entonces?
Gerente	Sí, ¿cómo no? ahora mismo.
Sandra	Muchas gracias.
Gerente	A usted.

gerente (m.) manager
residir to reside

en principio in principle
sacar to take out

quiero abrir una cuenta corriente I want to open a current account. The bank manager later explains that you can also have a **cuenta de ahorros**, savings account: for this you need a **libreta**, savings book.

solamente con tener la tarjeta de residencia es suficiente it's enough just to have a resident's card.

▶ **¿Y me puede facilitar un talonario?** And can you provide me with a cheque book?

la libreta de ahorros tiene más interés the savings account provides more interest (lit. the savings book has more interest).

La libreta de ahorros se mueve por otro sistema The savings book works in a different way (lit. moves through another system).

siempre puede retirar el saldo que tenga, bien en pesetas, que es la moneda nacional, o en divisas you can always withdraw the balance you have, either in **pesetas**, which is the national currency, or in foreign currency.

▶ **ahora mismo** right now.

Trabajos prácticos

10 First of all, a quiz. We give you the clues (all taken from dialogue 4); you provide the definitions. (Answers on page 209.)

a. Lo puedes obtener si tienes una cuenta corriente ....

b. El dinero que tienes en tu cuenta ....

c. Lo contrario a moneda nacional ....

d. En el banco puedes tener una cuenta corriente y también ....

....

e. Otra palabra para sacar ....

f. Si eres inglés y vives en España, necesitas ....

11 All these sentences have gone wrong! Can you re-order the words so that they make sense? They are slightly different from the version on page 142. (Answers on page 209.)

a. francés y cuenta soy abrir corriente una quiero.

....

b. ¿facilitar me un puede talonario?

....

c. la la es peseta nacional moneda.

....

d. ahorros libreta más tiene interés la de.

....

e. ¿retirar el de cuenta quiere saldo su corriente?

....

f. estipulada no ninguna hay cantidad.

....

g. ¿diferencia la es cuál?

....

12 For this speaking exercise, you go into a bank in Marbella to open an account. Ask the bank manager for details. Remember to call him **usted** (the polite form) or you may not get that account! Susan will prompt you.

Giros importantes

Un día de trabajo en la farmacia	A day's work in the chemist's
Comienzo a las nueve y media	I start at half past nine
Empiezas a atender al público	You begin to serve the public
Si tienes tiempo	If you have time
A la una y media cerramos	We close at half past one
Nos vamos a comer a la una y media	We go for lunch at half past one
Volvemos a revisarlo	We check it once again
Seguimos atendiendo al público	We carry on serving the public
Soy agente de viajes	I am a travel agent
He decidido instalarme por cuenta propia	I decided to set up on my own
Estoy muy satisfecho de . . .	I am very satisfied with . . .
Cada vez es mayor	It's getting bigger all the time
Actualmente me siento muy satisfecho	At the moment I feel very satisfied
¿Cuánto tiempo llevas trabajando aquí?	How long have you been working here?
Sobre unas veinte personas	About 20 people
¿Y qué horario tenéis?	And what hours do you work?
Y de vacaciones ¿qué tenéis?	And what is your holiday allowance?
Depende de la antigüedad de cada uno	It depends on each person's seniority
El último día que se trabaje de mes	The last working day in the month
¿Soléis hacer puentes festivos?	Do you take extra days at holiday time?
Depende de como te toque	It depends on whether it's your turn
Quiero abrir una cuenta corriente	I want to open a current account
¿Me puede decir lo·que hay que hacer?	Can you tell me what I have to do?
Solamente con tener la tarjeta de residencia es suficiente	It's enough just to have a resident's card
¿Necesito una cierta cantidad para abrir la cuenta?	Do I need a certain amount in order to open the account?
¿Me puede facilitar un talonario?	Can you provide me with a cheque book?
¿Cuál es la diferencia?	What's the difference?
La libreta de ahorros tiene más interés que la cuenta corriente	The savings account provides more interest than the current account
Siempre puede retirar el saldo que tenga	You can always withdraw your balance
Bien en pesetas, que es la moneda nacional, o en divisas	Either in pesetas, which is the national currency, or in foreign currency
Ahora mismo	Right now

Gramática

More about the subjunctive

(see also Units 5 and 6)
This unit contained another use of the subjunctive: do you remember **siempre puede retirar el saldo que tenga** (you can always withdraw the balance you have) and **depende de cómo te toque** (it depends on whether it's your turn)? In both these sentences, the second verbs, **toque** and **tenga**, are subjunctive. This is because they are expressing something uncertain or indefinite.

If you compare these two sentences you will be able to see the difference.

Busca a la chica que tiene pelo rizado He's looking for *the* girl who has curly hair; and

Busca a una chica que tenga pelo rizado He's looking for *a* girl who has curly hair.

In the first sentence, the verb **tener** is in the indicative (**tiene**) – because we know who she is – the girl with the curly hair. In the second sentence, the verb **tener** is in the subjunctive (**tenga**), because we're looking for any girl who's got curly hair – not a specific person.

13 Now study the following sentences and write down the reason why Spanish uses the subjunctive. The more examples you see, the more quickly you'll recognise when it is used. (Answers on page 209.)

a. **Escoge la que te guste.** Choose one that you like.
b. **¿Hay una habitación que tenga dos camas y cuarto de baño?** Is there a room with two beds and a bath?
c. **¿Conoces un libro que contenga esta información?** Do you know of a book that has this information?
d. **Aquellos que quieran recibo, que vengan por favor a recepción.** Would those who would like a receipt please come to reception.
e. **¿Sabes de algún chico español que quiera hacer un intercambio con un chico inglés?** Do you know of any Spanish boy who would like to do an exchange with an English boy?

More about verbs

In this unit there is a number of verbs which behave in a peculiar or irregular way. Let's have a closer look at some of them.

Deber & deber de

In practice, these two verbs are becoming rather confused: in dialogue 2, Ismael is not absolutely accurate about his usage! But strictly speaking, **deber**, without the preposition **de**, means 'owe', 'ought to':
¡debes estudiar más, hijo! you ought to study more, child!
Deber with the preposition **de** indicates you are supposing or putting forward a possibility:
debe de haber ido he must have gone.
debe de ser muy inteligente he must be very intelligent.

14 For this exercise, work out where to omit and where to insert that preposition **de**. (Answers on page 209.)

a. ¡**Debes** volver a casa a la hora!
b. **Debe** haber estudiado mucho tu hijo, ¿no?
c. **Debo** mucho a mis padres, lo reconozco.
d. **Debo** mil pesetas a mi hermano.
e. **Debe** estar ya en casa, ¿no te parece?

Seguir

Seguir, a radical-changing verb, normally means 'to follow':
sigue un curso de español en la universidad he's following a Spanish course at the university.
But **seguir** can also mean 'to continue (doing)' and in this case, it's followed by a present participle:
sigue escribiendo a su novia en Alemania he's still writing to his girlfriend in Germany.

15 Now practise what you have learnt by translating these sentences into English. (Answers on page 209.)

a. Los niños pequeños suelen seguir muy de cerca a sus madres.

....

b. ¡Esta niña sigue haciendo tonterías!

....

c. El partido comunista en España sigue la filosofía de Marx.

....

d. Sigue trabajando con su padre en el taller.

....

e. Seguimos viéndonos cada año en Navidades.

....

Volver

Finally, the verb **volver**. You should already know that it means 'to return' – but when followed by the preposition **a**, and another verb in the infinitive it means 'to do something again'.
Vuelvo a casa a las nueve I go home at nine o'clock. But,
Vuelvo a empezar I begin all over again.

16 Here are the words of a Spanish pop song. They are somewhat repetitive but they provide good examples of the two uses of the verb **volver**. Translate them, bearing this in mind. (Answers on page 209.)

Vuelvo a tu casa, vuelvo a tu calle ....

Vuelvo a los sitios donde yo te conocí ....

Pero no vuelvo a verte, no quieres amarme ....

Porque él vuelve de lejos – a él le quieres, sí . . . .

Lectura

The record shop that Marga visited also sells video equipment and cassette recorders. While we were there we picked up some publicity about one particular make of video. See how much you can understand – you may not find it too difficult because a lot of technical words are very similar to the English.

Congelación de imagen perfecta
Es posible una congelación de imágenes sin perturbaciones, con lo que se consigue una imagen fija perfectamente nítida.

Auto on
Puesta en marcha del vídeo de forma automática al introducir una cinta.

Programación
Posibilidad de programar la grabación de 4 programas de TV durante un período de tres semanas. También es posible la programación de los siete días de una semana a la misma hora.

Auto rebobinado
Cuando la cinta llega al final, se rebobinará totalmente de forma automática, quedando en disposición de ser extraída.

Selector de tono
Este selector le permitirá variar el tono del sonido de la cinta, haciéndolo más agudo (high), o más grave (low).

Búsqueda de imagen
Podrá mover su programa de vídeo en la pantalla del TV en ambos sentidos, hacia adelante y hacia atrás a una velocidad nueve veces superior a la normal, simplemente pulsando la tecla.

congelación (f.) freezing
perturbación (f.) flickering
nítido clear
cinta (f.) tape
grabación (f.) recording
rebobinar to rewind

extraer to extract
búsqueda (f.) finding, search
pantalla (f.) screen
pulsar to push
tecla (f.) button

17 What, in English, are the six facilities that the video recorder has to offer? (Answers on page 209.)

Before you go to Spain you will probably have to visit the bank to pick up your traveller's cheques. Here is a promotional piece for Thomas Cook about the facilities it provides for travellers abroad. See how much you can understand with the help of the vocabulary below, then answer the questions.

elección (f.) choice
preocupación (f.) worry
librar to free
riesgo (m.) risk
pérdida (f.) loss
divisa (f.) foreign currency

adecuado suitable
ahorrar to save
pago (m.) payment
cualquier any
solucionar to solve
reembolso (m.) refund

La Elección Correcta de Cheques de Viaje

Como llevar su dinero de viaje sin preocupación

Si va a viajar al extranjero, debe pensar en llevar cheques de viaje ETC Thomas Cook. Seguros, fáciles de usar, universalmente aceptados, le libran del riesgo de llevar dinero en efectivo, y en caso de pérdida o robo los Cheques de Viaje ETC Thomas Cook le son reembolsados de forma eficaz y rápida.

Elija la divisa más conveniente

No encontrará mayor variedad de divisas ni más apropiadas. Si selecciona la divisa adecuada para el país que va a visitar, podrá usar sus cheques como dinero en efectivo. Esto le ahorrará tiempo y pago de comisiones. ETC Thomas Cook le ofrece sus cheques de viaje en Dólares USA, Marcos Alemanes, Francos Franceses. Libras Esterlinas, Florines Holandeses, Dólares Canadá, Dólares Australia, Yenes Japoneses, Dólares Hong Kong. Francos Suizos y el de más reciente creación, la Peseta.

Un servicio de reembolso en todo el mundo

Con más 100,000 puntos de reembolso en todo el mundo, ETC Thomas Cook le proporciona un rápido y eficiente servicio de reembolso si sus cheques se pierden o se los roban. Todo lo que tiene que hacer es contactar con el servicio de reembolso de Thomas Cook, día o noche, en Norte América, Reino Unido y Europa, o cualquier oficina de Thomas Cook, Wagons lits o Hertz.

---

18 Here is a quiz to test how well you understood that extract. (Answers on page 209.)

a. Give three reasons why you should take Thomas Cook's travellers cheques on holiday with you ....

b. Name six different sorts of foreign currency ....
....

c. What do you do if you lose your cheques? ....

d. How many places are there where you can get a refund if you do lose your cheques? ....

e. Besides cashing your cheques, how else can you use them? ....
....

f. What two advantages does this method have? ....
....

Radio

The first radio extract is about taxi drivers on strike because their working hours have been restricted by the local council. The following vocabulary will help you to understand it. (Transcript on page 218.)

ovetense from Oviedo
concentrarse to gather
pleno (m.) general meeting
imponer to impose
descanso (m.) rest, break
industrial (m.) (here) worker

asimismo also
recurso (m.) appeal
medida (f.) measure
apoyar to support
partidario (m.) (here) in favour of
alcaldía (f.) mayor's office

19 Here's a translation of the report you have just heard with several pieces of information missing. See if you can supply the missing information in English. (Answers on page 210.)

Taxi drivers from Oviedo met at .... in front

of the .... , at the same time as a plenary

session of the town council was taking place, in order to protest

about .... of the corporation to enforce

.... on the taxi drivers. The taxi drivers

also presented .... , since they consider

this measure, on the part of the town council, to be ....

.... The taxi drivers who are affiliated to the

UGT .... as they are in favour of the Mayor's

decision on the new regulations about hours.

SER ¡La Radio!

The next radio extract is part of a phone-in programme. A young girl called María Ester has written to the presenter because she needs a job urgently: she's looking for a cleaning job or something in a restaurant. Hours must be compatible with the **academia** (private school) she attends in the evenings. You'll need the following vocabulary. (Transcript on page 218.)

independizarse to be independent
agobiar to overwhelm
cumplir con to fulfil, meet
  obligations
gasto (m.) cost
ofrecerse to offer oneself

siguiente following
ayudante (m.) helper
barra (f.) bar
portal (m.) porch, doorway
limpiar to clean

20 How much of María Ester's letter did you understand? Test yourself by answering the following questions in English. (Answers on page 210.)

a. What three possible jobs does the girl suggest?

    i ....

    ii ....

    iii ....

b. How many hours can she work per day? ....

c. What would her working hours be? ....

d. What time does she start at the school? ....

e. Why does she need the job so urgently? ....

Te toca a tí hablar

21 In this exercise we'd like you to tell us about your job. You might have to look up some specialized words in the dictionary to describe your particular situation; but try to concentrate on your hours (**el horario**), your conditions of work (**sueldo, vacaciones, puentes**), the size of your company (**empresa**), whether you work for yourself (**por cuenta propia**), and the advantages and disadvantages of your job. When you have decided what you want to say and described your job, Eloísa will tell you about hers. She's a teacher in an **instituto** (state secondary school).

22 Finally, you're applying for another job – in a travel agency. Work out the answers to the kind of questions you're likely to be asked:

¿Ha viajado usted mucho?
¿Tiene experiencia en este ramo?
¿Habla usted otros idiomas extranjeros?
¿Está dispuesto usted a trabajar bajo mucha presión?
¿Le importa trabajar muchas horas, sobre todo en enero y febrero?

When you've presented as favourable a picture of yourself as you can, turn on your tape and listen to Eloísa describing how well she could do the job.

10 Poderoso caballero es don dinero

What you will learn

- how to buy a **cassette radio**
- something about **videos** and **cameras**
- more about electrical equipment

... and what to do about your electricity charges!

Study guide

Diálogo 1
¿Cuál es tu máquina preferida?

Manolo   Me gusta la televisión en color por las imágenes, ¿no? porque se ve con claridad, y mucho mejor que la de blanco y negro – ésa es la que tengo yo en casa, la televisión.

Marga   Me encanta mi equipo de música, porque creo que realmente es bastante bueno. Eh . . . está compuesto por el tocadiscos, un sintonizador, un amplificador, una pletina y un ecualizador. Y creo que es realmente bueno porque reproduce muy bien las cassettes y los discos. ¡Me gusta mucho!

¿Y qué te gustaría comprar?

Ricardo   A lo mejor una moto.

Andrés   Un equipo completo de vídeo.

Gustavo   Pues yo me compraría un micro-computador.

Claudia   Yo me compraría un Betamax.

Daniel   Pensando en la familia, yo creo que a esta altura, con nuestras hijas listas para empezar a aprender computación, creo que decidiría en un computador.

claridad (f.) clarity	**ecualizador** (m.) equaliser
tocadiscos (m.) record player	**listo** ready
sintonizador (m.) tuner	**computación** (f.) computing
pletina (f.) deck	

Me gusta la televisión en color por las imágenes I like colour television because of the pictures. **Por** is a neat way of saying 'because of': you could also say **a causa de** if you were speaking more formally. As he is talking about a television set, Manolo should have said **el televisor** because, strictly speaking, **la televisión** means the service rather than the set. This is an example of Latin American usage creeping in.

ésa es la que tengo en casa that's the one I have at home.

▸ **Me encanta mi equipo de música** I love my stereo equipment (lit. it enchants me).

▸ **está compuesto por** it's made up of. Another use here of **por** meaning 'of' (**por** usually follows **compuesto**).

las cassettes: the cassette tapes; **el cassette** usually means radiocassette, the cassette recorder. But, because this is a recently introduced word, you'll find a lot of confusion about gender and spelling.

▸ **A lo mejor una moto** Probably a motorbike. **Una moto** is short for **motocicleta**; that's why it's feminine. **La foto** is a similar abbreviation.

Pensando en la familia Thinking about the family. But, **pensar** followed by **de** has a different meaning. **¿Qué piensas de la familia?** What's your opinion of the family?

Yo creo que a esta altura . . . I think that at this stage . . .

decidiría en I would opt for. It's more usual to use **por** than **en**.

Trabajos prácticos

1 Who likes what? Without looking back at the transcript, rewind and use the tape to help you to fill in the grid below. What are the interviewees' choices? (Answers on page 210.)

	Marga	Andrés	Manolo	Ricardo	Gustavo	Claudia	Daniel
micro-computador							
vídeo							
moto							
equipo de música							
televisor en color							
Betamax							
computador							

2 Now for some motives. Why do they choose these particular items? Write the answers, in Spanish, in the space below. (Answers on page 210.)

a. ¿Por qué quiere Daniel un computador para su familia?

....

b. ¿Por qué le gusta tanto a Marga su equipo de música?

....

c. ¿Por qué prefiere Manolo el televisor en color al de blanco y negro?

....

3 ¡**Enhorabuena!** Congratulations! You've just won a television competition. Your prize is a TV set (**un televisor**) – if you can think of a winning slogan. Pepe is acting as the television presenter and Susan will prompt you. See how you get on!

Diálogo 2
¿Por qué te compraste el Betamax?

Marga	¿Tienes vídeo?
Rafa	Sí, tengo vídeo.
Marga	¿Y qué sistema tienes?
Rafa	El Betamax.
Marga	¿Por qué te compraste el Betamax?
Rafa	Pues, porque es el más difundido en España.
Marga	Aha, y ¿sueles utilizarlo mucho en cuanto a grabaciones o sueles alquilar películas?
Rafa	Suelo hacer las dos cosas – en cuanto a grabaciones suelo grabar los dibujos animados.
Marga	¿Sí?
Rafa	Para mi hijo, porque los pide constantemente.
Marga	Y en cuanto a películas, ¿qué sueles alquilar, films, o . . . ?
Rafa	Sí, alquilamos películas en un vídeoclub.
Marga	¿Resulta barato o crees que es . . . ?
Rafa	No es demasiado barato pero tampoco es caro, o sea que está bien.
Marga	¿Y qué tipo de películas sueles alquilar?
Rafa	Bueno, normalmente son unas películas que han sido famosas alguna vez y que yo no he podido ver.
Marga	Sí.
Rafa	O cualquier otro tipo de películas que son por alguna cosa atractivas ¿no?
Marga	¿No crees que suele haber algún problema para conseguir buenas películas?
Rafa	Sí, y más en el sitio en donde estoy yo, donde es un sitio bastante pequeño.

- **difundido** widely available
  grabar to record
  alquilar to hire
  tampoco neither

- **cualquier** any
  conseguir (i) to obtain
  sitio (m.) place

¿Y qué sistema tienes? And what system do you have? Although sistema looks like a feminine word, it is in fact masculine: **un nuevo sistema** a new system.

¿Por qué te compraste el Betamax? Why did you buy (yourself) a Betamax? **Comprarse** to buy oneself: **Me compré un procesador de textos** I bought (myself) a word processor.

- **¿sueles utilizarlo mucho en cuanto a grabaciones?** do you use it a lot for recording? **en cuanto a** with regard to.

  los dibujos animados cartoons.

- **¿Resulta barato?** Does it work out cheaply?

  películas que han sido famosas alguna vez films that have been famous at some stage.

Trabajos prácticos

4 Listen to dialogue 2 again and see if you can find the Spanish equivalent of the following English phrases. (Answers on page 210.)

a. It's the most widely available. ....

b. It's a fairly small place. ....

c. I usually record cartoons. ....

d. Does it work out cheaply? ....

e. Do you usually rent films? ....

f. He's continually demanding them. ....

5 Read dialogue 2 again and then choose the correct answers to the questions below. (Answers on page 210.)

a. El Betamax es ☐ el sistema más difundido en España
☐ el sistema más distinto de España
☐ el sistema más desconocido en España

b. el precio de alquiler es ☐ muy caro
☐ muy barato
☐ módico

c. Rafa suele alquilar ☐ películas
☐ seriales
☐ telenovelas

d. ¿Qué suele hacer Rafa en cuanto al vídeo? ☐ grabar solamente
☐ alquilar solamente
☐ las dos cosas

6 You would like to buy a video, but your wife doesn't like the idea. Try to convince her with some really unbeatable arguments. Eloísa will play your wife and Susan will prompt you in English.

Escuche este video

Betahi-fi SONY

SL-HF 100

Diálogo 3
¿Cuál me recomendarías tú?

Marga	Buenas tardes.
Joven	Buenas tardes.
Marga	Mira, me gustaría comprarme un cassette.
Joven	¿Más o menos tienes una idea de cómo lo querías?
Marga	No. Quería que fuera un precio módico pero no tengo ninguna idea en especial.
Joven	Vamos a ver. Tienes el clásico radiocassette monogram, que parte de las siete mil pesetas, o cassettes estereofónicos a partir de quince mil, o aparatos copiadores de cintas que andarían sobre las treinta.
Marga	Eh bueno . . . ¿cuál me recomendarías tú?
Joven	Si eres una persona que copias cintas o te gusta copiar canciones para los amigos, quizás te venga mejor el radiocassette copiador.
Marga	Sí. ¿Tienes algún modelo más de este tipo?
Joven	Pues, de este tipo ahora mismo en las existencias no, pero se podría pedir uno ¿eh?
Marga	Mm. ¿Así que dices que son quince mil pesetas?
Joven	No, treinta mil pesetas el copiador y quince mil el estéreo normal.
Marga	Pues muy bien, gracias.
Joven	De nada.

¿Más o menos tienes una idea de cómo lo querías? Do you have some idea of how you wanted it? (**más o menos** means more or less). Notice how the young man addresses Marga as **tú**, although he doesn't know her. This is common among young people.

▶ **Quería que fuera un precio módico** I would like it to be reasonably priced. A subjunctive is used here after a verb of wishing (**querer**) when the subject of the sentence has changed from 'I' to 'it'. When there is only one subject, the second verb would be in the infinitive: **quería comprar el coche**, I wanted to buy the car.

no tengo ninguna idea en especial I haven't got any specific ideas.

▶ **a partir de las quince mil** from 15,000 (pesetas) upwards.

o aparatos copiadores de cintas or machines that copy tapes. The Spanish don't seem to have heard of copyright!

▶ **andarían sobre las treinta** they would be about 30 (thousand pesetas).

quizás te venga mejor el radiocassette copiador perhaps you'd be better off with the radiocassette that copies. Another subjunctive (**venga**) because the assistant is only suggesting a possibility.

▶ **en las existencias** in stock.

Trabajos prácticos

7 In this exercise some of the phrases that Marga and the assistant used in the shop in dialogue 3 have been changed slightly. Insert the original Spanish in the space provided. (Answers on page 210.)

a. Quisiera comprar un cassette ....

b. ¿Tiene otros modelos como éste? ....

c. ¿Sabes aproximadamente lo que quieres? ....

d. Has dicho que cuesta quince mil, ¿no? ....

e. Creo que para tí sería mejor el radiocassette copiador ....

....

f. No estoy muy segura de lo que quiero ....

8 Now back to basics. That dialogue contained a number of verb tenses which need to be examined a little more closely. Read dialogue 3 again and complete the exercise. (Answers on page 210.)

a. Find three examples of the conditional tense and write down their infinitives.

....

....

....

b. Find three examples of the present tense and write down their infinitives.

....

....

....

c. Find one example of a subjunctive and write down its infinitive.

....

d. Find an example of the imperfect tense and write down the third person form.

....

Is it different from the first person? ....

9 It's sales time in Spain – **los saldos**. You have some money to spend and there are some good buys in electronic equipment. Find out what's the best offer. Pepe will be the salesman and Susan will prompt you. You'll need to know **rebajado** reduced; **oferta** (f.) offer; **asequible** accessible.

Diálogo 4
¿Tienes un equipo de fotografía?

Gustavo Sí, tengo una cámara de 35mm, Nikon, con microprocesador. Es un modelo reciente de la Nikon que permite operación programada. Tengo un lente normal de 50mm y tengo un lente con zoom y teleobjetivo de 35 a 125mm. Desafortunadamente es un lente que requiere mucha luz, por la distancia focal. Tengo además un lente gran angular, de 28mm. Todo el equipo se puede operar también con flash electrónico y, por supuesto, poseo todos los aditamentos de limpieza que se requieren para mantener un equipo de fotografía en condiciones de operación.

teleobjetivo (m.) telephoto lens   **mantener** to maintain
además also, besides

Mi equipo de fotografía My photographic equipment. **Sacar una foto** to take a photograph. **Instantáneas** snapshots.

la Nikon names of companies are always feminine in Spanish. **Trabajo con la BBC** I work for the BBC.

que permite operación programada which allows programmed operation.

Desafortunadamente es un lente que requiere mucha luz Unfortunately, it's a lens which requires a lot of light.

un lente gran angular a wide-angled lens.

por supuesto poseo todos los aditamentos de limpieza que se requieren of course I own all the necessary cleaning equipment. Gustavo uses a more formal language here (**poseo** instead of **tengo**) as he's involved in a very technical subject. **Aditamentos** is a Latin American word meaning accessories. Spaniards would probably say **complementos**.

Trabajos prácticos

10 Dialogue 4 was full of technicalities about Gustavo's camera. Fill in as many details about each item as you can, in Spanish. (Answers on page 210.)

a. la cámara ....

....

b. el lente normal ....

....

c. el teleobjetivo ....

....

d. el lente gran angular ....

....

e. Gustavo también tiene ....

....

11 Now a little more vocabulary work. How skilled are you at forming nouns from verbs and vice versa? See whether you know, or can form, the noun or verb from the following words. If you can't, it's good practice to consult a dictionary and try to work out some of the endings which Spanish uses to given basic root words a variety of different meanings. (Answers on page 210.)

a. operar ....   **b.** permitir ....

c. poseer ....   **d.** limpieza ....

e. requerir ....   **f.** equipo ....

g. mantener ....

12 On tape you'll hear a simpler description of a camera and how to use it. Listen to it through once then see if you can repeat what was said. Below are some prompts to help you to remember the order in which things came. You will need to know: **pulsar el botón** to push the button, **enfocar** to focus, **tamaño** size and **cuenta con todos los medios** it has all the facilities.

marca (brand)   **imagen**
barato/caro   **quiere comprar otra**
sencillo/difícil de operar   **fotos sofisticadas**
aditamentos (accessories)

Giros importantes

Me gusta el televisor en color por las imágenes
I like colour television because of the pictures

Me encanta mi equipo de música
I love my stereo

Está compuesta por . . .
It consists of . . .

A lo mejor
Probably

Yo me compraría un micro-computador
I would buy (myself) a micro-computer

Pensando en la familia . . .
Thinking about the family . . .

Creo que decidiría por un computador
I think I would opt for a computer

¿Qué sistema tienes?
What system do you have?

¿Por qué te compraste el Betamax?
Why did you buy (yourself) the Betamax?

Es el más difundido
It's the most widely available

Suelo grabar los dibujos animados
I usually record the cartoons

¿Resulta barato?
Does it work out cheaply?

Tampoco es caro
It's not expensive either

¿Suele haber algún problema para conseguir buenas películas?
Is there usually a problem in obtaining good films?

Más o menos
More or less

Quería que fuera un precio módico
I'd like it to be reasonably priced

No tengo ninguna idea en especial
I haven't any specific ideas

Tienes el clásico radiocassette que parte de las siete mil pesetas
There is the ordinary radiocassette player, that starts at 7,000 pesetas

A partir de las quince mil
From 15,000

Andarían sobre las treinta
They would be about 30

¿Cuál me recomendarías tú?
Which would you recommend?

¿Tienes algún modelo más de este tipo?
Have you any others like this?

Quizás te venga mejor el radiocassette copiador
Perhaps the radiocassette that copies would suit you better

Ahora mismo en las existencias, no
Not in stock at the moment, no

Es un modelo reciente
It's a recent model

Tengo un lente normal
I have an ordinary lens

Un equipo de fotografía
Photographic equipment

Gramática

Por and para

For English speakers of Spanish, these two prepositions pose a lot of problems about when to use which one and where. Here are a few guidelines.

Por

Use **por** to mean 'because of':
Me gusta la televisión en color por las imágenes. I like colour television because of the pictures.

To mean 'by':
por avión by air or by plane.

When you want to say 'along' or 'through':
por la avenida de Santa Cruz along Santa Cruz Avenue.
por la ventana through the window.

When you're exchanging things:
dí mil libras por el coche. I gave a thousand pounds for the car;
gracias por tu carta thank you for your letter.

And in certain set expressions like:
por la mañana in the morning;
por supuesto of course.

Para

Use **para** to mean 'intended for' in expressions like **para usted**, for you, **para Carlos**, for Carlos.

And for destination:
el tren para Madrid the train to Madrid.

Use it with verbs when you can translate the phrase by the English phrase 'in order to':
Voy a España para comprarme un piso I'm going to Spain (in order) to buy a flat.

And in time expressions like:
la cita es para las dos the appointment is for two o'clock;
hazlo para mañana do it by tomorrow;

13 And now for a little practice. Here's a transcript of what Gustavo said about that video he bought last week in Gijón. Translate what he says, underline the phrases which use **por** and **para**, then try to work out why they're used here. (Answers on page 210.)

Bueno, la semana pasada fuimos a Gijón para pasar unos días con mis suegros. Fuimos por tren porque está el coche en el taller. Bueno pues, estuvimos paseando por la Avenida de Oviedo el sábado por la mañana, y vimos un vídeo muy rebajado en 'Videomania': entramos y lo compramos por setenta mil pesetas. La verdad es que lo compré para Isabel: hace meses que habla de comprarse uno. Lo vamos a usar para grabar películas que ponen muy tarde para luego verlas a una hora que nos vaya mejor.

Este, ese and aquel

You are probably quite familiar with these adjectives but you may be a little uncertain about exactly which to use when.

Este means 'this'

este café this coffee
estos cigarillos these cigarettes

esta botella this bottle
estas cerillas these matches

Ese means 'that'

ese hotel that hotel
esos bares those bars

esa cafetería that café
esas pensiones those boarding houses

Aquel means 'that over there'

aquel mar that sea
aquellos barcos those ships

aquella roca that rock
aquellas olas those waves

Remember that because **este**, **ese** and **aquel** are adjectives, they must agree with the nouns they describe. And if you want to turn them into pronouns (that is, use them on their own) you can do so easily:
Prefiero estos zapatos pero ésos son más cómodos. I prefer these shoes but those are more comfortable.

Used as pronouns, **éste**, **ése** and **aquél** must have accents.

14 Practise those adjectives by filling in the blanks below. It will also test whether you can remember the names of all that equipment in the dialogues! The first one has been done for you. (Answers on page 211.)

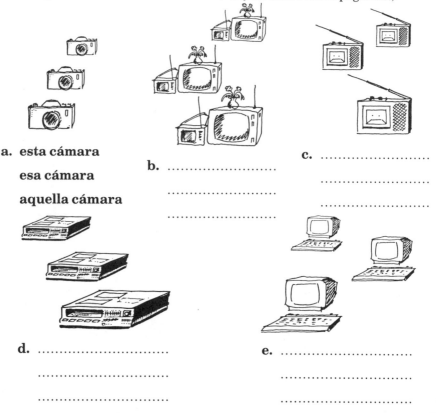

a. **esta cámara**

   esa cámara

   aquella cámara

b. ....

....

....

c. ....

....

....

d. ....

....

....

e. ....

....

....

Lectura

We've dealt with videos and cameras: now let's look at computers. This reading passage is part of some sales information about the Sinclair Spectrum. It's not too technical and a lot of the vocabulary is applicable in other areas. For example, **el teclado**, the keyboard, is used for a typewriter as well and **teclas** are keys on a piano, typewriter or computer.

El Ordenador de Todos Para Todo

El ordenador personal Sinclair ZX Spectrum ha batido (y sigue batiendo) todos los records de popularidad. Hoy por hoy, es un estándar en el hogar, el colegio y el trabajo. Éstas son sus principales características:

Color
Ocho colores disponibles para primer plano, fondo y borde (independientes entre sí). Control de intensidad de brillo.

Sonido
Orden BEEP con intensidad y duración variable. Altavoz interno que puede manejar 10 octavas.

Teclado
Teclas móviles de tamaño convencional de tacto agradable.

Memoria
Dos versiones 16K y 48K.

Gráficos
Alta definición.

Carácteres
Mayúsculas y minúsculas.

Grabación y carga
A alta velocidad.

Lenguaje
Basic Sinclair ampliado a 16K. Sistema exclusivo de entrada de comandos mediante una sola tecla.

Si el Spectrum es, en sí mismo, el microordenador más importante de la década de los ochenta, una de las razones sin duda más importantes es la cantidad de periféricos creados para aumentar su capacidad y utilidad.

---

batir to break (records)
estándar (m.) standard
hogar (m.) home
primer plano (m.) foreground
fondo (m.) background
borde (m.) edge
altavoz (m.) loudspeaker
manejar to handle

móvil moveable
tamaño (m.) size
tacto (m.) touch, feel
mayúscula (f.) capital letter
minúscula (f.) small letter
carga (f.) load
ampliado widened, upgraded
mediante by means of

15 Now fill in the blanks. To help you, the English translations of the words appear in brackets. (Answers on page 211.)

a. Hoy por hoy es un estándar en el .... (home, school, work).

b. Ocho colores disponibles para .... (foreground, background and edge).

c. Orden BEEP con .... (variable intensity and length).

d. Teclas móviles de .... (standard size).

e. Gráficos de .... (high definition).

f. Sistema exclusivo de entrada de comandos ....

.... (via a single key).

Here is a less technical piece about several films that have just been released as videos. See what you can make of this extract.

El último tango en París

El último tango en París ya está al alcance de todos los videoaficionados. A la vuelta del trabajo o con el carrito de la compra, sólo es necesario pasarse por un club para alquilar el film de Bertolucci. En casa, frente al televisor, e incluso con sus hijos, descubriremos que no es más que una bella historia de amor, escéptica y con final dramático. Eso sí: el cuerpo de María Schneider puede hacernos recurrir al manual del vídeo para aprender a congelar la imagen. Sigue valiendo la pena. La Warner juega fuerte, en pleno verano presenta doce nuevas películas con *El tango* a la cabeza. *Verano del 42* es una película entrañable sobre el descubrimiento del amor de un adolescente de quince años en una colonia de verano en las playas de Nueva Inglaterra. *El ojo de la aguja*, protagonizada por Donald Sutherland, es una historia de espionaje durante la segunda guerra, basada en el libro de Ken Follet, *La isla de las tormentas*.

al alcance within reach
el carrito de la compra
  (m.) shopping trolley
incluso even
cuerpo (m.) body
recurrir to have recourse to

valer la pena to be worthwhile
entrañable appealing
aguja (f.) needle
protagonizado starring
espionaje (m.) espionage
tormenta (f.) storm

16 Answer these questions in English. (Answers on page 211.)

a. How many films are mentioned? ....

b. What are their English titles? ....

....

c. What is the title of Ken Follet's book? What does it mean?

....

d. Where does the action of *Verano del 42* take place?

....

e. What kind of film is *El ojo de la aguja?* ....

f. When does it take place? ....

Radio

The first radio extract is taken from Charito's phone-in programme. María Isabel has rung in to complain about the cost of installing electrical wiring in the house she's just had built in the country. It's going to cost her a lot more than it cost her neighbour – and she wants to know why. You'll need the following vocabulary. (Transcript on page 218.)

cerquina very close
casina (f.) small house
luz (f.) light
¡caramba! goodness me!
pertenecer (a) to belong (to)
enganchar to hook up

palo (m.) pole
presupuesto (m.) estimate
¡qué barbaridad! how terrible!
contestación (f.) answer
fuerza (f.) power

17 Now complete the phrases below. Listen carefully to the text and fill in the blanks. (Answers on page 211.)

a. Mire, es que hice una casina en un pueblo y me cuesta la luz

....

b. Yo quería saber por qué hace................................... lo pusieron

otros vecinos y les costaron ....

c. Y a mí me falta muy poco para ....

d. O sea .... de Coyoto.

e. Y de donde me tienen que enganchar a mi casa, hay

....

f. ¡Qué ....! ¿Y lo consultó usted esto?

The next radio extract is from the same programme. Charito reads a letter requesting a cooker – it doesn't have to be new, but should be in good condition, **en buen uso**. You'll need the following vocabulary. (Transcript on page 219.)

demás others
cariñoso loving
cocina (f.) cooker
carbón (m.) coal

agradecer to thank
aldea (f.) village
firmar to sign

18 Listen to that recording again and list the order in which Charito read out the following remarks. (Answers on page 211.)

a. ☐ Le agradecería llame a este teléfono
b. ☐ Un saludo cariñoso para todos
c. ☐ Se nos despide con un saludo esta amiga
d. ☐ Sois estupendos
e. ☐ Desearía encontrar una cocina de carbón
f. ☐ Es para llevar a una casita a la aldea
g. ☐ Demás componentes del programa Escandalera

And finally, a short advertisement for a shop called Gailo. It sells **frigoríficos** (refrigerators), **lavadoras** (washing-machines) and **cocinas** (cookers). Just listen to it, to get the flavour of Spanish advertisements on the radio.

Te toca a tí hablar

 19 You've got a piece of equipment for sale. It could be a camera, a stereo or an old black and white television. Work out how you would set about selling it to someone who answers your advertisement in the classified column of your local paper. Then listen to how Eloísa goes about selling her stereo equipment.

20 ¡Éxito! Success! You've got rid of that outdated equipment and you've got some money to spend. What would you most like to buy and why? Eloísa, of course, has some quite original ideas.

11 Más ruido que nueces

What you will learn

- something about Spanish **radio** programmes
- and about how radio is financed
- more about reading habits in Spain and the types of **newspapers** that Spaniards buy

... and the problems of learning a **foreign language**

Study guide

Diálogo 1
¿Tienes un programa preferido?

Marga	Sí, Sin Prisa, un programa de música lenta.
Verónica	De música selecta.
Carmen	Me gusta escuchar música por la noche cuando estoy estudiando.
Rafa	Prefiero escuchar los informativos.
Eduardo	Un programa Directo Directo.
Martín	Mm, no sé, temas musicales, y temas deportivos y telediarios.
Gustavo	Generalmente tengo la radio sintonizada en la Radio Nacional que divulga constantemente música clásica.
Claudia	Yo la tengo en una emisora que se llama la emisora Montserrat, que solamente es música romántica.
Daniel	Normalmente, si no estoy muy cansado, me gustan los programas informativos.

deportivo sport

▶ **Sin Prisa** In no hurry (lit. without hurry).

selecta fine, choice or especially chosen, select.

Prefiero escuchar los informativos I prefer to listen to the news. Notice that **escuchar** means to listen *to* so doesn't need to be followed by **a**.

Directo Directo is a very popular magazine-type radio programme which combines interviews, news, comment and features.

telediarios Martín is referring here to the television news; he's forgotten that he was asked about the radio.

tengo la radio sintonizada en I have the radio tuned to . . . **Sintonía** (f.) can mean either tuning or a signature tune.

que divulga constantemente música clásica which broadcasts non-stop classical music. **Divulgar** is rather a formal word for **emitir**, to broadcast.

me gustan los programas informativos. I like news programmes. **Los informativos** is the usual word for the news.

Trabajos prácticos

1. How well did you understand the interviews about radio preferences in dialogue 1? On the grid below indicate what programmes people liked, bearing in mind that some people had more than one preference. (Answers on page 211.)

	Classical music	Easy listening	News	Sports	Magazine programmes
Eduardo					
Martín					
Carmen					
Daniel					
Rafa					
Verónica					
Claudia					
Marga					
Gustavo					

2. Now for some practice with adjectives. Which words were used to describe the following items in dialogue 1? (Answers on page 211.)

a. música ....

b. temas ....

c. radio (Careful with this one, it comes from a verb). ....

....

d. programas ....

3. You're an interviewer for a research firm that's been asked to find out which programmes are most popular on Cadena Libre Antena. Susan will prompt you in English. Use the **usted** form. The following phrases may be of help:
¿suele . . . ? ¿qué tipo de . . . ? ¿qué le parecen . . . ?

Diálogo 2
La prensa se lee bastante

Marga Háblame de la prensa por favor.

Redactor Yo voy a hacer una comparación entre la prensa regional y la prensa nacional. Como vamos a decirles a todos aquí, que en Asturias se halla aproximadamente un millón, cien mil habitantes y que aquí tenemos cuatro periódicos diarios, una revista mensual, otra semanal, varios bimensuales. Aquí se lee bastante el periódico, dentro de lo que cabe, aunque no es la tónica general en toda España. Aproximadamente, el periódico de mayor tirada tiene cuarenta y cinco mil ejemplares, calculando que puedan leer el periódico cinco personas por ejemplar. Es una media bastante importante de cara al resto del país. La cultura media en Asturias es importante, por lo tanto los periódicos se leen. Hay que decir también, respecto a la prensa por ejemplo en nuestra región, es que hay un periódico importante, dedicado única y exclusivamente a la región, que tiene además la competencia de la prensa nacional, que esta prensa nacional llega a la vez, al mismo tiempo, aquí a Asturias, y por lo tanto, ha de luchar contra ellos. La prensa se lee bastante ahora, más que nada dentro de esta nueva etapa de gobierno que en la etapa anterior, en la dictadura.

tirada (f.) circulation
ejemplar (m.) copy

▶ **media** (f.) average
competencia (f.) competition

Redactor This means either a writer or editor: our interviewee writes and presents radio programmes for Radio Cadena SER, one of the biggest commercial radio stations in Spain. He has a 'journalistic' style even when giving an informal 'off-air' interview.

hacer una comparación to do a comparison of.

en Asturias se halla . . . un millón . . . de habitantes there are a million inhabitants in Asturias. You can use **hallarse** or **encontrarse** (both of which mean literally to find oneself) to substitute for more common verbs like **hay** or **estar**.

▶ **una revista mensual, otra semanal, varios bimensuales.** One monthly magazine, another weekly one and several which appear twice a month. All these adjectives can be used on their own: **un mensual** a monthly magazine.

▶ **La prensa se lee bastante ahora** newspapers are quite widely read now. (For use of reflexives, see Units 2 and 4.)

dentro de lo que cabe as much as one can expect.

▶ **no es la tónica general** it's not the norm.

Es una media bastante importante de cara al resto del país. It's quite a high average when compared with the rest of the country.

La cultura media en Asturias es importante. The general level of education in Asturias is high.

respecto a la prensa with regard to the press.

dedicado única y exclusivamente devoted entirely and exclusively. If you have two adverbs that end in **mente** following one another you can omit the first **mente**. For formation of adverbs, see page 177.

por lo tanto, ha de luchar contra ellos. Therefore, it has to fight against them.

Trabajos prácticos

4 Tick the correct answer. (Answers on page 211.)

a. Asturias tiene
- ☐ dos millones de habitantes
- ☐ cien mil habitantes
- ☐ un millón y medio de habitantes

b. En Asturias hay
- ☐ cuatro diarios
- ☐ cinco diarios
- ☐ cuarto diarios

c. La prensa se lee
- ☐ menos que antes
- ☐ más que antes
- ☐ igual que antes

d. Un periódico es leído por
- ☐ tres personas
- ☐ cinco personas
- ☐ cincuenta personas

e. La prensa nacional llega
- ☐ a la misma hora que la prensa regional
- ☐ antes que la prensa regional
- ☐ una hora después de la prensa regional

f. La cultura media en Asturias es
- ☐ alta
- ☐ inferior
- ☐ normal

5 Here are translations of some of the phrases which the radio presenter used. Find the Spanish equivalent and write it down in the space provided. (Answers on page 211.)

a. In Asturias there are about a million inhabitants.

....

b. Therefore, it has to compete against them.

....

c. This new phase of government.

....

d. It's a fairly high average. ....

e. It's not the norm throughout Spain..................................

f. It also faces competition from the national press.

....

6 You've just met a radio journalist and you've questioned him about the press in Spain. Now it's his turn to ask you about the press in the UK. Here are some words that might help: **cotilleo** gossip; **culto** highbrow; **la familia real** the royal family. Susan will prompt you in English.

Diálogo 3
Los jóvenes compran revistas

Marga	¿Qué periódicos son los que tienen más venta?
Eduardo	Bueno, a nivel regional, *La Nueva España*, y algo también *La Voz de Asturias*. A nivel nacional, *El País*.
Marga	¿Y qué personas suelen inclinarse por determinado tipo de prensa?
Eduardo	Sobre todo, la gente mayor se inclina, o bien por la prensa regional, *La Nueva España*, que tiene muchas noticias locales, y de algunas zonas de la provincia y luego, el *ABC*. Y la gente de menos edad se inclina sobre todo por *El País*.
Marga	¿Suelen comprar muy a menudo los jóvenes, periódicos?
Eduardo	No con mucha frecuencia. Los jóvenes más bien compran revistas científicas, de deportes, automovilismo.
Marga	¿Y existen juegos con revistas para ordenadores?
Eduardo	Sí, también, hay además una cantidad grande de títulos a lo largo de publicaciones mensuales, semanales, que son los que compran principalmente la gente joven.
Marga	¿Y qué tipo de prensa prefieres tú? ¿qué sueles leer?
Eduardo	Bueno, yo habitualmente leo siempre *La Nueva España* como periódico regional y hojeo más que leo la prensa, el resto de la prensa nacional.

a menudo often
▶ **más bien** rather

¿Qué periódicos son los que tienen más venta? Which newspapers have the greatest sales?

a nivel regional on a regional level.

¿Y qué personas suelen inclinarse por determinado tipo de prensa? And which people usually opt for a certain kind of press?

▶ **la gente mayor se inclina, o bien por . . .** older people opt either for . . .

¿Y existen juegos con revistas para ordenadores? And do the computer magazines come with games? **Ordenador** is another word for **computador**, computer.

a lo largo de publicaciones mensuales throughout monthly publications.

yo habitualmente leo I usually read. A variant on **yo suelo leer**.

▶ **hojeo más que leo** I glance through rather than read (**hojear** to skim, leaf).

Trabajos prácticos

7 That conversation (dialogue 3) was about reading habits in a Spanish provincial capital. See whether you can remember what the trends were that the shopkeeper had observed among his clients by completing the following grid. (Answers on page 211.)

	El País	ABC	Nueva España	revistas	Voz de Asturias
la gente joven suele leer					
la gente mayor suele leer					
Eduardo suele leer					
periódicos con más venta i **a nivel local** ii **a nivel nacional**					

8 Some of dialogue 3 is transcribed here again – but a few of the phrases and structures have been changed. Underline the phrases that are different, and jot down the original version. Listen to your tape again to remind you. (Answers on page 211.)

Marga ¿Qué periódicos son los que se venden más?

Eduardo En cuanto a periódicos regionales, *La Nueva España* y hasta cierto punto *La Voz de Asturias*. Hablando de diarios nacionales, *El País*.

Marga ¿Y quiénes optan por determinado tipo de prensa?

Eduardo Los mayores se deciden por la prensa regional, *La Nueva España*, o que informa sobre noticias locales y de unas regiones de la provincia – luego el *ABC*. Los más jóvenes tienden a comprar *El País*.

Marga ¿La gente joven compra los periódicos con frecuencia?

Eduardo No muy a menudo. Los menores compran publicaciones de ciencias, de deportes o de coches.

9 For this speaking exercise, you're comparing notes with Pepe about reading habits in Spain and the UK. Follow Susan's prompts in English.

Diálogo 4
Para mí es bastante difícil

Marga Estoy estudiando inglés desde hace un año y medio aproximadamente y lo estoy haciendo porque realmente me gusta, no porque lo necesite para mi trabajo, ya que en el trabajo solamente utilizamos un inglés técnico y no es imprescindible conocer un inglés coloquial. Eh, para mí es bastante fácil traducir del inglés al español; lo que ocurre es que cuando intentas hablar en inglés, no dispones de esa fluidez que tienes en tu propio idioma. Y digamos que se te ponen un poco las cosas cuesta arriba. Y también es bastante difícil para mí coger las frases en voz pasiva inglesa. ¡Es realmente difícil!

imprescindible necessary   **propio** own

▶ **Estoy estudiando inglés desde hace un año** I've been studying English for a year. There is more about this construction in our grammar section on page 177.

no porque lo necesite para mi trabajo not because I (might) need it for my work. Marga uses the subjunctive here because she's expressing uncertainty after a negative.

▶ **ya que en el trabajo** given that at work. **Ya que** is a useful 'linking' word. **Dado que** and **puesto que** can be used in the same way.

lo que ocurre es cuando intentas hablar en inglés what happens is when you try to speak in English. Marga uses the **tú** form of **intentar**, to try, in much the same way as we do in English. It is very colloquial.

▶ **no dispones de esa fluidez** you don't have that fluency (lit. you don't have that fluency at your disposal).

▶ **digamos que se te ponen un poco las cosas cuesta arriba.** Let's say things get a bit difficult for you. **Cuesta arriba** means uphill.

es bastante difícil para mi coger las frases en voz pasiva inglesa. It's quite difficult for me to pick up English phrases in the passive. **Coger** is a portmanteau word which means here 'to pick up' or 'catch'. **No lo cogí** I didn't catch it. Notice that Marga has a problem with the passive because Spanish tries to avoid using it and prefers an active verb instead. So, for example, 'newspapers are read' would be rendered in Spanish not as **periódicos son leídos** but **se leen los periódicos**, using the reflexive **se** construction. Look back at dialogue 2 for more examples. For more on reflexives, see Units 2 and 4.

Trabajos prácticos

10 In this exercise, find the answers using the following clues. The initial letters of the answers form a word that describes Marga's feelings about English! (Answers on page 212.)

a. periódico que sale todos los días ☐ ....

b. se habla en Estados Unidos ☐ ....

c. lo contrario a difícil ☐ ....

d. una lengua ☐ ....

e. una forma hablada del idioma ☐ ....

f. optar por ☐ ....

g. tipo de música ☐ ....

☐ ....

11 Make sure you know all the verbs which Marga uses by jotting down the first person singular of each one in the space provided. Give the ordinary present indicative. (Answers on page 212.)

a. estoy estudiando ....

b. lo estoy haciendo ....

c. no es imprescindible *conocer* ....

d. no dispones de ....

e. y digamos que ....

f. se ponen difíciles las cosas ....

g. es fácil *traducir* ....

h. es difícil *coger* ....

¡**Cuidado!** (Careful!) Most of those verbs are irregular. If you got them wrong, revise them from the verb tables on page 225.

12 Here's your chance to air your frustrations with the Spanish language! Tell Eloísa exactly what you feel are the problems. Susan will prompt you in English. You may need the following vocabulary: **extenso** extensive, **sonido** sound, and **fuerte** strong.

Giros importantes

Sin prisa	Without haste
Prefiero escuchar	I prefer to listen to
los informativos	the news
programas de música lenta	'easy listening' programmes
temas musicales	music programmes
temas deportivos	sports programmes
música romántica/clásica	romantic/classical music
Tengo la radio sintonizada en	I have the radio tuned to Radio
Radio Nacional	Nacional
La prensa regional/nacional	Regional/national press
En Asturias se halla un millón de	In Asturias there are a million
habitantes	inhabitants
Periódicos diarios	Daily newspapers
Revistas mensuales	Monthly magazines
semanales	weekly magazines
bimensuales	twice-monthly magazines
No es la tónica general	It's not the norm
El periódico de mayor	The newspaper with the largest
tirada	circulation
Es una media bastante	It's quite a high average
importante	
Respecto a la prensa	With regard to the press
Por lo tanto	Therefore
¿Qué periódicos son los que	Which newspapers have the
tienen más venta?	greatest sales?
A nivel regional/nacional	On a regional/national level
La gente mayor se inclina o bien	Older people opt either
por . . . o por . . .	for . . . or for . . .
Revistas científicas	Science magazines
Revistas con juegos para	Magazines with computer
ordenadores	games
A lo largo de	Throughout
Yo habitualmente leo	I usually read
Hojeo más que leo	I skim rather than read
Estoy estudiando inglés desde	I have been studying English for a
hace un año	year
No porque lo necesite para mi	Not because I need it for my
trabajo	work
Ya que en el trabajo	Given that at work
Un inglés técnico/coloquial	Technical/spoken English
Es difícil/fácil traducir del inglés	It's difficult/easy to translate from
al español	English to Spanish
No dispones de esa fluidez	You haven't got that fluency
Se te ponen las cosas cuesta	Things get a bit difficult for
arriba	you
Es difícil coger las frases	It's difficult to catch the phrases

Gramática

Hacer

Here is some more information about time expressions with **hacer**.

- Use it to mean 'ago' in sentences like:
  Hace un mes, fui a Barcelona A month ago, I went to Barcelona.
  La ví aquí, hace un rato. I saw her here a moment ago.

- Use it to mean 'for' in sentences like:
  Trabajo en Correos desde hace cuatro años. I've been working at the Post Office for four years.
  Vivo en Bilbao desde hace veinte años. I've lived in Bilbao for 20 years.

- You can change the order of these sentences and put **hace** at the beginning, missing out **desde**: **Hace cuatro años que trabajo en Correos. Hace veinte años que vivo en Bilbao.**

- The thing to remember with this type of sentence is that both verbs are used in the same tense:
  Hacía dos años que la conocía I had known her for two years (Imperfect).
  Hace muchos meses que tengo este dolor de espalda I've had this back trouble for many months (Present).

  (Note that Spanish uses the Imperfect where English uses the Pluperfect, and the Present where English uses the Perfect.)

13 In this exercise you are given two components to make into sentences using either **desde hace** or **hace . . . que**. Be careful not to confuse the constructions! The first one has been done for you. (Answers on page 212.)

a. un año   estudiar   *Estudio desde hace un año/Hace un año que estudio.*

b. un momento   estar aquí   ....

c. varios años   leer la Prensa   ....

d. unos meses   aprender español   ....

e. algunos días   tener la gripe   ....

f. una semana   esperar una carta   ....

Adverbs

Adverbs tell you how things are done: well, badly, slowly, quickly. To form an adverb in Spanish, start with the feminine form of the adjective (if there is one) and add the ending **mente**. If there is no feminine form, add **mente** to the masculine, e.g. **valiente ▶ valientemente; feroz ▶ ferozmente.**
Conduce estupendamente. He drives fantastically.
Sabe inglés perfectamente. He knows English perfectly.

If the **mente** form is too long, or sounds awkward, you can substitute it for a phrase with **con**.
Viene con frecuencia. He comes here frequently.
Hace todo con mucha calma. He does everything very calmly.

Or, if you want to be more colloquial, you can stick with the adjective.
Dijo ella, tranquila. She said, calmly.

Be careful with **malo** and **bueno.** They are not adverbs but adjectives. The adverbial forms are **mal** and **bien.**

La comida era muy mala. The meal was very poor.
Salimos a comer pero comimos muy mal. We went out for a meal, but we ate very badly.

Habla bien el español. He speaks Spanish well.
Su español es muy bueno. His Spanish is very good.

14 Turn adjectives into adverbs. Here is a series of pictures, each with a short description. Make up your own sentences, based on these, but using the verb given. (Answers on page 212.)

a. un coche de carreras rápido

corre ....

b. un cocinero perfecto

cocina ....

c. unos estudiantes diligentes

estudian ....

d. un torero valiente

torea ....

e. una tirada difícil

lo coge con ....

f. un mastín feroz

ladra ....

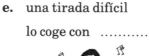

g. unos cantantes estupendos

cantan ....

h. una de sus novelas anteriores

lo escribió ....

i. una carta reciente

la recibió ....

j. una modelo exclusiva

trabaja para Dior ....

Lectura

Now that you're so far ahead in your study of Spanish, you might like to sign up for a course in Spain. Read the following letter from an Association of Language Schools and see whether they offer you what you want.

Hispalen
San Miguel 16
Zaragoza

Muy señores nuestros:

Somos una organización dedicada a la enseñanza del español como idioma extranjero. Contamos con más de catorce centros distribuídos por las principales ciudades españolas y con una gran experiencia en la enseñanza de idiomas.

A continuación, les facilitamos una información detallada sobre nuestros cursos. Debido a la gran variedad de los mismos, confiamos que los estudiantes no tengan problema alguno en elegir el más conveniente para su nivel de conocimiento de la lengua española y que los programas se ajusten a sus particulares necesidades y preferencias.

Mención especial merece la obtención de 'credits' por varias universidades españolas; Zaragoza, Madrid y Salamanca si los estudiantes estuviesen interesados.

Para más información o en caso de cualquier duda, rogamos se pongan en contacto con la dirección arriba indicada.

Esperando que encuentren el curso que desean y tenerles pronto entre nosotros.

Les saluda atentamente,

Juan Carreras Muñoz

enseñanza (f.) teaching	**elegir (i)** to choose
contar con (here) to have	**nivel** (m.) level
a continuación later	**merecer** to deserve
facilitar to provide	**duda** (f.) doubt
debido a due to	**rogar (ue)** to ask, beg
confiar to trust	**dirección** (f.) address

15 How much of that passage did you understand? Answer the questions below in English to test yourself. (Answers on page 212.)

a. What two 'trump cards' does the Association have to offer?

....

b. What must you do if you have any queries?

....

c. Do you have to work for 'credits'? ....

d. How can you be sure you'll get the level of class you want?

....

e. How flexible are the syllabuses? ....

f. What two things does the Association wish for its future students?

....

Spanish teachers need courses too! What does the following programme have to offer?

---

1. Nivel de conocimientos. Los participantes deben poseer ya un buen dominio de la lengua española.

2. Contenidos. Perfeccionar el conocimiento práctico del español: información sobre métodos y técnicas lingüísticos: prácticas basadas en la elaboración y análisis de unidades docentes.

3. Sesiones de trabajo en grupos. La mayoría de las sesiones consistirá en reuniones por grupos con el fin de elaborar materiales, desarrollarlos en una clase y luego evaluarlos. Se utilizarán grabaciones mediante vídeo. Análisis de materiales aportados por los participantes o por el profesor. Visitas a zonas de interés en los alrededores, tanto por razones de entorno geográfico como social.

4. Estructura de los cursos. Los cursos constarán de dos sesiones diarias sobre temas troncales y de una tercera sesión en la cual se podrá elegir entre dos opciones.

5. Actividades complementarias. Conferencias/excursiones/asistencia a diversas actividades culturales y folklóricas/facilidades para desplazarse a la playa.

6. Residencia. Todos los participantes se alojarán, en regimen de pensión completa y en habitaciones individuales.

7. Matrícula. El precio de la matrícula es de 64.000 pesetas por el curso y el alojamiento (excepto cena de sábados y domingos).

---

elaboración (f.) production	**constar de** to consist of
docente teaching	**troncal** (m.) core, basic
desarrollar to develop	**elegir (i)** to choose
grabación (f.) recording	**conferencia** (f.) lecture
mediante via	**asistencia** (f.) attendance
aportar to bring	**desplazarse** to travel
tanto por . . . como both for . . . as	**alojarse** to stay
los alrededores vicinity	**matrícula** (f.) fee
entorno (m.) surroundings	

16 Now for a true/false exercise. Which of the following statements are true (**verdad**) or false (**mentira**)? (Answers on page 212.)

	verdad	mentira
a. All meals are included in the price.	☐	☐
b. There will be opportunities for discussing your own material.	☐	☐
c. Beginners can take part in the course.	☐	☐
d. There are two main work sessions per day.	☐	☐
e. Audio-visual equipment will be available.	☐	☐
f. Lectures will also be arranged.	☐	☐

Radio

The first radio extract is an advertisement for a newspaper, *La Nueva España*, one of the local newspapers published in Asturias. Although very fast, it's not very long, and it's very clearly enunciated, so you shouldn't have any problems in understanding it. (Transcript on page 219.)

fiabilidad (f.) reliability
difusión (f.) circulation
realizar to accomplish
esfuerzo (m.) effort
recoger to collect
al tanto de in touch with
actualidad (f.) current affairs

por supuesto of course
cuanto (here) everything
villa (f.) small town
acontecimiento (m.) event
sabroso daring, racy
protagonizar to star in
suceso (m.) event

17 We've transcribed some of the advertisements – but left some spaces. Rewind your cassette and see if you can supply the missing information. (Answers on page 212.)

Los grandes periódicos lo son por .... y por su

fiabilidad, como .... , el periódico

de Asturias. Líder en .... prestigiado por

su .... Para figurar en ese ....

.... *La Nueva España* realiza ....

un esfuerzo .... El periódico

recoge .... las opiniones de ....

prestigiados y plurales, informaciónes de lo que ocurre ....

.... selectivas y suficientes para estar ....

.... Las últimas y más contrastadas

....y, por supuesto, cuanto ocurre en

.... y en los pueblos asturianos. Y esos .... que

protagonizan los famosos, ... y los

episodios humanos ....se

comentan en casa ....

The last radio extract is taken from a short talk by our journalist about the station that he works for, Radio Asturias Cadena SER. You'll need the following vocabulary. (Transcript on page 220.)

emisora (f.) radio station	**estatal** state
pertenecer to belong	**plantilla** (f.) staff
generar to generate	**corto** short: (here) small
comercio (m.) business	**sitio** (m.) place
subvención (f.) subsidy	**sobre todo** above all

18 In what order did the journalist make the following statements? (Answers on page 212.)

a. ☐ Tiene una plantilla corta.

b. ☐ Tiene una vocación sobre todo regional.

c. ☐ Es totalmente comercial.

d. ☐ Es una emisora privada.

e. ☐ No tiene ninguna subvención estatal.

f. ☐ Está dedicada a todo tipo de información.

19 And can you fill in the following numbers? (Answers on page 212.)

a. Funciona desde el año ....

b. Es la .... emisora de España.

c. Tiene una plantilla corta, como de .... trabajadores.

d. No hay trabajadores que lo hagan en .... sitios a la vez.

Te toca a tí hablar

20 Which newspapers and magazines do you read? Why? Have you any particular favourites? Do you read the foreign press? Have you noticed any difference between the press in Spain and the British press? Say as much as you can about your preferences before listening to Pepe talking about his likes and dislikes.

12 *El mundo da muchas vueltas*

What you will learn

- something about **regional self-government**
- something about the 'noble art' of **boxing**
- how **pollution** has affected one city in Northern Spain
- ... and something about the changing face of **officialdom**

The tree of Guernica, symbol of Basque independence

Study guide

Diálogo 1
¿Ha cambiado algo en Asturias?

Marga ¿Ha cambiado algo en Asturias desde que ésta tiene su propia autonomía?

Francisco Monge Callejo Creo sinceramente que ha cambiado bastante y además ha cambiado para bien. En general han mejorado la calidad y la cantidad de los servicios prestados por la Administración pública al administrado desde que ha tenido lugar el proceso autonómico, ya que la administración está más cerca del administrado y permite conocer mejor y más directamente sus propios problemas y sus necesidades, aplicando las soluciones más exactas y correctas. En lo que se refiere a turismo, puedo opinar con pleno conocimiento de causa, y la prueba de ello es que hemos mejorado las tareas de propaganda, de información y de atención al turista. Hemos aumentado la red hotelera y otras muchas actuaciones que la falta de tiempo me impide continuar.

mejorar to improve
tarea (f.) task
aumentar to increase
red (f.) network
actuación (f.) action
▶ **falta** (f.) lack
impedir (i) to prevent

Plaza de la Escandalera, Oviedo

¿Ha cambiado algo en Asturias desde que ésta tiene su propia autonomía? Has anything changed in Asturias since it's had its own self-government? There is more about forming the perfect tense (**ha cambiado**) on page 193. In the past few years Spain has been devolving power to the regions; this is called **autonomía**. There are now 17 autonomous regions in Spain.

los servicios prestados por la Administración pública al administrado services provided by the public Administration to the citizen (lit. the administrated person). **Prestado** literally means lent.

▶ **desde que ha tenido lugar el proceso autonómico** since the process of autonomy has taken place. **Tener lugar** to take place.

▶ **En lo que se refiere a turismo puedo opinar con pleno conocimiento de causa** As for tourism, I can make a judgement with full knowledge of the facts. A rather pompous turn of phrase!

la prueba de ello the proof of it. **Ello** is a neuter form – it does not refer to any specific noun so is neither masculine nor feminine.

Trabajos prácticos

1 All those perfect tenses in dialogue 1 have been changed into the present continuous. Put them back into the original without looking at the transcript. If you've forgotten what was said, listen to your tape again. (Answers on page 212.)

a. ¿Está cambiando algo en Asturias? ....

....

b. Está mejorando la calidad de los servicios prestados ....

....

c. Estamos aumentando la red hotelera ....

....

d. Está teniendo lugar el proceso autonómico ....

....

e. Creo sinceramente que está cambiando para bien ....

....

2 Find the answers to the following definitions – most of them are words that occurred in dialogue 1. The initial letters of the answers spell the answer to the last question. (Answers on page 212.)

a. región en el norte de España

b. unos – otros

c. trabajos, labores

d. – – – – – muchas actuaciones

e. palabra negativa

f. tener una opinión

g. contrario a empeorar

h. dificultar, estorbar

i. independencia de las regiones

PRINCIPADO DE ASTURIAS

FRANCISCO MONGE CALLEJA
JEFE DEL SERVICIO DE ORDENACION
Y PROMOCION DEL TURISMO

Plaza España, 2 Bajo
Teléfono 25 48 56

33007 · OVIEDO

3 Now you ask Señor Monge how things have changed in his office since autonomy came to the regions. Pepe will play Señor Monge and Susan will prompt you in English.

Diálogo 2
Es un deporte de los más sanos que hay

Ricardo Bueno, pues, la verdad es que yo no conozco la mala fama del boxeo pero no sé por qué la leyenda esa, ya que yo lo considero un deporte de los más sanos y más verdaderos que hay, puesto que en ningún momento los boxeadores pues se hacen ninguna picia, es conocido como un noble deporte y si hay alguna leyenda negra, pues es extra-deportiva. Los años que llevo de afición al boxeo, pues la verdad es que no he visto nada de ese tipo y yo lo considero siempre pues muy limpio y muy honrado.

Susan ¿Es sano?

Ricardo Totalmente, ya que exige un, una gimnasia y un footing que se hace por la mañana y después por la tarde pues se dedica de hora y media a dos horas de gimnasia o sea, que el deporte es totalmente sano . . .

Susan ¿No hace daño al boxeador?

Ricardo El boxeo en sí no, porque como le dije antes, eh, requiere un footing por la mañana y una gimnasia por la tarde, entonces después, si se refiere a los golpes que puedan llevar durante el combate, con una buena preparación se elimina todo ese daño que puedan recibir.

fama (f.) reputation	**exigir** to demand
sano healthy	**requerir (ie)** to demand
limpio clean	**preparación** (f.) training
honrado honourable	**eliminar** to avoid

no sé por qué la leyenda esa I don't know why that legend. Ricardo should have added a verb like **existe** here, to complete the sentence.

puesto que en ningún momento los boxeadores se hacen ninguna picia since at no time do the boxers do each other any harm.

▶ **si hay alguna leyenda negra** if there is any 'black legend'. **La leyenda negra** refers to the notoriety Spaniards acquired in Europe during the Inquisition.

es extradeportivo it's nothing to do with the sporting aspect.

▶ **los años que llevo de afición al boxeo** the years I've been a boxing fan.

una gimnasia y un footing gymnastics and jogging. **El gimnasio** is a gymnasium; the word 'jogging' is now replacing 'footing' in Spanish.

El boxeo en sí, no Boxing in itself, no.

si se refiere a los golpes que puedan llevar if you are referring to the blows that can be sustained. **Puedan** is subjunctive, used here to convey uncertainty (see page 81.)

todo ese daño que puedan recibir all the harm they could suffer. **Puedan** is again in the subjunctive; Ricardo doubts very much that they do suffer.

Trabajos prácticos

4 How would you translate the following phrases? (Answers on page 212.)

a. I have not seen anything of that kind ....

b. I always consider it to be very clean and very honourable ....
....

c. It is known as a noble sport ....

d. I am unaware of boxing's bad reputation ....

e. The sport is completely healthy ....

f. It demands gymnastics and jogging in the morning........................
....

g. With good training, there's no risk of their getting hurt.................
....

5a. **Boxeo** is the sport, and **boxeador** the sportsman. What are the people who practise the sports listed below called? You may have to refer to a dictionary. (Answers on page 213.)

    i fútbol ....

    ii tenis ....

    iii natación ....

    iv gimnasia ....

    v ciclismo ....

    vi equitación ....

b. How many words can you find in this **sopa de letras** (word scramble)? They all come from the dialogue you've just studied.

s	o	n	a	s	m	u	y	g
e	x	t	r	a	o	s	e	i
u	a	e	k	e	m	o	s	m
q	d	g	r	d	e	n	e	n
r	a	i	r	t	n	a	d	a
o	n	x	y	a	t	y	a	s
p	u	e	s	t	o	l	e	i
a	r	g	e	n	e	u	q	a

....

....

....

....

....

....

....

....

6 You don't like boxing, but Pepe does. Ask him to justify his views – and try to justify yours. Susan will prompt you in English. You'll need to know the words **bárbaro** barbaric and **aguante** endurance.

Diálogo 3
Contaminación en Avilés

Marga   ¿Es cierto que hay una excesiva contaminación en Avilés?
Redactor Efectivamente, porque Avilés tiene tres de las industrias más
contaminantes de nuestro país, que son la siderurgia: tiene una
siderúrgica integral, tiene una fábrica de aluminio y tiene fábricas
de abonos. La cantidad de polución de azufre sobre todo y de
partículas contaminantes que lanzan al espacio estas industrias
hace que Avilés tenga una especie de neblina permanente que afecta
considerablemente a la salud de los propios avilesinos. En Avilés
hay un número importante de enfermos de asma, de enfermedades
respiratorios. Eh, lo bueno que tiene Avilés en este instante es que
el gobierno ha aprobado un plan para luchar contra la
contaminación. Existen unas oficinas y existen también unos puntos
donde se mide diariamente la contaminación que se lanza al cielo, y
también se ha obligado a la mayoría de las industrias a instalar, por
sus propios medios, medidas anticontaminantes, que en un plazo
más o menos corto, darán resultado.

contaminación (f.) pollution	**lanzar** to throw
siderurgia (f.) iron and steel industry	**enfermo** (m.) sick person
siderúrgica (f.) iron and steel plant	**enfermedad** (f.) illness
fábrica (f.) factory	**aprobar (ue)** to approve
abono (m.) fertilizer	**luchar** to struggle, fight
azufre (m.) sulphur	**medir (i)** to measure

hace que Avilés tenga una especie de neblina permanente makes
Avilés have a sort of permanent fog. Note the subjunctive **tenga** after **hace
que**.

los propios avilesinos the people of Avilés themselves.

▶ **Lo bueno que tiene Avilés** The good thing about Avilés. More about the
use of neuter pronouns on page 193. **Lo malo** would mean 'the bad thing
about . . .'

▶ **por sus propios medios** by their own means.

medidas anticontaminantes anti-pollution measures.

en un plazo más o menos corto, darán resultado will be effective in the
fairly short term.

Trabajos prácticos

7 Here are a few questions on dialogue 3 to see if you understood it all. Answer in Spanish. (Answers on page 213.)

a. ¿Cuáles son las tres industrias más contaminantes, según el redactor?

i ....

ii ....

iii ....

b. ¿Cuáles son las dos enfermedades que padecen los avilesinos?

i ....

ii ....

c. ¿Qué dos medidas ha tomado el gobierno central?

i ....

ii ....

d. Hay dos sustancias que lanzan al aire estas industrias. ¿Qué son?

i ....

ii ....

8 Dialogue 3 contained a number of adjectives. We've kept the nouns, but omitted the adjectives used to describe them. Fill in the blanks. Don't forget that adjectives must agree in gender and number! (Answers on page 213.)

a. Sus .... medios.

b. Enfermedades ....

c. Partículas ....

d. Una siderúrgica ....

e. Medidas ....

f. Una especie de neblina ....

g. Hay un número .... de enfermos.

h. Un plazo más o menos ....

i. Una .... contaminación.

9 You want to go on holiday to Gijón in the north of Spain – but it's quite close to Avilés and you're worried about pollution. Ask Pepe if the problem is as bad as you've heard it is. Susan will prompt you in English.

Diálogo 4
Una reacción espontánea

Andrés Las autonomías son una reacción espontánea a un fenómeno que ha ido sucediendo durante los últimos cuarenta años.

Carmen Sí, y además también ha servido para agilizar toda la burocracia, ¿no? Cualquier gestión burocrática es ahora mucho más rápida, porque hay cierta independencia de la administración del gobierno central.

Andrés Pero el hecho de crear en cada autonomía unos parlamentos nuevos y unos gobiernos nuevos, ¿no ha aumentado o incrementado los costos al Estado?

Carmen Sí, es posible, pero pienso que vale la pena, porque además también ha servido para revalorizar todas las costumbres populares y el folklore y todo eso.

Andrés Pero sigo pensando que las autonomías, en algunas regiones de España, no han llegado a cumplir su papel. El papel que un pueblo está . . .

Carmen Ah, te refieres al País Vasco ¿verdad?

Andrés Sí, el País Vasco y a otras autonomías u otras regiones como Galicia y Cataluña.

gobierno (m.) government   **incrementar** to increase
hecho (m.) fact, deed

un fenómeno que ha ido sucediendo a phenomenon which has been occurring.

ha servido para agilizar toda la burocracia it has served to speed up the entire bureaucracy.

Cualquier gestión burocrática Any bureaucratic business.

◆ **Pero sigo pensando** But I still think (lit. I continue thinking).

◆ **no han llegado a cumplir su papel** they haven't yet accomplished their rôl

te refieres al País Vasco, ¿verdad? you mean the Basque Country, don't yo

Trabajos prácticos

10 Match the following phrases from dialogue 4 with their English equivalents. (Answers on page 213.)

a. ☐ Sigo pensando que las autonomías no han llegado a cumplir su papel.

b. ☐ Te refieres al País Vasco ¿verdad?

c. ☐ ¿No han aumentado los costos al Estado?

d. ☐ Ha servido para revalorizar las costumbres populares.

e. ☐ Cualquier gestión burocrática es ahora mucho más rápida.

f. ☐ Pienso que vale la pena.

g. ☐ Hay cierta independencia de la administración del gobierno central.

a. You mean the Basque Country, don't you?
b. I think it's worthwhile.
c. Any official business is much faster now.
d. Haven't the costs to the State increased?
e. I still think they haven't achieved their goal.
f. It's served to revitalise popular customs.
g. There is a certain amount of independence from central government.

11 Andrés gave two reasons why he wasn't altogether in favour of regional independence, and Carmen responded with several reasons why she felt **autonomía** was working on the whole. Can you marshal their arguments in Spanish? (Answers on page 213.)

En pro .... **En contra** ....

....

....

....

....

....

....

12 What are **autonomías**? How different are they from local government in Britain? What differences have they made to life in the Spanish provinces? You're still not entirely clear about all this, so here's your chance to get Eloísa to help you to sort it out. Susan will prompt you in English. You'll need to know the following vocabulary: **confuso** confused, **libertad** (f.) freedom, **ley** (f.) law and **poder** (m.) power.

Giros importantes

¿Ha cambiado algo en Asturias?	Has anything changed in Asturias?
Creo sinceramente	I sincerely believe
Sí, bastante y para bien	Yes, quite a lot and to the good
Han mejorado la calidad y la cantidad de los servicios	The quality and the quantity of the services have improved
Desde que ha tenido lugar el proceso autonómico	Since autonomy has taken place
En lo que se refiere a autonomías	As far as autonomies are concerned
Puedo opinar que	I am of the opinion that
La prueba de ello es . . .	The proof of this is . . .
Yo lo considero	I consider it
Ya que	Given that
Puesto que	Given that
Es conocido como . . .	It is known as . . .
Si hay alguna leyenda negra	If there is any 'black legend'
Es extradeportivo	It's nothing to do with the sporting aspect
Los años que llevo de afición al boxeo	The years I've been a boxing fan
Una gimnasia y un footing	Gymnastics and jogging
Si se refiere a . . .	If you are referring to . . .
¿Es cierto que?	Is it true that?
Hace que Avilés tenga una especie de neblina permanente	Makes Avilés have a kind of permanent fog
Hay un número importante de . . .	There is a large number of . . .
Lo bueno que tiene Avilés . . .	The good thing about Avilés is . . .
Lo malo	The bad thing
Por sus propios medios	With their own means
Medidas anticontaminantes	Anti-pollution measures
En un plazo más o menos corto	In the fairly short term.
Ha servido para agilizar	It has managed to speed up
Cualquier gestión burocrática es más rápida	Any bureaucratic business is faster
El hecho de crear	The fact of creating
¿Han aumentado los costos al Estado?	Have the costs to the State increased?
Es posible que . . .	It's possible that . . .
Pienso que vale la pena	I think it's worthwhile
Sigo pensando que . . .	I still think that . . .
No han llegado a cumplir su papel	They haven't yet accomplished their rôle
¿Te refieres al País Vasco?	You mean the Basque Country?

Gramática

The perfect tense

Here's a brief summary of what the perfect tense means and when to use it.

Use the perfect tense where in English you would say: I have (done, written, left): in other words, for events which have only just taken place.

To form the perfect, you need the auxiliary verb **haber**, to have.

he	**hemos**	
has	**habéis**	plus the past participle.
ha	**han**	

The past participle is formed, for **ar** verbs, by adding **ado** to the stem; and for **er** and **ir** verbs, by adding **ido** to the stem. So:

Ha sacado unas fotos muy buenas She has taken some very good photos.
He salido esta mañana I have been out this morning.
Mis vecinos han vendido su casa My neighbours have sold their house.

13 Now for some practice. Here is a manager, talking about life on the road with his superstar client. He is talking about how things were: we'd like you to update what he says by changing those preterite (far back in the past) tenses into the perfect. The first one has been done for you. (Answers on page 213.)

a. Tuvo dos o tres depresiones fuertes. *Ha tenido* dos o tres . . .

b. Hubo muchos momentos emocionantes en su vida ....

c. Mucha gente vino para ofrecerme dinero ....

d. Pero siempre dije que no..

e. Siempre creí en él..

f. Recorrimos América de arriba abajo ....

g. Trabajamos en los mejores sitios – y en los peores ....

h. Carlos llegó allí, cantó y procuró distraer a la gente ....

i. Este tipo de vida me fue muy bien ....

As we saw in dialogue 1, you can also use past participles as adjectives, by making them 'agree' with their noun. Thus, if you use one to describe a masculine plural noun, the past participle is also masculine and plural. So:
servicios prestados services rendered;
el boxeo es muy honrado boxing is very honourable.

Neuter forms

If you're talking about something in general, an idea or opinion, you will probably have to use a neuter form. This is because you aren't referring to anything specifically masculine or feminine. The most common neuter forms are **esto** this, **eso** that, and **aquello** that (more remote than **eso**). So:

Esto no me gusta I don't like this.
Si tengo la culpa de algo – es de eso If I'm guilty of anything, it's that.

Lo can also be used in this way – either by itself:
No quiso comprar lo que vió He wouldn't buy what he saw;
or with an adjective:
**Lo bueno del pescado es que lo puedes comer todos los días sin llegar
a cansarte** The good thing about fish is that you can eat it every day
without getting tired of it.

14 Here are some more examples of neuters together with their English
translations. See if you can match them up. (Answers on page 213.)

a. Esto es lo único que me preocupa ....

b. Me gusta tener éxito en lo que hago..

c. Y eso es lo que me pasó a mí ....

d. Imagínate de lo que es capaz ese hombre ....

e. Y eso no es todo ....

f. Lo extraño de todo eso es que ni la madre se dio cuenta ....

g. Lo cierto es que González sigue con vida ....

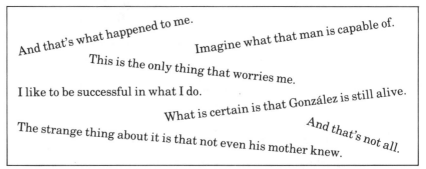

And that's what happened to me.

Imagine what that man is capable of.

This is the only thing that worries me.

I like to be successful in what I do.

What is certain is that González is still alive.

The strange thing about it is that not even his mother knew.

And that's not all.

Propio

And finally, a short note about the meaning of **propio**.
It can mean 'your very own' as in:
La ví con mis propios ojos I saw her with my own eyes.
It can mean 'himself' or 'herself':
Me lo dijo el propio ministro. The minister himself informed me.
And it can mean 'characteristic of':
Un vino propio de la región A wine characteristic of the region.

15 What does **propio** mean in these phrases? (Answers on page 213.)

a. El vestido que tienes puesto no es propio para ir a misa, hija.

....

b. Desde el año pasado tiene casa propia. ....

c. La tela esta es propia del verano. ....

d. ¡Estuve hablando con el propio director del colegio!.......................

Lectura

Unemployment (**el paro**) is as great a problem in Spain as it is in the rest of Europe. The following news item tells how some young Spaniards are beginning to overcome their own problems of unemployment with help from local authority funds.

---

167 jóvenes sin trabajo han creado 35 empresas en los últimos seis meses.

Un total de 167 hombres y mujeres desempleados, menores de 30 años, han creado sus propios puestos de trabajo en 35 empresas diferentes, a través de los planes de promoción de empleo juvenil, puestos en marcha por la Comunidad de Madrid. Equipos de asesoramiento orientan a los jóvenes sobre la viabilidad de los proyectos presentados y les procuran los fondos económicos necesarios, sea en forma de subvenciones o de préstamos a bajo interés. La Dirección General de Juventud se ha encargado de la creación de cuatro equipos de asesoramiento.

---

empresa (f.) firm
desempleado unemployed
puesto (m.) post
a través de via, through
puesto en marcha set up
equipo (m.) team
asesoramiento (m.) counselling

orientar to counsel
procurar to find
fondos (m.pl.) resources
subvención (f.) subsidy
préstamo (m.) loan
juventud (f.) youth
encargarse to undertake

16 First of all, some numbers. From the news item you have just read, fill in as much information as you can about each one in English. (Answers on page 213.)

a. 167 ....

b. 35 ....

c. cuatro ....

Now for some vocabulary. Expand the words given into phrases and then translate them into English. The first one has been done for you. (Answers on page 213.)

d. Préstamos *a bajo interés* .... *low interest rates* ....

e. Los últimos ....

f. Los fondos ....

g. Puestos ....

h. Equipos ....

i. Planes ....

j. Empleo ....

The second reading passage is a letter written to a magazine about **la mili** (national service). National (military) service is still compulsory in Spain, and much resented among young people. See how Pedro Moreno reacts to a previous letter published by the magazine and what his feelings are about **la mili**.

Me ha causado verdadero estupor, o quizá horror, leer la carta de Enrique Herrera Rodriguez. Me parece muy bien que usted, Señor Herrera, haya sido aplicado en el servicio militar y que le hayan ocurrido cosas maravillosas en él, pero tratar de generalizar este cuento de hadas para la mayoría de los reclutas es tergiversar y falsear la realidad. Usted justifica la mili porque aprendió en ella un oficio; para su conocimiento, le diré que hoy, para ser mecánico o electricista, existen las escuelas de Formación Profesional.

Yo por el contrario, conozco a cientos de personas que no tienen que dar las gracias a la mili. Por ejemplo: las familias de aquellos reclutas que durante la mili se suicidaron, de aquellos que murieron en estúpidos accidentes y todos aquellos jóvenes que tenemos que sacrificar un año precioso de nuestras vidas, sobre todo los que pierden su trabajo (¿por servir a la patria?).

Pedro Moreno
Sevilla

estupor (m.) astonishment
aplicado (m.) a good student
cuento de hadas (m.) fairy story

recluta (m.) recruit
tergiversar to distort
oficio (m.) trade
formación (f.) training

17 Pedro Moreno gives one advantage of compulsory military service and four disadvantages. Can you list them all below in English? (Answers on page 213.)

a. ventaja ....

b. desventaja ....

c. desventaja ....

d. desventaja ....

e. desventaja ....

And why is the only advantage of military service no longer valid?

f. ....

Radio

The first radio broadcast is about schooldays of yore – the nostalgia and the bitter reality. Life in the village school was hard: in those days, Spaniards believed in the proverb **la letra con sangre entra** which loosely translates as 'spare the rod and spoil the child'. The following vocabulary should help you to understand the extract. (Transcript on page 220.)

palo (m.) stick
rezar to pray
párvulo (m.) infant
castigo (m.) punishment
reglazo (m.) rap with the ruler
arrugado wrinkled
niñez (f.) childhood
decepción (f.) disappointment
recogido collected

pedagogo (m.) teacher
aula (f.) classroom
llevar a cabo to carry out
fracaso (m.) failure
angustia (f.) anguish
envolver (ue) to surround
tinta (f.) ink
pluma de garbanzo ordinary pen
evangelio (m.) gospel

18 Now test your comprehension by answering these questions in English. (Answers on page 213.)

a. What was the book by Nelson Méndez called? ....

b. Did he actually write it? ....

c. Give three elements which **siempre envolvió la antigua escuela**.

....

d. How many school teachers does the speaker recall? ....

e. And how does he describe them? ....

f. What three things did the little boy learn in the infant school? ......

....

g. How many times did he have to recite **debo ser educado**? ....

....

h. What are the only things that he wants to remember about those

early days? ....

Asturias is the most important mining area in Spain and inevitably the newspapers and radio programmes reflect this by giving a great deal of coverage to what is happening within the industry. In our next radio broadcast we have a report about a miner who has been lost underground. You will need the following vocabulary. (Transcript on page 220.)

rescate (m.) rescue
picador (m.) faceworker
brigada de salvamento
   (f.) rescue team
técnico (m.) expert
tarea (f.) task
creciente growing
central (f.) plant, headquarters
exigir to demand

rigor (m.) strictness
cumplimiento (m.) fulfilment
familiares (m.pl.) relations
dar de alto to 'sign on'
Seguridad Social (f.) Social
  Security
descartar to dismiss
sepultado buried

19 Here are some English phrases. Listen to the news item as many times as you need, and match the English version with its equivalent in Spanish. (Answers on page 213.)

a. The work of rescuing the miner Juan Antonio Medio is still continuing. ....

b. The rescue work could go on for a number of hours.

....

c. In view of the growing number of accidents at work.

....

d. It is not yet known exactly where the body of the miner lies.

....

e. In the Santa Fe mine, serious irregularities have been brought to light. ....

Te toca a tí hablar

20 And finally, what has happened recently in Britain or the United States that has seriously worried or angered you? You could talk about pollution, increasing centralization – or the growing drug problem among young people. Say as much as you can about the topic – and then listen to Eloísa talk about what has seriously troubled her about life in modern Spain.

Answers to exercises

Unit 1 Hoy por mí, mañana por tí

Exercise 1
a. me gusta/prefiero bailar b. me gusta/prefiero ir de bares/ir de copas
c. me gusta/prefiero salir a caminar/pasear d. me gusta/prefiero ir a cenar
fuera e. me gusta/prefiero conversar con mis amigos f. me gusta/prefiero ir
a escuchar (oír) música g. me gusta/prefiero ir a una discoteca

Exercise 2
a. mujer b. mujer c. hombre d. mujer e. hombre f. mujer

Exercise 4
a. *i* Portraits of our Times *ii* Portraits of Women in the Court of King Juan
Carlos *iii* The Spanish Labyrinth *iv* The Thorn Birds b. *i* Travel
ii Adventure c. *i* binding is cheaper *ii* they are adventure and travel
stories

Exercise 5
a. The Lover b. The Name of the Rose c. The Tenth Man d. The Jewel in
the Crown e. The Greek Myths

Exercise 7
a. Por la tarde *jugáis* al parchís b. Sí, señora, *jugamos* al parchís c. *Hemos
estado* hasta las cuatro d. *Oye* una cosa, pero me *dijeron* de que ellos *suelen*
hacer trampas e. ¡ *son* unos tramposos! f. *Dicen* que *sacaron* una ficha y no
la *sacaron*, que *salieron* con cinco

Exercise 8
¡Pues yo no puedo creer eso de mi padre!
Sí ¿no? Puedes creerlo de tu padre y de mi marido, vamos, que como si fuera
tu tío.
¿Y Paco?
Tan tramposo, lo que pasa es que ése habla menos – las mata callando.

Exercise 9
M ¿Jugáis al parchís todos los sábados?
A Sí, casi todos los sábados echamos una partida.
M ¿Y cuánto tiempo jugáis?
A Muchas horas, hemos estado jugando hasta las tres de la madrugada.
M ¿Es cierto? ¿Cómo podéis estar jugando tanto tiempo?
A Porque nuestros maridos son unos tramposos y nosotras queremos ganar la
   partida.
M ¡Ojo! ¡mi padre no es un tramposo!
A A que sí, y Carlos también.
M ¡No puedo creer eso de mi tío!
A Pues puedes creértelo. Son unos mentirosos.

Exercise 10
a. una playa grande b. una playa intermedia c. una playa pequeña
d. estar en la arena e. estar en las rocas f. estar en un prado g. hay menos
nubes h. el sol parece que calienta más

Exercise 11
a. *i* tranquilo *ii* peligrosa *iii* un tanto peculiar
b. *i* el mar te lleva *ii* hay menos nubes
c. *i* apenas se nota *ii* bastante tranquilo *iii* hasta cierto punto peligrosa
iv siempre despeja

Exercise 13
a. Me gusta escuchar música b. Pero (a él) le gusta charlar en la taberna
c. Me gusta caminar d. Pero (a él) le gusta bailar en la discoteca e. Me
gusta leer libros serios f. Pero (a él) le gusta leer novelas de aventuras

Exercise 14

a. hablo español bastante bien **b.** estoy trabajando en Madrid **c.** estudio español en una clase nocturna **d.** se está vendiendo muy bien **e.** tengo este libro de Vázquez Figueroa **f.** el mar te puede arrastrar mientras que te estás bañando **g.** estoy escuchando la radio

Exercise 15

a. se sienta **b.** enciende la luz **c.** se despierta **d.** nieva **e.** quiere éste **f.** pierde el monedero

Exercise 16

a. 20 years ago **b.** Mother Courage **c.** In the Thirty Years' War **d.** She has nothing left to sell

Exercise 17

Activities: grass skiing, riding, squash, photography, making an F.M. radio *When*: 1–15 August *Where*: Cadi mountain range in the Pyrenees *Price*: 16,000 pesetas *Includes*: full board and all activities *Telephone numbers*: 442 98 75 and 265 42 01

Exercise 18

Si busca una bicicleta a su medida, búsquela en Deportes el Rosín. Usted llega a una máquina única en Asturias, que proporciona las medidas exactas de la bicicleta que usted necesita. Deportes el Rosín, Ronda de la Cámara, 5, Avilés, y a rodar a medida.

Exercise 19

a. cheeses **b.** shopping centres **c.** at the weekend **d.** charcuterie, cheese, delicatessen **e.** cheeses, cold meats and starters **f.** Friday **g.** to the country

Exercise 20

d, b, g, e, f, a, c

Unit 2 Coser y cantar

Exercise 1

a. ¿Cuál es el trabajo que menos te gusta realizar? **b.** ¿Tú piensas que es un trabajo muy poco remunerado? **c.** Ya sabía que iba a ser ama de casa. **d.** Desventajas, pues claro, estás siempre en casa. **e.** El que menos me gusta es el cocinar.

Exercise 2

c, e, d, b, a, f.

Exercise 4

a. *i* road construction machinery *ii* excavators *iii* machinery for collecting wood from the mountains **b.** You have all your equipment to hand **c.** *i* changes his clothes *ii* goes into the workshop *iii* does his work **d.** Manolo repairs machinery

Exercise 5

a. motor **b.** obras **c.** taller **d.** máquina **e.** averiado **f.** comodidades

Exercise 7

a. en el centro de control/ después de desayunar **b.** para discutir los resultados de las pruebas **c.** para mirar cómo varía la conducta del modelo **d.** por las tardes/ para tratar de ajustar mis trabajos teóricos a los trabajos del laboratorio

Exercise 8

Me voy/ hago experiencias/ ordenador/ normalmente/ hablar/ comentar/ experimentos/ según/ charla/ regreso/ desarrollo/ ver/ diferentes/ normalmente/ hasta las doce/ después de las dos/ unos trabajos bibliográficos/ intentar/ prácticos

Exercise 9

a. Desayuno y voy a la universidad **b.** Hago unos experimentos en el laboratorio **c.** Hago revisiones bibliográficas **d.** Para ajustar la parte teórica a la parte técnica **e.** Discutimos los resultados de las pruebas

Exercise 10

a. *me suelo levantar* sobre las ocho **b.** *suelo llegar al taller* sobre las nueve y media **c.** *tengo que encargarme* de atender al teléfono **d.** *mantenerlo todo bien es bastante difícil*, porque el teléfono esta sonando sin parar **e.** *a la una* siempre tengo.que pasar por el banco

Exercise 11

a. 1 **b.** 5 **c.** 4 **d.** 3 **e.** 6 **f.** 2

Exercise 12

a. me levanto a las siete de la mañana **a.** sí, normalmente voy al taller **b.** atiendo al teléfono **c.** a la una **a.** normalmente sí

Exercise 13

a. (yo) me levanto **b.** (tú) te sientas **c.** (ellos) se van **d.** (él) se quita **e.** (él) se ducha **f.** (ella) se baña **g.** (ellas) se ponen **h.** él se acuesta

Exercise 14

a. tengo que estar en el taller a las nueve **b.** ¡tú tienes que estudiar mucho más! **c.** ¿no tienes que cambiarte ahora? **d.** no tiene que hacer la reparación aquí **e.** tiene que hacer las primeras pruebas

Exercise 15

suelo soler/ suena sonar/ cuesta costar/ encuentro encontrar/ vuelvo volver/ me acuerdo acordarse/ puedo poder/ me acuesto acostarse

Exercise 16

a. después de ir al cine, comentamos la película **b.** para llegar a ser médico, hay que estudiar mucho **c.** voy a decírselo a tu padre **d.** la costumbre de echar la siesta es una cosa muy latina **e.** sin verle a él, no te lo puedo decir **f.** antes de hacer tus deberes, acuérdate de lo que dijo el profesor

Exercise 17

a. verdad **b.** mentira **c.** mentira **d.** verdad **e.** verdad **f.** verdad **g.** mentira

Exercise 18

a. actualizar **b.** cifras **c.** modificar **d.** pulsar **e.** revolver **f.** respuesta **g.** poner orden

Exercise 19

a. pink, blue, yellow, orange, beige **b.** any colour **c.** yellow **d.** sallow person **e.** ginger-haired and freckled person

Exercise 20

a. *i* 287619 *ii* 289763 **b.** *i* 10.000 pesetas *ii* 5.000 pesetas *iii* 15.000 pesetas *iv* 20.000 pesetas *v* 35.000 pesetas

Unit 3   Acá y allá

Exercise 1

a. mentira **b.** verdad **c.** mentira **d.** mentira **e.** mentira **f.** mentira

Exercise 2

Hola buenos días. Buenos días, señorita, ¿qué *deseaba*? Mire, es que *me gustaría* alquilar un coche. Voy a *estar* aquí unos días. Me gustaría que *fuera* un coche pequeño. Bueno, *vamos* a ver. *Tenemos* varias tarifas pero *creo* que la mejor es la de Europcar. Bueno, yo creo que el Ford Fiesta *estaría* bien. La tarifa del Ford Fiesta *sería* por semana. Si lo *alquila* una semana, *tiene* derecho a kilometraje ilimitado.

Exercise 4
a. costoso **b.** desarrollada **c.** espesa **d.** diseñados **e.** navegable

Exercise 5
a. el transporte por carretera es costoso porque la topografía de Colombia es espesa **b.** la aviación es *i* la más antigua del mundo *ii* bastante desarrollada **c.** *i* los aeropuertos son mal diseñados **d.** *i* Los ferrocarriles son muy deficientes **e.** *i* El sistema por mar, por río, es en épocas del año

Exercise 7
el parabrisas, the windscreen/ el limpiaparabrisas, the windscreen wipers/ la ventanilla, the window/ el escape, the exhaust/ el techo, the roof/ el maletero, the boot/ el asiento delantero, the front seat

Exercise 8
a. *ii* **b.** *i* **c.** *iv* **d.** *iii*

Exercise 10
a. me perdieron mi equipaje **b.** realmente ocurrió **c.** llegué a Manchester y mi equipaje no aparecía **d.** fui a reclamarlo **e.** me dijeron de que estaba en Amsterdam **f.** Me quedé realmente sorprendida **g.** Me dijeron que mandarían un telex **h.** al final mi equipaje llegó **i.** no tenía absolutamente nada que ponerme **j.** fue algo un poco realmente asqueroso.

Exercise 11
a. rapidez/en menos de 24 horas . . . **b.** alta frecuencia/más de 100 trenes diarios . . . **c.** regularidad/sus envíos salen y llegan a destino puntualmente **d.** comodidad/usted mismo puede facturar sus envíos . . . **e.** transporte de todo tipo de envíos/desde un paquete con impresos . . . **f.** le esperamos hasta última hora/usted puede efectuar su envío hasta una hora antes de la salida del tren **g.** doble seguridad/ seguridad de la mercancía y para usted y su empresa

Exercise 13
a. a mí **b.** a él **c.** detrás de ella **d.** delante de ellos **e.** conmigo

Exercise 14
detrás de mí/ conmigo/ contigo/ de mí/ a mí/ conmigo/ de ella/ delante/ por tí/a mí/ ¿Y a tí?/ para mí/ con ella

Exercise 15
a. fue **b.** cogió **c.** reaccioné **d.** bajé **e.** quité **f.** apagué **g.** vió **h.** ví

Exercise 16
a. iría **b.** viajaría **c.** alquilaría **d.** tomaría el sol **e.** enviaría

Exercise 17
pintaría/ vendería/ compraría/ iría/ pasaría

Exercise 18
a. she has lost her luggage **b.** running round in circles **c.** yes **d.** claim compensation **e.** that she won't have lost everything if she gets it **f.** when she has more news

Exercise 19
a. RENFE offices **b.** families of three and more **c.** one **d.** children between four and 12 **e.** 100 pesetas

Exercise 20

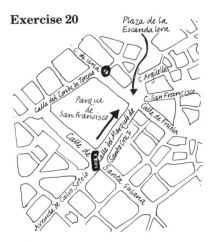

Exercise 21
a. mentira **b.** verdad **c.** mentira **d.** mentira **e.** mentira

Unit 4 Las fiestas donde quisieras

Exercise 1
Vertical: además/ toma/ maíz/ ritmo/ ensayan *Horizontal*: calle/ fiesta/ día/
harina/ echa/ corona/ tiempo

Exercise 2
a. coronamos **b.** escogemos **c.** suponemos **d.** echamos **e.** preparamos **f.** se
mira **g.** se toma **h.** se ensaya **i.** se baila **j.** se canta

Exercise 4
Horizontales **1.** toros **2.** háblame **3.** quincena **4.** lo **5.** sol **6.** el **7.** plazas
Verticales **1.** tí **2.** vaquilla **3.** soga **4.** mes **5.** meses **6.** no **7.** no **8.** al

Exercise 5
a. propiamente **b.** consiste en **c.** corral **d.** el centro de la ciudad **e.** especie
de **f.** característica **g.** soltar **h.** peligroso **i.** de uno en uno

Exercise 7
a. No me apetece mucho, la verdad **b.** Sí, me gustaría ver la nueva película
en el cine Rex **c.** Ir a pasear y mirar escaparates **d.** No, prefiero cenar antes

Exercise 10
a. 2 **b.** 1 **c.** 6 **d.** 3 **e.** 4 **f.** 5

Exercise 11
puedes ver una película/ puedes escuchar una conferencia/ puedes asistir al
teatro/ puedes comer en el restaurante/ puedes beber en el bar/ puedes
escuchar música clásica.

Exercise 13
a. se habla inglés **b.** se sale por aquí **c.** se prohibe fumar **d.** se entra por
aquí **e.** se cierra 2–5

Exercise 14
a. pesadísimo **b.** lindísimo **c.** malísima **d.** feísimo **e.** gordísimo

Exercise 15
a. 1 **b.** 3 **c.** 4 **d.** 6 **e.** 2 **f.** 5

Exercise 16
El último viaje

Exercise 17
a. Luisito **b.** El Naútico **c.** Apolo **d.** El Cafetín **e.** El Cafetín **f.** Luisito **g.** El Cafetín **h.** El Naútico

Exercise 18
Brooklyn Uno: La gran ruta hacia China/ 5.30, 10.30/ autorizada para todos
Brooklyn Dos: La academia de conductores/ 5.00, 7.45, 10.30/ autorizada para todos *Clarín Uno:* Los comancheros/ 5.00, 7.30, 10.30/ autorizada para todos *Clarín Dos:* Frankenstein el monstruo/ 18+

Exercise 19
dan/ esté/ tachado/ tire/ es/ vamos/ haber/ buscaremos/ haya/ proyecta/ acaba/ dado/ preguntará/ queremos

Unit 5 Beberás y vivirás

Exercise 1
pescado/ atrasado, se lo cobraron caro; comida mejicana/ muy picante; sopa/ se la tiró encima; paella/ fría y grasienta; gazpacho/ fuerte, sabía a vinagre

Exercise 2
a. me la tiró por encima **b.** nos lo cobraron caro **c.** no lo quisieron cambiar **d.** me pusieron un gazpacho que sabía a vinagre **e.** fuimos a un restaurante **f.** la comida peor que comí **g.** fuimos a comer en la zona de Luarca

Exercise 3
a. Ricardo Salas **b.** Manolo González **c.** Charo Jiménez **d.** Jorge Cantero **e.** Carolina Menéndez

Exercise 4
a. cebollas **b.** huevos cocidos **c.** sal y pimienta **d.** limón **e.** pimientos **f.** gambas **g.** aceite de oliva **h.** ajo **i.** arroz **j.** pollo

Exercise 5
a. primero calientas el aceite **b.** luego fríes el ajo **c.** luego se añade el pollo **d.** se mezcla todo otra vez **e.** por taza de arroz, dos de agua **f.** se decora con gambas

Exercise 6
a. 7 **b.** 5 **c.** 1 **d.** 3 **e.** 4 **f.** 6 **g.** 2

Exercise 7
everyone prefers the supermarket, except Claudia who prefers the plaza de mercado, Araceli who likes the small shop when she's in a hurry, and Paqui who prefers her village shop because she knows the people.

Exercise 8
small shop: you know the people, it's better when you're in a hurry; *supermarket:* better choice, you can buy everything at once, people don't bother you, you don't have to queue, better variety and more goods.

Exercise 10
a. gastronomía **b.** reprimir **c.** protegerse **d.** pertenecer **e.** ritos **f.** matriarcado **g.** local

Exercise 11
a. Una forma de defenderse *de las mujeres* **b.** Las mujeres estamos aquí reprimiendo *a los hombres* **c.** ¿Qué es una *sociedad gastronómica?* **d.** ¡Eso sí que *tiene gracia!* **e.** La gastronomía es una de *las aficiones más importantes* **f.** Es un local que *los hombres alquilan* **g.** Solamente pueden *entrar hombres*

Exercise 13
a. 4 b. 1 c. 5 d. 3 e. 6 f. 2.
freír, vestirse, medir, servirse, competir, pedir

Exercise 14
a. No te vayas hasta que llegue yo b. Cuando vayas a casa di a tu madre que no volveré hasta las siete c. Tu padre trabaja para que comamos todos d. Mientras que viva no volveré a verte e. Aunque haga sol no iré a la playa – tengo demasiado que hacer f. Antes de que te pongas a estudiar, arregla tu habitación (**a.** negative command; after **hasta que** – action in the future **b.** After **cuando**, to express uncertainty **c.** To express action in the future after **para que** **d.** To express an uncertain length of time after **que e.** To express uncertain future action **f.** To express uncertain future action. Hasta que/ para que/ mientras que/ aunque/ antes de que.)

Exercise 15
a. en su punto, álgido b. la pulpa c. por fuera d. seco e. skimmed g. los niños se los toman sin sentir g. hacer una cura de salud

Exercise 16
Bertran i *Serra, 20 Barcelona*. Cierre *domingos y festivos*. Dueños *Rosa* y *Javier Grau*. Especialidades *setas y guisos de toro*. Ensaladas aliñadas con vinagres de *Modena* y de *Jerez* con aceites *vírgenes de oliva*. Menú del día: entremeses: *erizos de mar*; carnes: *foiegras a vino añejo, carré de lechal*.

Exercise 17
alone, with sugar or with honey

Exercise 18
sopa vichyssoise, aguacates rellenos, mousse de verduras y de pescado, salmón ahumado, langosta fría a la parisienne, salmón Bella Vista, lubina Bellaeaso, cigalas al vapor, solomillo Wellington, silla de ternera, tierna de cerdo ahumado, fruta, queso, helado de almendra

Unit 6 Una vez al año no hace daño

Exercise 1
a. pastillas b. cabeza c. recomendó d. sal e. bebiese f. dio g. cansada
The key word is **tensión**.

Exercise 2
tenía/ sufro/ dijeron/ ví/ me sentía/ informó/ salí/ no me decidía a/ insistió/ terminar/ repitió/ había que/ me encuentro/ aconsejó/ comiese/ durmiera

Exercise 4
Lo que sí hace Carmen: es cuidadosa con el tipo de comida que toma/ toma frutas, verduras frescas, ensaladas/ hace un poco de ejercicio: yoga, y a veces juega al squash
Lo que no hace Carmen: no hace mucho para mantener la salud/ no toma mucha grasa/ no tiene mucho tiempo para practicar deportes

Exercise 5
a. mantenerte b. cuidadosa c. practicas d. procuro e. ejercicio f. a veces

Exercise 7
The customer has: dolor de cabeza, inflamación, picores. *She does not have*: fiebre, dolor de estómago. *She sometimes has*: malas digestiones

Exercise 8
a. Son pastillas para quitar picores; hay que tomar tres al día. b. Es pomada para los picores. Hay que ponerla durante dos o tres días. c. Es manzanilla para el estómago y para malas digestiones.

Exercise 10
a. picores b. dolor de huesos c. glóbulo ocular amarillo d. cara amarilla
e. cuerpo cansado

Exercise 11
a. *i* catching a cold *ii* rich food b. *i* smell of food *ii* smell of cigarettes
c. Marga was in bed for two months d. he sent her for some tests e. that
she had hepatitis

Exercise 13
a. tomaba b. iba c. recogía d. estaba e. estudiaba f. bailaba g. vivía

Exercise 14
hiciera, se cansara, tuviera (all appear after the verb **aconsejar** – a verb of
ordering or commanding): fuese (after **para que**): despertara (after **sin
que**): valiera (after a conditional, plus **una persona**, an indeterminate):
fuera (after a conditional, plus **otro sitio**, an indeterminate): hubiera hecho
(a hypothetical statement): hubiese estado casada (after **si** – a conditional
clause).

Exercise 15
a. crema b. agua y jabón c. pinza d. el segundo día

Exercise 16
sweat more/ drink more/ are thirstier/ get drunk/ kidney problems

Exercise 17
cebada de grano/ azúcar de caña/ zumo de limón – this makes lemon barley
water

Exercise 18
sienta/ desnatada/ desnatada/ alimentará/ engordará/ desnatada/ proteínas/
grasa/ Asturias

Exercise 19
el de la edad/ curar/ mantener/ vitaminas/ minerales/ *alimentos indicados*:
fruta, verduras, aceites crudos/ *alimentos contraindicados*: leche, alimentos
fritos, alimentos de cerdo, grasas cocinadas

Unit 7 El día de la raza

Exercise 1
a. to fall out of the frying pan into the fire b. man proposes, God disposes c.
Rome was not built in a day d. a bird in the hand is worth two in the bush
e. all that glisters is not gold f. better late than never

Exercise 2
The proverb is: cada oveja tiene su pareja.
a. compañero b. Asturias c. diré d. andas e. cocina f. vecino
g. embarques h. j i. algún

Exercise 4
a. Latin American b. Latin American c. Latin American d. Spaniard
e. Spaniard

Exercise 5
nosotros/ ciudadano/ carro/ importante/ oír

Exercise 6
1 c. 2 e. 3 b. 4 d. 5 a.

Exercise 7
a. pelota b. tenis c. ciclismo d. fútbol e. natación

Exercise 8
a. Ballesteros **b.** Princess Anne **c.** Mohammed Ali **d.** Chris Evert-Lloyd **e.** Bjorn Borg

Exercise 10
a. rozarse los dedos: ¿cuánto vale?
b. hasta la coronilla: hasta acá arriba
c. soltar un beso: una cosa que te gusta mucho
d. dar palmadas en la cara: ¡tiene una cara!
e. formar un círculo con los dedos: está perfecto

Exercise 11
a. das un beso **b.** me tienen hasta acá arriba **c.** hay mucha gente **d.** los dedos unidos **e.** ¿cuánto vale? **f.** gran cantidad

Exercise 13
Don't let your children play in the washrooms.
Respect the plants and trees.
Turn off your radio before midnight.
Respect others. Turn down your radio.
Keep the campsite clean. Use the rubbish bins.
Don't pour water onto the plants.
Don't bring guests in without permission.
Don't wash or wash up in the drinking fountains.

Exercise 14
a. nunca voy al cine/ no voy nunca al cine **b.** nadie te llamó/ no te llamó nadie **c.** no estoy listo para salir **d.** no ví ni a mi padre ni a mi hermana **e.** no quiero ninguna **f.** no tengo nada en la mano **g.** seeing is believing **h.** you never miss the water 'til the well runs dry **i.** no man is born wise

Exercise 15
a. mentira **b.** verdad **c.** mentira **d.** verdad **e.** verdad **f.** verdad

Exercise 16
El día *18*/ en *Bilbao*/ gigantes y *cabezudos*/ corridas en *Vista Alegre*/ juegos *infantiles*/ fuegos *artificiales*/ toros de *cohetes*

Exercise 17
a. cheese sandwiches **b.** 10,000 **c.** town crier **d.** oldest shepherdess in the region **e.** Bulnes **f.** from the eastern part of the area

Unit 8 Día de mucho, víspera de poco

Exercise 1
a. Sí, estuve de vacaciones unos días en el mes de julio **b.** Fui a Barcelona **c.** Fui con mi marido y otro matrimonio **d.** Me ha parecido muy grande y ruidosa **e.** Me ha parecido estupendo **f.** Sí, tengo dos amigos allí **g.** He estado dos días **h.** Sí, marché con pena

Exercise 2
a. ¿Estuviste de vacaciones el año pasado? **b.** ¿Y llevaste a tus hijos contigo? **c.** ¿Y cómo te ha parecido Marbella? **d.** ¿Y el clima? **e.** ¿Tienes algunos amigos allí? **f.** ¿Cuántos días estuviste?

Exercise 4
Colorado, red/ Nevada, snowy/ Rio Tinto, red river/ Florida, flowery/ Los Angeles, the angels/ Las Vegas, the plains/ Rio de la Plata, silver river/ Rio Grande, big river/ Santa Fe, holy faith

Exercise 5
a. preciosa **b.** fenomenales **c.** fantástica **d.** bonito **e.** fantástica **f.** económico **g.** interesante

Exercise 7

ríos asturianos: pesca de salmón/ San Isidro y Pajares: el esquí, deportes de nieve/ Naranjo de Bulnes: alpinismo

Exercise 8

a. La temporada de pesca del salmón en nuestros ríos asturianos. **b.** Se puede practicar el esquí y todos los deportes de nieve. **c.** Hay dos estaciones, una en San Isidro y otra en Pajares. **d.** El Naranjo de Bulnes tiene una pared vertical de 600 metros que se la convertido en uno de los grandes mitos de los montañeros.

Exercise 10

a. 6 **b.** 1 **c.** 7 **d.** 4 **e.** 2 **f.** 3 **g.** 5

Exercise 11

a. Ismael mencionó tres excursiones **b.** El Gaitero fabrica sidra **c.** Se las visita a la vuelta **d.** No, sólo se visita parte de la basílica **e.** No, lleva incluído el almuerzo **f.** La excursión más importante es a Covadonga y Lagos

Exercise 13

b. la basílica más grande de España **c.** la fábrica más famosa de Villaviciosa **d.** los picos más altos de Europa **e.** los lagos más bellos del norte de España **f.** San Isidro y Pajares, las estaciones más elegantes de Europa

Exercise 14

a. Acabábamos de llegar a la estación cuando salió el tren **b.** ¡Si acabamos de llegar! **c.** Acababan de salir de la casa cuando sonó el teléfono **d.** Acaban de perder el tren **e.** No está. Acaba de salir **f.** Acabo de abrir este paquete

Exercise 15

a. una aldea **b.** Puente Poncebos **c.** León **d.** la roca **e.** descansamos

Exercise 16

a. *i* stroll *ii* walk *iii* climb **b.** *i* in winter *ii* by the west face *iii* through sheets of ice **c.** *i* Holy Rock *ii* Treasurer **d.** *i* rest *ii* to spend the night **e.** explore the Cares gorge **f.** *i* green waters *ii* steep rock faces

Exercise 17

zoológico/ hoy/ conoce/ mirar/ vendedor/ ambulante/ fulanazo/ patea/ busca/ hecho/ sacra/ matar/ pimiento

Unit 9 Trabajar para la vejez, discreción es

Exercise 1

a las nueve y media comienzo a atender al público/ por la mañana corrijo y coloco pedidos, reviso algún albarán, hago formulas magistrales/ a la una y media, damos pedidos al almacén, cerramos y vamos a comer/ a las cuatro revisamos pedidos, reponemos las faltas y seguimos atendiendo al público/ a las siete y media cerramos

Exercise 2

a. 5 **b.** 3 **c.** 2 **d.** 1 **e.** 6 **f.** 3

Exercise 4
a. satisfecho y muy feliz **b.** cierto ánimo de superación **c.** mejor, mayor
d. tremendo **e.** importante

Exercise 5
I decided to set up on my own: he decidido instalarme por cuenta propia/ I
was right: estaba en lo acertado/ at the moment I feel very satisfied:
actualmente me siento muy satisfecho/ the work I'm doing: la labor que
estoy realizando/ the number of clients is growing: la clientela cada vez es
mayor

Exercise 7
a. tres años **b.** una veintena **c.** treinta **d.** no **e.** tres

Exercise 8
a. Trabajo en esta empresa desde hace dos años **b.** Somos 10 en esta
sucursal **c.** Sí, tres: en Madrid, Pamplona y San Sebastián
d. Tengo cuatro semanas al año, una en navidades y tres en verano
e. El último viernes del mes

Exercise 10
a. un talonario **b.** el saldo **c.** divisas **d.** una cuenta de ahorros **e.** retirar
f. una tarjeta de residencia

Exercise 11
a. soy francés y quiero abrir una cuenta corriente **b.** ¿me puede facilitar un
talonario? **c.** la peseta es la moneda nacional **d.** la libreta de ahorros tiene
más interés **e.** ¿quiere retirar el saldo de su cuenta corriente? **f.** no hay
ninguna cantidad estipulada **g.** ¿cúal es la diferencia?

Exercise 13
All the verbs are subjunctive because the thing or person involved is not
specific – we do not know which specific room, book, boy or whatever is
being referred to.

Exercise 14
The only sentences which need **de** are **b.** and **e.**

Exercise 15
a. little children usually follow their mothers closely **b.** this girl is still
being stupid! **c.** the communist party in Spain follows a Marxist
philosophy **d.** he is still working with his father in the workshop **e.** we go
on seeing one another every year at Christmas

Exercise 16
I return to your house, I return to your street
I return to the places I knew you . . .
But I don't see you again, you don't want to love me
Because he returns from afar – and you love him . . .

Exercise 17
The video machine has: picture freeze, automatic start, automatic
programming, automatic cassette ejection, automatic tuning, image finder

Exercise 18
a. safe/ easy to use/ universally accepted/ you don't need to carry cash/ you
are reimbursed if you lose them **b.** US dollars/ marks, French francs/
sterling/ Dutch florins/ Canadian dollars/ Australian dollars/ Japanese yen/
Hong Kong Dollars/ Swiss francs/ pesetas **c.** you go to their office or contact
their refund service **d.** more than 100,000 **e.** as cash **f.** you save time and
commission.

Exercise 19
Half past six this afternoon/ town hall/ the unilateral decision/ weekly rest periods/ a formal complaint; appeal/ arbitrary/ did not attend the gathering

Exercise 20
a. *i* working in a cafeteria or restaurant, *ii* cleaning offices or entrances, *iii* looking after a child **b.** seven **c.** 9 am – 4 pm **d.** 5 pm **e.** because of economic problems within the family

Unit 10 Poderoso caballero es don dinero

Exercise 1
micro-computador: Gustavo/ vídeo: Andrés/ moto: Ricardo/ equipo de música: Marga/ televisor en color: Manolo/ Betamax: Claudia/ computador: Daniel

Exercise 2
a. porque sus hijas están listas para aprender computación **b.** porque reproduce muy bien las cassettes y los discos **c.** por las imágenes que se ve con claridad

Exercise 4
a. es el más difundido **b.** es un sitio bastante pequeño **c.** suelo grabar los dibujos animados **d.** ¿resulta barato? **e.** ¿sueles alquilar películas? **f.** los pide constantemente

Exercise 5
a. el Betamax es el sistema más difundido en España **b.** el precio de alquiler es módico **c.** Rafa suele alquilar películas. **d.** Rafa suele hacer las dos cosas

Exercise 7
a. me gustaría comprarme un cassette **b.** ¿tienes algún modelo más de este tipo? **c.** ¿más o menos tienes una idea de como lo querías? **d.** ¿Así que dices que son quince mil pesetas? **e.** quizás te venga mejor el radiocassette copiador **f.** no tengo ninguna idea en especial

Exercise 8
a. me gustaría (gustar), quería (querer), andarían (andar), recomendarías (recomendar), se podría (poder) **b.** eres, son (ser), vamos (ir), tienes, tengo (tener), parte (partir), gusta (gustar), dices (decir), copia (copiar) **c.** fuera (ser), venga (venir) **d.** quería (querer), no

Exercise 10
a. la cámara de 35mm, Nikon, con microprocesador, modelo reciente, operación programada **b.** el lente normal de 50mm **c.** el teleobjetivo de 35 a 125mm, requiere mucha luz **d.** el lente gran angular de 28mm **e.** Gustavo también tiene todos los aditamentos de limpieza

Exercise 11
a. operación **b.** permiso **c.** posesión **d.** limpiar **e.** requerimiento **f.** equipar **g.** mantenimiento

Exercise 13
Well, last week we went to Gijón to spend a few days with my in-laws. We went by train because my car is in the garage. As we were walking along Avenida de Oviedo on Saturday morning, we saw a video at a very reduced price in Videomania. We went in and bought it for 70,000 pesetas. Actually, I bought it for Isabel: she's been talking about buying one for months. We're going to use it to tape late-night films so that we can see them at a time that suits us better.

para pasar: (in order) to spend/ fui por tren: I went by train/ por la Avenida de Oviedo: along Oviedo Avenue/ lo compramos por: we bought it (in exchange) for; lo compré para Isabel: I bought it (intended) for Isabel/ para grabar: (in order) to tape/ para verlas: (in order) to see them

Exercise 14
b. estos televisores, esos televisores, aquellos televisores c. este radiocassette, ese radiocassette, aquel radiocassette d. estos vídeos, esos vídeos, aquellos vídeos e. este computador, ese computador, aquel computador

Exercise 15
a. el hogar, el colegio y el trabajo b. primer plano, fondo y borde
c. intensidad y duración variable d. tamaño convencional e. de alta definición f. mediante una sola tecla

Exercise 16
a. Three b. Last Tango in Paris, Summer of '42, The Eye of the Needle
c. La isla de las tormentas / Storm Island d. New England e. a spy thriller
f. during the Second World War

Exercise 17
a. medio millón de pesetas b. cuatro años/ veintidos mil pesetas c. medio millón d. está el pueblo cerquita e. seis palos f. barbaridad!

Exercise 18
a. 5 b. 2 c. 7 d. 3 e. 4 f. 6 g. 1

Unit 11 Más ruido que nueces

Exercise 1
Eduardo: magazine programmes/ Martín: news and sports programmes/ Carmen: easy listening (music); she does not specify/ Daniel: news programmes/ Rafa: news/ Verónica: classical music/ Claudia: easy listening (romantic music)/ Marga: easy listening (slow music)/ Gustavo: classical music

Exercise 2
a. lenta, selecta, clásica, romántica b. musicales, deportivos
c. sintonizada d. informativos

Exercise 4
a. cien mil habitantes b. cuatro diarios c. más que antes d. cinco personas e. a la misma hora que la prensa regional f. alta

Exercise 5
a. En Asturias se halla aproximadamente un millón habitantes b. Por lo tanto, ha de luchar contra ellos c. Esta nueva etapa de gobierno d. Es una media bastante importante e. No es la tónica general en toda España f. Tiene además la competencia de la prensa nacional

Exercise 7
la gente joven suele leer *El País* y revistas/ la gente mayor suele leer *La Nueva España*, y el *ABC*/ Eduardo suele leer *La Nueva España*/ Los períodicos con más venta *i* a nivel local son *La Nueva España* y *La Voz de Asturias* *ii* a nivel nacional, *El País*

Exercise 8
tienen más venta/ bueno, a nivel regional/ algo también/ a nivel nacional/ ¿qué personas suelen inclinarse por?/ la gente mayor se inclina/ tiene muchas/ algunas zonas/ la gente de menos edad se inclina sobre todo por/ ¿suelen comprar a menudo los jóvenes periódicos?/ no con mucha frecuencia/

los jóvenes más bien compran revistas científicas, de deportes,
automovilismo

Exercise 10
a. diario **b.** inglés **c.** fácil **d.** idioma **e.** coloquial **f.** inclinarse por **g.**
ligera (or lenta). Whole word is 'difícil'

Exercise 11
estudio/ hago/ conozco/ dispongo de/ digo/ pongo/ traduzco/cojo

Exercise 13
b. estoy aquí desde hace un momento/ hace un momento que estoy aquí
c. leo la prensa desde hace varios años/ hace varios años que leo la prensa
d. aprendo español desde hace unos meses/ hace unos meses que aprendo
español **e.** tengo la gripe desde hace algunos días/ hace algunos días que
tengo la gripe **f.** espero una carta desde hace una semana/ hace una semana
que espero una carta

Exercise 14
a. corre rápidamente **b.** cocina perfectamente **c.** estudian diligentemente
d. torea valientemente (con valor) **e.** lo coge con dificultad **f.** ladra
ferozmente **g.** cantan estupendamente **h.** lo escribió anteriormente **i.** la
recibió recientemente **j.** trabaja para Dior exclusivamente

Exercise 15
a. it has more than 14 centres and experienced teachers **b.** write to their
address **c.** no, but they may do so if they wish **d.** there are many different
levels **e.** very flexible **f.** that students will find the right course and that
they will sign up for one

Exercise 16
a. mentira **b.** verdad **c.** mentira **d.** verdad **e.** verdad **f.** verdad

Exercise 17
el número de sus lectores/ *La Nueva España*/ difusión/ objetividad
informativa/ selecto grupo de periódicos líderes/ día a día/ al servicio del
público/ a diario/ articulistas/ en España y en el mundo/ al tanto de la
actualidad/ noticias de deportes/ las villas/ acontecimientos más sabrosos/
los sucesos/ que después de leídos/ y las reuniones de amigos.

Exercise 18
a. 4 **b.** 6 **c.** 2 **d.** 1 **e.** 3 **f.** 5

Exercise 19
a. 1926 **b.** cuarta **c.** unos veinte **d.** dos

Unit 12 El mundo da muchas vueltas

Exercise 1
a. ha cambiado **b.** ha mejorado **c.** hemos aumentado **d.** ha tenido lugar
e. ha cambiado

Exercise 2
a. Asturias **b.** u **c.** tareas **d.** otras **e.** no **f.** opinar **g.** mejorar
h. impedir **i.** autonomía

Exercise 4
a. no he visto nada de ese tipo **b.** lo considero siempre muy limpio y muy
honrado **c.** es conocido como un noble deporte **d.** no conozco la mala fama
del boxeo **e.** el deporte es totalmente sano **f.** requiere un footing y una
gimnasia por la mañana **g.** con una buena preparación se elimina todo ese
daño que puedan recibir

Exercise 5
a. *i* futbolista *ii* tenista *iii* nadador *iv* gimnasta *v* ciclista
vi jinete **b.** muy/ extra/ nada/ gimnasia/ puesto/ ropa

Exercise 7
a. *i* siderurgia integral *ii* fábrica de aluminio *iii* fábricas de abonos
b. *i* asma *ii* enfermedades respiratorias **c.** *i* ha establecido unos puntos
para medir la contaminación *ii* ha obligado a las industrias a instalar
medidas anticontaminantes **d.** *i* azufre *ii* partículas contaminantes

Exercise 8
a. propios **b.** respiratorias **c.** contaminantes **d.** integral
e. anticontaminantes **f.** permanente **g.** importante **h.** corto
i. excesiva

Exercise 10
a. e **b.** a **c.** d **d.** f **e.** c **f.** b **g.** g

Exercise 11
En pro: agiliza la burocracia y revaloriza el folklore y las costumbres
populares; *En contra:* han aumentado los costos al Estado y algunas
regiones no han llegado todavía a cumplir su papel autonómico

Exercise 13
b. ha habido **c.** ha venido **d.** he dicho **e.** he creído **f.** hemos recorrido
g. hemos trabajado **h.** ha llegado, ha cantado y ha procurado **i.** ha ido

Exercise 14
a. Esto es lo único que me preocupa: this is the only thing that worries
me **b.** Me gusta tener éxito en lo que hago: I like to be successful in what I
do **c.** Y eso es lo que me pasó a mí: and that's what happened to me
d. Imagínate de lo que es capaz ese hombre: imagine what that man is
capable of! **e.** Y eso no es todo: and that's not all **f.** Lo extraño de todo
eso, es que ni la madre se dio cuenta: the strange thing about it is that not
even his mother knew **g.** Lo cierto es que González sigue con vida:
what is certain is that González is still alive

Exercise 15
a. suitable **b.** own **c.** characteristic of **d.** (the headteacher) himself

Exercise 16
a. 167 young people under 30 without work **b.** 35 companies have been
created **c.** four teams of counsellors have been set up **e.** los últimos seis
meses (the last six months) **f.** los fondos económicos necesarios (the
necessary economic resources) **g.** puestos de trabajo (jobs) **h.** equipos de
asesoramiento (counselling teams) **i.** planes de promoción (promotion
plans) **j.** empleo juvenil (youth employment)

Exercise 17
a. you can learn a trade **b.** depression can lead to suicide **c.** you risk dying
in stupid accidents **d.** you have to sacrifice a year of your life **e.** you lose
your job **f.** other institutions can now provide training

Exercise 18
a. I accuse you, teacher **b.** No, it was a compilation **c.** fear, sadness, failure,
silence, anguish **d.** Two **e.** old and wrinkled **f.** to sing, to pray and to
cry **g.** at least 100 **h.** the noise, the ink, the gospels

Exercise 19
a. continúan realizándose los labores del rescate del picador Juan Antonio
Medio **b.** las tareas del rescate podrían prolongarse durante varias
horas **c.** ante el creciente número de accidentes laborales **d.** se desconoce
aún en qué punto exacto se encuentra el cuerpo del minero **e.** en la mina
Santa Fe se han detectado graves irregularidades.

Transcripts of radio programmes

These may be used in various ways. If you understand fairly easily, try not to look at the transcripts until after you have done the exercises. Otherwise, read the transcripts through before listening, or listen and read at the same time.

Unit 1 exercise 18

Si busca una bicicleta a su medida, búsquela en Deportes El Roxin. Usted llega a una máquina única en Asturias, proporciona las medidas exactas de la bicicleta que usted necesita. Deportes El Roxin, Ronda de la Cámara 5, Avilés, y a rodar a medida.

Unit 1 exercise 19

¡Hola, amigas, buenos días! Pues, se va acercando el fin de semana otra vez. Es que hoy estamos a viernes y claro la compra diaria se incrementa, se incrementa porque vamos a necesitar muchos más artículos para salir al campo, para ir a la playa, a la piscina, y porque además es fácil que tengamos algún invitado. Ya saben que en verano siempre vienen parientes y amigos de fuera a visitarnos, cuando menos se les espera, y además pues se les recibe con alegría y con cariño, y lógicamente debemos estar preparadas para recibirlos como se merecen. Por eso, hoy, nuestras visitas a los centros comerciales Tenderina y Lugones con nuestro carro de la compra serán muy especiales. Visitaremos la sección de charcutería y quesería para proveernos de los aperitivos, entremeses variados de primera calidad, y lo mismo en quesos, quesos de bola, quesos para sandwich, manchegos, azules, cabrales, asturianos etcétera, y ¡a qué precios! Es algo que deben tener muy en cuenta.

Unit 1 exercise 20

Y si hoy empezábamos la hora deportiva con una buena noticia para el fútbol, pues hay que seguir con una mala noticia para el fútbol – concretamente para el fútbol juvenil – en ese mundial que España está jugando en Tiflis, en la Unión Soviética. La selección de Brasil ha derrotado esta tarde a la de España, por dos goles a cero, cero a cero en la primera parte, el partido correspondiente al grupo B de ese mundial, su 19 de fútbol, que se ha disputado hoy en el estadio central de Tiflis ante unos 25 mil espectadores. Los goles fueron marcados en el minuto 49 por Luciano en una jugada personal y el dos a cero en el minuto 64, obra de Valalo, un disparo a media altura que no pudo atajar el guardameta español, Unzúe.

Unit 2 exercise 19

Te habrán vestido de rosa si niña, de azul si niño, de amarillo si la madre previsora no quiso pensar en colores, o de cualquiera si la madre era moderna y se burlaba de las primeras diferenciaciones por razón del sexo. El color de tu piel y de tu pelo te marcan para el resto de tus días. Seguro que tienes una amiga pecosa y panocha que, vestidita de naránja, parece una botella de butano, o esa otra de mal color que con una maravillosa camisa color beige no podría distinguirse de un tipo de galleta.

Unit 2 exercise 20

Hola buenos días.
Dígame, buenos días.
Buenos días.
Sí. ¿Cuál es su teléfono?
287619.
Sí.

o 289763.

9763. Adelante.

Vamos a ver, vendemos una habitación de dos camas de uno cinco, [Sí] dos mesitas completas, comodín, armario de cuatro cuerpos con somieres y colchones. Todo ello en treinta y cinco mil pesetas.

En treinta y cinco mil. ¿Algo más?

Sí, vendemos una máquina de coser Siemens, con un mueble, esto está semi nuevo, en veinte mil pesetas.

Con mueble, en veinte mil pesetas.

Una mesa de comedor para doce comensales, con seis sillas tapizadas en marrón, en quince mil pesetas.

¿Cuántas sillas, perdón?

Seis.

Seis sillas. Tapizadas. Sí.

¿El precio?

En quince mil, todo.

Quince mil.

Vendemos una vitrina de comedor y un trinchero en cinco mil pesetas.

En cinco mil.

Y un frigorífico.

Frigorífico.

En diez mil pesetas.

En diez mil. ¿Queda alguna cosa más?

No, nada más.

Suerte en estas ventas y repito sus teléfonos. 287619 y 289763.

Exactamente.

De acuerdo.

Gracias.

Adiós.

Adiós.

Unit 3 exercise 20

Un minuto para las once de la mañana. Vamos a recordar a todos los conductores que se acerquen hoy a la ciudad de Oviedo y también a los propios ovetenses, que han entrado en vigor nuevas normas en algunas calles de la ciudad, nuevas normas de tráfico. Vamos a repetirlas una vez más: queda en dirección única descendente la Calle Marqués de Santa Cruz: se prohibe el giro a la izquierda de Argüelles a Fruela y ya están en funcionamiento los semáforos del entronque Santa Susana, Calvo Sotelo y Santa Cruz. Para completar esta primera fase de la reordenación del tráfico en Oviedo, sólo falta el cambio de sentido de la calle de San Francisco y la regularización de los semáforos en la Plaza de la Escandalera. Rogamos a todos los conductores, por favor, que se fijen en la señalización y que estén atentos a las direcciones de tráfico y también a las directivas de los guardias de la policía municipal.

Unit 3 exercise 21

La comisión que investiga el accidente aéreo del Boeing 747 japonés ha emitido su primer informe oficial en el que no se precisan las causas del accidente. Hasta el momento los datos de la caja negra y de las grabaciones del piloto sólo han podido determinar que doce minutos después del despegue se produjo un gran estruendo en la parte trasera del avión. A partir de ese momento la trayectoria del aparato, según el informe, fue errática, hasta que se estrelló contra el monte Okura, a treinta y dos minutos después de haber salido de Tokio.

Unit 4 exercise 18

Las nueve horas y treinta y dos minutos. Y hoy con el día que hace, vamos a invitarles a ir al cine y vamos a invitarles a ir al Cine Brooklyn Uno, una sala climatizada donde a las cinco treinta y a las diez treinta, pues proyectan la gran aventura *La gran ruta hacia China*, espectacular, divertida, emocionante, autorizada para todos los públicos, toda la familia puede acercarse al Cine Brooklyn Uno.

En el Brooklyn Dos, pues todavía es su segunda semana y sigue el éxito del estreno más divertido a las cinco, siete cuarenta y cinco y diez treinta. *La academia de conductores*, también autorizada para todos los públicos. Y bueno, pues en el Clarín Uno, también autorizada para todos los públicos, ahora en estreno a las 5.00, 7.30 y 10.30, para uno de los mejores westerns de la historia del cine, *Los comancheros*. Y en el Brooklyn, en el Clarín Dos, queremos decir, pues una película sólo para mayores de dieciocho años, porque claro, todo no va siempre tan bien para toda la familia. También hay que tener películas para los mayores. *Frankenstein el monstruo*, solamente para mayores de 18 años. Ya sabe, él que ama la vida va al cine y si hace mal tiempo, mucho mejor.

Unit 4 exercise 19

Ricos y menos ricos, parados y mujeres aburridas, pensionistas y representantes de comercio, políticos y gentes del espectáculo, todos, absolutamente todos le dan al cartoncito. El que esté libre de no haber tachado algún cartón en su vida, que tire la primera piedra. Mi propósito es que hoy vamos a pasar nuestra tarde de ocio en este templo de vicio. Tras haber sacado nuestra tarjeta, buscaremos una mesa en la que haya jugadores. En frente, una pantalla de vídeo proyecta casi siempre las mismas escenas de alguna película que no acaba nunca. La vendedora, tras haber dado los cartones, por riguroso turno, a nuestros compañeros de mesa, nos preguntará cuántos queremos. Rechazaremos la oferta con la máxima educación. Nunca llegamos a la tentación. Hemos venido a observar. Los acompañantes de nuestra mesa nos recibirán con una mirada ambigua, una mirada que igual quiere decir ¿para qué te sientas aquí? o, este tipo es gafe. La señora de la izquierda con un bolígrafo multicolor en la mano derecha, no para de pasar las cuentas de un rosario que tiene en la otra mano. Un señor calvo y con bigote de oficinista de posguerra, le comenta a su compañero que ya van tres veces que se quedan por el diez.

Unit 5 exercise 17

Para hacer diferente la comida de cada día, tenemos nuestro gran postre, CUAJADA DANONE, tan natural y deliciosa como marca la tradición: tan exquisita sola, como con azúcar o con miel. CUAJADA DANONE, nuestro gran postre.

Unit 5 exercise 18

Para que se hagan una idea de cómo se debe atender a los invitados cuando organicen una cena en su casa, vamos a darles cuenta del menú con que se despidieron anoche de las autoridades locales los reyes de España. Primero, las entradas: sopa vichyssoise bien fría, crema de aguacate y ensaladas variadas. Luego aguacates rellenos, mousse de pescado y mousse de verduras, pâtés y salmón ahumado. Después, los pescados: langosta fría a la parisienne, salmón Bella Vista, lubina Bellaeaso, dentón al horno, y cigalas al vapor. Pasando a las carnes, solomillo Wellington, cordon bleu a la mallorquina, silla de ternera a la Rodicieux, pechugas de poularde rellenitas de turrón y pierna de cerdo ahumada. Al final, vienen los postres con quesos variadísimos, frutas, repostería fina y helado de almendras de Andratx que ya saben que es el sitio de moda esta temporada. Vale, ya pueden irse a cenar con su señora si es que aún les quedan ganas.

Unit 6 exercise 18

En verano ¡qué bien sienta leche desnatada La Polesa! Leche desnatada La Polesa. Te alimentará y no te engordará. Leche desnatada La Polesa, con todas las proteínas, pero sin grasa. ¡La Polesa! La leche de Asturias.

Unit 6 exercise 19

Bueno, ella me está escuchando ahora ¿no?
Ella está en la cama.
Ah, está en la cama. Bueno ya sabe que, claro, aquí el único problema que tenemos es el de la edad. Ese es uno de los problemas que no es problema, sino simplemente hay que aceptarlo porque es así, la edad es así.
Ya.
Entonces, lo que hay que hacer es mantener, nunca, en este caso nunca hay que pretender curar, sino tratar de mantener ese organismo. Entonces, para mantener su organismo lo que hay que hacer es, eh, a base de vitaminas y minerales. Las vitaminas y los minerales los encuentra en todos los vegetales: por lo tanto esta persona deberá de tomar mucha fruta y deberá de comer muchas verduras. Está totalmente contraindicado que tome leche, que tome alimentos fritos, que tome alimentos de cerdo o alimentos cocinados, grasas cocinadas y deberá de recurrir siempre a las grasas crudas. Es decir, a los aceites crudos.

Unit 7 exercise 18

También se ha cerrado con gran éxito el décimoquinto certamen del queso Cabrales en Arenas de Cabrales en el cual se han repartido gratuitamente diez mil bocadillos de este fabuloso queso. El pregón corrió a cargo de Eduardo Méndez Riestra y seguidamente se proclamó la anciana Naranjo de Bulnes. Se rindió homenaje a la pastora mayor de Los Picos de Europa, Domitila Campillo Martínez, natural de Bulnes, que cuenta ochenta y dos años de edad. El festival del queso Cabrales cuenta con una extraordinaria clientela prácticamente de toda la zona oriental de la región.

Unit 8 exercise 18

A nuestro zoológico veraniego tenemos hoy al ticketero. Ya verán como lo conoce. Según como se quiera mirar, el ticketero es también una especie de vendedor playero ambulante, aunque no consienta la condición de autónomo de aquél del que ayer les hablaba. Este fulanazo, es eso sí, pero es que también se patea la arena en busca de incautos. El hecho de que usted quiera o no quiera, según su sacra santa voluntad, matar el tiempo nocturno en una discoteca, a él le importa más bien un pimiento. A él le mete el ticket por las narices como si se tratase de la raja aquella de sandía que les decía la otra tarde. El ticketero está mayormente fuera de la ley, pero eso también le importa un rábano, lo mismo que a su jefe de la discoteca en cuestión. Que ése sí es uno de los personajes más molestos de la presente fauna veraniega. Porque a pesado no le gana absolutamente nadie. Y es que claro, los garbanzos famosos los tiene duros el muchacho. Y así las cosas, por la mañana en la playa repartiendo sus papelillos, y por las noches en la puerta de la discoteca haciendo lo propio. Es el encargado de decir aquello que antiguamente se estilaba, pasen y vean. El ticketero suele ser un chaval joven y normalmente delgadito, quizá por las puñaladas esas, por las cornadas que dicen da el hambre.

Unit 9 exercise 19

Los taxistas ovetenses se concentraron a las seis y media de esta tarde ante el ayuntamiento de la ciudad, coincidiendo con la celebración de un pleno municipal para protestar por la decisión unilateral de la corporación, de imponer descansos semanales a los industriales del taxi. Así mismo, los taxistas presentaron un recurso, ya que consideran esta medida municipal como arbitraria. Los industriales del taxi afiliados al UGT, no apoyaron la concentración a ver demostrarse partidarios de la decisión de la alcaldía de la nueva reglamentación para el descanso.

Unit 9 exercise 20

Soy una chica joven, seria y con responsabilidad, que necesito independizarme a causa de algunos problemas familiares y económicos que me están agobiando, pero para dar este paso, necesito un trabajo que me sea compatible para cumplir con los gastos de independencia, al menos económicamente. Bueno, yo me ofrezco para trabajar por siete horas a partir de las nueve de la mañana hasta las cuatro de la tarde, y quiero insistir sobre este horario por la siguiente razón; de que a partir de las cinco entro a una academia. Me ofrezco para ayudante de cocina y barra en cafetería o restaurante; también cogería cuatro o cinco oficinas o portales para limpiar, y también cuidaría un niño.

Unit 10 exercise 17

Hola, buenas tardes.
Buenas tardes.
¿Con quién hablo? ¿Con quién hablo, por favor?
Con María Isabel.
María Isabel ¿de Oviedo?
De Coyoto, pero es para un pueblo, eh, muy cerquina.
Bueno, pero usted está en Coyoto.
Sí.
Pues, ala, adelante María Isabel.
Mire, es que hice una casina en un pueblo.
Sí.
Y me cuesta la luz medio millón de pesetas.
¡Caramba!
Siempre cuando, que no hacían poco más que decir que había no sé cuántos millones para la electrificación rural.
Mm.
Y yo quería saber por qué hace cuatro años lo pusieron otros vecinos, y les costaron veintidos mil pesetas.
¿Y a usted cuánto me dijo?
Y a mí me falta muy poco para medio millón.
Para medio millón.
A ver si alguien me da una contestación, a ver, derecho, a esto.
O sea, está el pueblo cerquita de Coyoto.
Bueno, pertenece a Siero.
Pertenece a Siero.
De donde me tienen que enganchar a mi casa, hay seis palos, lo mismo que a este otro señor.
Sí.
Que hace cuatro años, o cinco, que se lo pusieron y le costó veintidos mil. Y a

mí me cuesta la entrada de mi casa cuatrocientas mil, más luego, llegarlo lo poco que hay, que hacen pasar por su terreno, alrededor de medio millón. ¡Qué barbaridad! ¿Y lo consultó usted esto en el departamento allí en el ayuntamiento?

Yo llamé a lo de la luz y me dijeron, cuando lo fueron a mirar, que me costaría ciento ochenta mil pesetas. Cuando me mandan el presupuesto, me mandan con cuatrocientas mil. Y fui a consultar y nada. No te dan contestación.

Unit 10 exercise 18

Carta que nos envían desde Lentrega. Dice, Señorita Charito Laguna y demás componentes del programa Escandalera. Un saludo cariñoso para todos. Sois estupendos. Os escucho siempre que puedo. Desearía encontrar una cocina de carbón a precio de programa. Si alguna persona la tuviera, le agradecería llame a este teléfono 344009, 344009, que es en Gijón. Dice: es para llevar a una casita a la aldea, por tanto, no necesita estar nueva pero sí en buen uso. Bueno, pues nada, y se nos despide con un saludo esta amiga que firma Maruja.

Unit 11 exercise 17

Los grandes periódicos lo son por el número de sus lectores y por su fiabilidad, como *La Nueva España*, el periódico de Asturias. Líder en difusión, y prestigiado por su objetividad informativa. Para figurar en ese selecto grupo de periódicos líderes, *La Nueva España* realiza día a día un esfuerzo al servicio del público.

El periódico recoge a diario las opiniones de articulistas prestigiados y plurales, informaciones de lo que ocurre en España y en el mundo, selectivas y suficientes para estar al tanto de la actualidad. Las últimas y más contrastadas noticias de deportes y, por supuesto, cuanto ocurre en las villas y los pueblos asturianos.

Y esos acontecimientos más sabrosos que protagonizan los famosos, los sucesos y los episodios humanos que después de leídos, se comentan en casa y las reuniones de amigos.

Unit 11 exercise 18

Radio Asturias es una emisora privada. Tiene su juego de administración, pertenece a una familia, funciona desde el año mil novecientos veintiseis. Es la cuarta emisora de España, que se créo en España. En España comenzó la radio en mil novecientos veinticuatro. Es totalmente comercial y se financia única y exclusivamente con la publicidad que generan los comercios, las industrias etcétera, de nuestra región. No tiene ninguna subvención estatal – tiene una plantilla corta, como de unos veinte trabajadores, la mayoría de ellos dedicados también única y exclusivamente a la radio. No hay trabajadores que lo hagan en dos sitios a la vez, sino simplemente en Radio Asturias. Está dedicada a todo tipo de información y tiene una vocación sobre todo regional. Se dedica única y exclusivamente a la región.

Unit 12 exercise 18

Palo, maestro, uno, dos, tres, a, e, i, o, u. Fue un día lluvioso. El tiempo pasaba y yo sabía cantar, rezar y llorar. Mi primer curso de párvulos – castigos, reglazos, y 'debo ser educado' lo menos cien veces. Mis maestras, dos viejas arrugadas y que parecían no haber tenido niñez.

Hay muchas decepciones con la escuela. Estas palabras de alumnos, y recogidas por Nelson Méndez en un hermoso libro, *A tí, profesor, yo te acuso:* manual que en la generación de los nuevos maestros o pedagogos circulaba hace unos años, con mucha difusión por las aulas: ideas, proyectos de utopía bastante difícil de llevar a cabo, diga, diría uno que imposible. Se habla de la escuela vieja, de la letra con sangre entra, de la escuela autoritaria, la de deseos no cumplidos, de caminos cerrados, y al final, al final, el miedo, la tristeza, el fracaso, el silencio, la angustia, que siempre envolvió a la antigua escuela, aunque uno tan sólo quiera acordarse ahora de lo bonito del pasado, del babel, de la tinta de la pluma aquella de garbanzo o de las copias del evangelio.

Unit 12 exercise 19

Buenos días, a las once y tres minutos, información regional en Radiocadena Española, en el Principado. Continúan realizándose en la mina Santa Fe las labores del rescate del picador Juan Antonio Medio. Los trabajos de salvamento que llevan a cabo las brigadas de HUNOSA presentan gran dificultad y, según ha informado hace escasos minutos un técnico que participa en los mismos, se desconoce aún en qué punto exacto se encuentra el cuerpo del minero. Las tareas del rescate podrían pues prolongarse durante varias horas. Ante el creciente número de accidentes laborales registrados en lo que va de año en la minería asturiana, las centrales sindicales, SOMO, UGT y Comisiones Obreras han exigido a la administración regional un mayor rigor en el cumplimiento de las normas de seguridad e higiene. Por su parte, familiares de Juan Antonio Medio se han reafirmado en su acusación de que en la mina Santa Fe se han detectado graves irregularidades. Así, en la inspección de trabajo, se ha revelado que hasta ayer no fueron dados de alta en la Seguridad Social el minero sepultado y otro compañero, por lo que no se descarta que estas anomalías administrativas pueden extenderse a otros trabajadores de minas de montaña.

Grammar list

Verbs and verb tables

This section is divided into four parts: first, regular verb tables where you will find all the forms of the three verb types **-ar**, **-er** and **-ir**. Then comes a section on radical-changing verbs, followed by another on verbs which have special spelling changes. Finally, there is an alphabetical list of the more common irregular verbs and verbs which have special meanings or take certain prepositions.

Radical-changing verbs which occur in this list have their changes marked in brackets. We'll only indicate the irregularities in the verb – other forms will be as normal. Derivative verbs won't be included because they behave just like their 'parent': for example, **convenir** to agree, behaves like **venir** to come and won't be listed separately. Remember that in Spanish **ll**, **ñ** and **ch** are letters in their own right and occur immediately after **l**, **n** and **c** respectively.

Abbreviations:

inf. = infinitive	pp. = past participle
rc. = radical changing	pr. subj. = present subjunctive
pret. = preterite tense	fut. = future tense
imp. subj. = imperfect subjunctive	fam. command = familiar command
pres. = present tense	for. command = formal command

Regular verbs

	-ar	-er	-ir
infinitive	hablar *to speak*	aprender *to learn*	vivir *to live*
present participle	hablando *speaking*	aprendiendo *learning*	viviendo *living*
past participle	hablado *spoken*	aprendido *learned*	vivido *lived*
present	*I speak, am speaking, do speak* hablo hablas habla hablamos habláis hablan	*I learn, am learning, do learn* aprendo aprendes aprende aprendemos aprendéis aprenden	*I live, am living, do live* vivo vives vive vivimos vivís viven
imperfect	*I was speaking, used to speak, spoke* hablaba hablabas hablaba hablábamos hablabais hablaban	*I was learning, used to learn, learned* aprendía aprendías aprendía aprendíamos aprendíais aprendían	*I was living, used to live, lived* vivía vivías vivía vivíamos vivíais vivían
preterite	*I spoke, did speak* hablé hablaste habló hablamos hablasteis hablaron	*I learned, did learn* aprendí aprendiste aprendió aprendimos aprendisteis aprendieron	*I lived, did live* viví viviste vivió vivimos vivisteis vivieron
future	*I shall speak, I will speak* hablaré hablarás hablará hablaremos hablaréis hablarán	*I shall learn, I will learn* aprenderé aprenderás aprenderá aprenderemos aprenderéis aprenderán	*I shall live, I will live* viviré vivirás vivirá viviremos viviréis vivirán

	-ar	-er	-ir
conditional	*I would speak, I should speak*	*I would learn, I should learn*	*I would live, I should live*
	hablaría	aprendería	viviría
	hablarías	aprenderías	vivirías
	hablaría	aprendería	viviría
	hablaríamos	aprenderíamos	viviríamos
	hablaríais	aprenderíais	viviríais
	hablarían	aprenderían	vivirían
perfect	*I have spoken*	*I have learned*	*I have lived*
	he hablado	he aprendido	he vivido
	has hablado	has aprendido	has vivido
	ha hablado	ha aprendido	ha vivido
	hemos hablado	hemos aprendido	hemos vivido
	habéis hablado	habéis aprendido	habéis vivido
	han hablado	han aprendido	han vivido
pluperfect	*I had spoken*	*I had learned*	*I had lived*
	había hablado	había aprendido	había vivido
	habías hablado	habías aprendido	habías vivido
	había hablado	había aprendido	había vivido
	habíamos hablado	habíamos aprendido	habíamos vivido
	habíais hablado	habíais aprendido	habíais vivido
	habían hablado	habían aprendido	habían vivido
familiar commands (positive)	*speak*	*learn*	*live*
	habla	aprende	vive
	hablad	aprended	vivid
familiar commands (negative)	*don't speak*	*don't learn*	*don't live*
	no hables	no aprendas	no vivas
	no habléis	no aprendáis	no viváis
formal commands	*speak*	*learn*	*live*
	hable	aprenda	viva
	hablen	aprendan	vivan
present subjunctive	*I (may) speak*	*I (may) learn*	*I (may) live*
	hable	aprenda	viva
	hables	aprendas	vivas
	hable	aprenda	viva
	hablemos	aprendamos	vivamos
	habléis	aprendáis	viváis
	hablen	aprendan	vivan

	-ar	-er	-ir
imperfect subjunctive (-ra form)	*I (might) speak*	*I (might) learn*	*I (might) live*
	hablara	aprendiera	viviera
	hablaras	aprendieras	vivieras
	hablara	aprendiera	viviera
	habláramos	aprendiéramos	viviéramos
	hablarais	aprendierais	vivierais
	hablaran	aprendieran	vivieran
imperfect subjunctive (-se form)	*I (might) speak*	*I (might) learn*	*I (might) live*
	hablase	aprendiese	viviese
	hablases	aprendieses	vivieses
	hablase	aprendiese	viviese
	hablásemos	aprendiésemos	viviésemos
	hablaseis	aprendieseis	vivieseis
	hablasen	aprendiesen	viviesen

Radical-changing verbs

1 **-ar** and **-er** verbs: $o \rightarrow ue$

contar (ue) to count
present cuento, cuentas, cuenta: contamos, contáis, cuentan
present subjunctive cuente, cuentes, cuente: contemos, contéis, cuenten
formal commands cuente, cuenten

2 **-ar** and **-er** verbs: $e \rightarrow ie$

perder (ie) to lose
present pierdo, pierdes, pierde: perdemos, perdéis, pierden
present subjunctive pierda, pierdas, pierda: perdamos, perdáis, pierdan
formal commands pierda, pierdan

3 **-ir** verbs: $e \rightarrow i$

pedir (i, i) to ask for
NB: Where there are two changes, the first is for the present, the second for the preterite and present participle.
present participle pidiendo
present pido, pides, pide: pedimos, pedís, piden
preterite pedí, pediste, pidió: pedimos, pedisteis, pidieron
present subjunctive pida, pidas, pida: pidamos, pidáis, pidan
imperfect subjunctive pidiera (-se), pidieras, pidiera: pidiéramos, pidierais, pidieran
formal commands pida, pidan

4 **-ir** verbs: $o \rightarrow ue, o \rightarrow u$

dormir (ue, u) to sleep
present participle durmiendo
present duermo, duermes, duerme: dormimos, dormís, duermen
present subjunctive duerma, duermas, duerma: durmamos, durmáis, duerman
imperfect subjunctive durmiera (-se), durmieras, durmiera: durmiéramos, durmierais, durmieran
formal commands duerma, duerman

5 **-ir** verbs: $e \rightarrow ie, e \rightarrow i$

sentir (ie, i) to feel sorry, to regret, to feel
present participle sintiendo
present siento, sientes, siente: sentimos, sentís, sienten
preterite sentí, sentiste, sintió: sentimos, sentisteis, sintieron
present subjunctive sienta, sientas, sienta: sintamos, sintáis, sientan
imperfect subjunctive sintiera (-se), sintieras, sintiera: sintiéramos, sintierais, sintieran
formal commands sienta, sientan

Spelling changing verbs

1 Verbs ending in **-gar:**

pagar to pay for
preterite pagué, pagaste, pagó: pagamos, pagasteis, pagaron
present subjunctive pague, pagues, pague: paguemos, paguéis, paguen
formal commands pague, paguen

Other verbs like **pagar** are **jugar** to play and **llegar** to arrive.

2 Verbs ending in **-car:**

explicar to explain
preterite expliqué, explicaste, explicó: explicamos, explicasteis, explicaron
present subjunctive explique, expliques, explique: expliquemos, expliquéis, expliquen
formal commands explique, expliquen

Other verbs like **explicar** are **tocar** to touch, **equivocarse** to make a mistake, **sacar** to take out, **secar** to dry and **marcar** to dial.

3 Verbs ending in **-ger** or **-gir**:

coger to take hold of (things)
present cojo, coges, coge: cogemos, cogéis, cogen
present subjunctive coja, cojas, coja: cojamos, cojáis, cojan
formal commands coja, cojan

Other verbs like **coger** are **dirigirse** to go towards, **escoger** to choose and **recoger** to pick up.

4 Verbs ending in **-zar**:

cruzar to cross
preterite crucé, cruzaste, cruzó: cruzamos, cruzasteis, cruzaron
present subjunctive cruce, cruces, cruce: crucemos, crucéis, crucen
formal commands cruce, crucen

Other verbs like **cruzar** are **aterrizar** to land, **comenzar** to begin, **empezar** to begin and **organizar** to organize.

5 **-er** and **-ir** verbs with stem endings in **a**, **e** and **o**:

leer to read
present participle leyendo
past participle leído
preterite leí, leíste, leyó: leímos, leísteis, leyeron
past subjunctive leyera (-se), leyeras, leyera: leyéramos, leyerais, leyeran

Other verbs like **leer** are **caer** to fall, **creer** to believe, **oír** to hear and **traer** to bring.

6 Verbs ending in **-cer** or **-cir** preceded by a vowel:

conocer to know
present conozco, conoces, conoce: conocemos, conocéis, conocen
present subjunctive conozca, conozcas, conozca: conozcamos, conozcáis, conozcan
formal commands conozca, conozcan

Other verbs like **conocer** are **aparecer** to appear, **nacer** to be born, **ofrecer** to offer, **parecer** to seem, **pertenecer** to belong to and **reconocer** to recognize.

Irregular verbs, verbs with special meanings, verbs + prepositions

abrir	to open **he abierto** (perfect)
acabar de	+ inf. to have just. Use this verb in the present tense: **acabo de llegar** I've just arrived, or in the imperfect: **acababa de llegar** I had just arrived
acordarse de	to remember (rc: **ue**)
acostarse	to go to bed (rc: **ue**)
alegrarse de	to be happy to
andar	to walk **anduve** etc. (pret.) **anduviera** etc. (imp. subj.)
aprender a	to learn how to
apretar	to tighten (rc: **ie**)
asistir a	to be present at
atender	to attend, pay attention, look after (rc: **ie**)
atravesar	to cross (rc: **ie**)
ayudar a	to help someone to
conducir	to drive **conduzco, conduces** etc. (pres.), **conduje** etc. (pret.), **conduzca** (for. command)
contar	to count (rc: **ue**)
costar	to cost (rc: **ue**)
cubrir	to cover **cubierto** (pp.)
dar	to give **doy, das** etc. (pres.), **di, diste, dio** etc. (pret.), **dé, des, dé** etc. (pr. subj.)
decidirse a	to decide to
decir	to say **digo, dices, dice, decimos, decís, dicen** (pres.), **dije, dijiste,**

dijo, dijimos, dijisteis, dijeron (pret.), **diré, dirás** etc. (fut.), **he dicho** (perf.), **di, decid** (fam. command)

despertarse	to wake up (rc: **ie**)
doler	to be painful (rc: **ue**) **me duele el pie** my foot hurts
dormir	to sleep (rc: **ue**)
dormirse	to fall asleep

empezar a	to begin to (rc: **ie**)
encantar	to enchant **me encanta** I like it very much
encender	to light, switch on (rc: **ie**)
encontrar	to find (rc: **ue**)
enseñar a	to teach
entender	to understand (rc: **ie**)
escribir	to write **escrito** (pp.)
estar	to be **estoy, estás** etc. (pres.), **estuve, estuviste** etc. (pret.)

faltar	to be missing **falta Juan** John's missing
freír	to fry **frito** (pp.) **huevos fritos** fried eggs

haber	to have (auxiliary) **he, has, ha, hemos, habéis, han** (pres.), **hube** etc. (pret.), **he, habed** (fam. command), **hay** there is/are, **había** there was/were
hacer	to do/make **hago, haces** etc. (pres.), **hice, hiciste, hizo, hicimos, hicisteis, hicieron** (pret.), **haré, harás** etc. (fut.), **hecho** (pp.), **haz, haced** (fam. command)

importar	to matter **no importa** it doesn't matter
interesar	to interest **no me interesa** I'm not interested
invitar a	to invite
ir	to go **voy, vas, va, vamos, vais, van** (pres.), **fui, fuiste, fue, fuimos, fuisteis, fueron** (pret.), **iba, ibas** etc. (imp.), **vaya, vayas** etc. (pr. subj.), **ve, id** (fam. command), **he ido** etc. (perf.)
irse	to go off, to go away

llover	to rain (rc: **ue**) **está lloviendo** it's raining

morir	to die (rc: **ue**) **muerto** (pp.)
mostrar	to show (rc: **ue**)
mover	to move (rc: **ue**)

nevar	to snow (rc: **ie**) **está nevando** it's snowing

oler	to smell (rc: **ue**) **huelo, hueles** etc. (pres.), **huele a cebolla** it smells of onions, **huela, huelas, huela, olamos, oláis, huelan** (pr. subj.)
olvidarse de	to forget to

pensar	to think (rc: **ie**) **pensar en** to think about
perder	to lose (rc: **ie**)
persuadir a	to persuade
poder	to be able (rc: **ue**) **podré** etc. (fut.), **pude** etc. (pret.)
poner	to put **pongo, pones** etc. (pres.), **pondré** etc. (fut.), **puesto** (pp.), **puse, pusiste** etc. (pret.), **pon, poned** (fam. command)
ponerse	to put on **me pongo el abrigo** I put on my coat
	to become **se puso pálida** she went pale
preferir	to prefer (rc: **ie**)
probar	to try (rc: **ue**)

quedar	to stay, be left **no me queda dinero** I've no money left
querer	to want (rc: **ie**) **querré** etc. (fut.), **quise** etc. (pret.)
quitarse	to take off **se quitó los zapatos** he/she took off his/her shoes

romper	to break **roto** (pp.)

saber	to know **sé, sabes** etc. (pres.), **sabré** etc. (fut.), **supe** etc. (pret.), **sepa** etc. (pr. subj.)
saber a	to taste of
salir	to go out **salgo, sales** etc. (pres.), **saldré** etc. (fut.), **sal, salid** (fam. command)

sentarse	to sit down (rc: **ie**)
sentir	to feel (rc: **ie**) **lo siento** I am sorry
ser	to be **soy, eres, es, somos, sois, son** (pres.), **sea, seas, sea** etc. (pr. subj.), **fui, fuiste, fue, fuimos, fuisteis, fueron** (pret.), **era, eras, era, éramos, erais, eran** (imp.), **sé, sed** (fam. command)
servir	to serve (rc: **ie**)
servirse	to help oneself ¡**sírvase!** help yourself!
soler	to be accustomed to (rc: **ue**) **suelo venir a España todos los años** I usually come to Spain each year
sonar	to ring (rc: **ue**)
sonar a	to sound like
tener	to have (rc: **ie**) **tengo, tienes** etc. (pres.), **tendré, tendrás** etc. (fut.), **tuve, tuviste** etc. (pret.), **ten, tened** (fam. command)
tener que	+ inf. to have to
traer	to bring **traigo, traes** etc. (pres.), **traje, trajiste** etc. (pret.), **traído** (pp.)
tratar de	to try to
tratarse de	to be about **en la película se trata de la guerra civil** the film is about the civil war
valer	to be worth ¿**cuánto vale?** how much is it? **vale** OK **val, valed** (fam. command)
venir	to come (rc: **ie**) **vengo, vienes** etc. (pres.), **vendré** (fut.), **vine, viniste** etc. (pret.), **ven, venid** (fam. command)
ver	to see **veo, ves, ve** etc. (pres.), **veía, veías** etc. (imp.), **visto** (pp.)
volver	to go back (rc: **ue**), **vuelto** (pp.)
volver a	+ inf. to do something again

Vocabulary
Spanish – English

A

abajo below
abonar to pay; subscribe to
abono *m.* fertilizer
abrigo *m.* coat
abrir to open
abrupto steep
aburrido boring
acabar to finish
academia *f.* private college
acampada *f.* campsite
aceite *m.* oil
acercar to draw near
acertado right; correct
aconsejar to advise
acontecimiento *m.* event
acordarse (ue) to remember
acorde *m.* agreement
acostarse (ue) to go to bed
actuación *f.* performance; conduct
actualidad present time
actualizar to bring up to date
actualmente nowadays
acuerdo *m.* agreement, **de acuerdo** agreed
adelante forward
además besides
aderezado prepared; seasoned
aditamento *m.* accessory
adonde to where
adquirir to acquire
aéreo air
aeropuerto airport
afición *f.* fondness; liking for
aficionado fan
agilizar to speed up
aglomerado massed together
agobiar to burden; weigh down
agosto August
agotado tired out; sold out
agradable agreeable
agradecer to thank
agricultor *m.* farmer
agua *f.* water
aguacate *m.* avocado
aguardiente *m.* rum
agudo sharp; high
aguijón *m.* sting
aguja *f.* needle
ahí there
ahora now
ahorros *m.pl.* savings
ahumado smoked
aire *m.* air
ajillo *m.* garlic sauce
ajo *m.* garlic
ajustar to adjust
ala *f.* wing
albarán *m.* invoice
albaricoque *m.* apricot
alcance *m.* reach, **al alcance de** within reach
alcanzar to reach

aldea *f.* town
alegrarse to be happy, cheerful
alegre happy, extrovert
alegría *f.* happiness
alejar to remove, move away
alemán German
Alemania Germany
aleta *f.* wing
álgido chilly; most prolific
algo something
algún some
alimentar to feed
alimentos *m.pl.* food
aliñado dressed (salads)
allá over there
allí there
almacén *m.* store
almendra *f.* almond
almuerzo *m.* lunch
alojamiento *m.* lodging
alojarse to lodge
alquilar to rent; hire
alquiler *m.* rental
alrededor around
alrededores vicinity
altavoz *m.* loudspeaker
alto high
altura *f.* height
ama de casa *f.* housewife
amante *m.* lover
amar to love
amarillento yellowish
amarillo yellow
ambientado setting (novels)
ambiente *m.* atmosphere
ambulante walking; travelling
ameno pleasant; agreeable
amigo *m.* friend
amor *m.* love
amo *m.* master; boss
ampliado widened
añadir to add
anciano *m.* old man
andar to walk
angustia *f.* anguish; distress
angustioso distressing
animar to enliven; encourage
ánimo *m.* soul; courage
anoche last night
anotar to take notes
ante before
antelación *f.* advance, **con antelación** in advance
antena *f.* aerial; antenna
antes before
anticipado in advance
anticontaminante anti-pollutant
anticuado antiquated; out of date
antiguo old; classic
antigüedad *f.* antiquity
añejo mellow (of wine)
año year
aparecer to appear

apariencia f. appearance
apenas hardly
apertura f. opening
apetecer to crave, long for
aportar to bring
aprender to understand
aprobar to approve; pass (exam)
aquel that
aquí here
arena f. sand
arriba above
arroz rice
arrozada f. rice feast
asegurarse to assure oneself
así thus; in that way
asma f. asthma

B
bailar to dance
baile m. dance
bajar to go down
bajo under
bañarse to bathe
banco m. bank
banda f. band
bandeja f. tray
baño m. bath
barato cheap
barbaridad f. outrage, ¡qué
   barbaridad! how terrible!
barba f. beard
barco m. boat; ship
barra f. bar
barro m. mud
bastante enough
bastar to be enough; sufficient
batalla f. battle
batir to whip up, beat
bebé m. baby
beber to drink
beca f. scholarship
becario scholarship-holder
belleza f. beauty
bello beautiful
besar to kiss
beso m. kiss
besugo m. sea-bream
biblioteca f. library
bicicleta f. bicycle
bien well
bigote m. moustache
billete m. ticket
blanco white
boca f. mouth
bocadillo m. sandwich
boda f. marriage
bodega f. wine-cellar; bar
bola f. ball (small)
bolera f. bowling alley
bolígrafo f. biro
bonito pretty; nice
borde m. edge
borrachera f. drunkenness

botella f. bottle
boxeador m. boxer
boxeo m. boxing
brasileño m. Brazilian
bravo wild; rough
brillo m. shine
bueno good
bulto m. luggage; package
burlarse to mock
busca search, en busca de in
   search of
buscar to search
búsqueda f. search

C
caber to fit in
cabeza f. head
cabezudo big-headed
cabo m. end; cape
cada each
cadena f. chain
caja f. box; till
calamares m.pl. squid
caldereta f. fish or meat stew
calentar to warm, heat
calidad f. quality
caliente hot
caliza f. limestone
calor m. heat
calvo bald
calladito quiet
callarse to keep quiet
calle f. street
cama f. bed
cámara f. camera
camarero waiter
cambiar to change
cambio m. change; exchange
caminar to walk
camino m. path
camisa f. shirt
campamento m. camp; encampment
campeonato m. championship
campesino m. peasant
campo m. field; countryside
canción f. song
cansar to tire, grow weary
cantar to sing
cantidad f. quantity
cantinera f. barmaid
canto m. song
caña f. sugar-cane
capaz capable of
caprichoso capricious
¡caramba! heavens!
carambola f. trick; ruse
caramelo m. sweet
carbón m. coal
carga m. load
cargar to load
cariño m. affection
cariñoso affectionate
carnavales m.pl. carnival time

carne f. flesh; meat
caro expensive
carrera f. career; race
carreta f. wagon; cart
carretera f. road
carretilla f. trolley
carrito m. trolley
carro m. cart; car (Latin America)
carroza f. coach; carriage
carta f. letter
cartoncito m. card
casa f. house
casarse to get married
casco m. helmet; city centre
casero home-made
casi almost
casina f. little house
casita f. little house
caso m. case
cassette m./f. cassette
castigo m. punishment
caza f. chase; hunt
cebada f. barley
cebolla f. onion
ceja f. eyebrow
cena f. dinner
cenar to dine
centro m. centre
cerca near
cerdo m. pig
cerilla f. match
cero m. zero
cerrar (ie) to close
certamen m. competition
cesta f. basket
cicliturista bicycle tourer
cielo m. sky
ciencia f. science
científico scientific
ciento hundred
cierto sure; certain
cifra f. number; statistic
cigala f. lobster
cigarrillo m. cigarette
cima f. top; peak
cine(matógrafo) m. cinema
cinta f. tape
cita f. date
ciudad f. city
claro clear
clase f. class
clientela f. clientele
clima m. climate
cobrar to charge
coche m. car
cochecito m. pram
cocido m. stew
cocina f. kitchen
cocinar to cook
cocinero m. cook
coger to catch; take
cohete m. rocket; kite
cola f. queue

colchón m. mattress
colectivo collective
colegio m. school
colina f. hill
colocar to put, place
coloso colossus
columpio m. swing
combate m. combat
comedor m. dining room
comensal m. guest
comenzar to begin
comer to eat
comercio m. shop; commerce; trade
comida f. meal; food
comité m. committee
cómodo m. comfortable
comodín gadget
compañero m. companion
compañía f. company
comparación f. comparison
comparsa f. procession
competencia f. responsibility
complacer to please
complementos m.pl. accessories
completo full
comportar to bear, endure
compra f. shopping
comprar to shop
compuesto composed of
computador m. computer
con with
concluir to conclude
concretamente specifically
concurrido crowded
condenado condemned
conducir to drive
conducta f. behaviour
conductor m. driver
conferencia f. lecture
confiar to entrust
congelación f. freezing
congelar to freeze
congreso m. meeting; conference
conocer to know
conocido well-known
conocimiento m. knowledge
conquistado conquered
consabido well-known
conseguir (i) to obtain
consejo m. advice
consentir (i) to agree
consistoriales m.pl. town council
constar to be clear from, consta que
  it is clear that . . .
contabilidad f. book-keeping
contaminante pollutant
contar to count
contener to contain
contenido m. contents
contestación f. answer
contestar to reply
contra against
contraindicado not recommended

contrario contrary, **al contrario** on the contrary
conveniente convenient; suitable
conversar to talk; converse
convertidor *m.* convertor
convenir to agree
copa *f.* glass
copia *f.* copy
copiador *m.* copier
copiar to copy
coraje *m.* courage; valour
corona *f.* crown
coronar to crown
coronilla *f.* top of head, **hasta la coronilla** up to here
corral *m.* pen (for livestock)
corregir (i) to correct
Correos Post Office
correr to run
corrida *f.* bullfight
corriente current
cortado cut; sliced
corte *m.* cut
corto short
cosa *f.* thing
cosecha *f.* harvest
coser to sew
costa *f.* coast
costar to cost
costo *m.* cost
costoso costly
costumbre *f.* custom
crear to create
creciente growing
creer to believe
crema *f.* cream
crimen *m.* crime
crucero *m.* cruiser
crudo raw
crudeza *f.* rawness
cruz *f.* cross
cruzar to cross
cuajada *f.* junket
cual which
cualquier (a) any
cuando when
cuánto how much
cuarto quarter; room
cuerpo *m.* body
cueva *f.* cave
cuidar to look after
cuidado look out! careful!
culpa *f.* guilt, **tener la culpa** to be guilty
cumbre *m.* peak
cumpleaños *m.* birthday
cumplir to accomplish, **cumplir años** to have a birthday

CH
charcutería *f.* delicatessen
chaval *m.* lad
chico boy

chorizo *m.* spicy sausage

D
dado *m.* dice
daño *m.* harm, **hacer daño** to hurt
danza *f.* dance
danzar to dance
dar to give
datos *m.pl.* data; facts
deber to owe; to have to
debido a due to
década *f.* decade
decepción *f.* disappointment
decidir to decide
décimo tenth
decir to say
dedo *m.* finger
defensa *f.* defence
deficiente lacking
dejar to leave
delante in front of
delantero front
delgado slim; thin
demás others; the rest
demasiado too much
demora *f.* delay
demostrar (ue) to show
dentro inside
depender to depend
depilar to depilate; remove hair
deporte *m.* sport
deportivo sporty; sporting
derecha right, **a la derecha** on the right
derecho straight
derrame *m.* overflow; discharge
derrotar to beat; overcome
desafortunadamente unfortunately
desarrollar to develop
desarrollo *m.* development
desarticular to separate; take apart
desayunar to have breakfast
descansar to rest
descanso *m.* rest
descarga *f.* unloading
descartar to discard; lay aside
descender to descend; go down
desconocer to be unfamiliar with
describir to describe
descubrimiento *m.* discovery
descubrir to discover
descuento *m.* discount
desde since
desear to desire
desempleado *m.* unemployed
deseo *m.* desire; wish
desesperado desperate
desfiladero *m.* pass; gorge
desfile *m.* parade
desnatado skimmed
despacho *m.* dispatch
despedirse (i) to say goodbye
despegar to take off

despejar to clear up
despertarse (ie) to wake up
desplazarse to move
después afterwards; after
destacar to stand out
desventaja *f*. disadvantage
detallado detailed
detener to delay; detain
detrás behind
devolver (ue) to devolve
día *f*. day
diario daily
diario *m*. daily newspaper
diariamente daily
dibujo drawing
dictadura *f*. dictatorship
dieta *f*. diet
difícil difficult
dificultad *f*. difficulty
difundido diffused; spread
difusión *f*. diffusion
dinero *m*. money
Dios *m*. God
dirección *f*. address
director manager; boss
dirigir to direct
disco *m*. record
discoteca *f*. discothèque
discutir to discuss
diseñado designed
diseño *m*. design
disfraz *m*. disguise
disparar to shoot
disparo *m*. shooting; shot
disponer to arrange; dispose
disponible available; on hand
dispuesto prepared to
disputar to argue; dispute
distinguirse to be distinguished; differ
  from
distinto different
distraer to distract
diverso diverse; different
diversión *f*. amusement
divertido amusing
divisas *f.pl*. foreign currency
divulgar to spread; circulate
docente educational
dolencia *f*. pain; sorrow
dolerse (ue) to be in pain; to hurt
dolor *m*. pain
domingo *m*. Sunday
dominio *m*. dominion; power
don *m*. gift; courtesy title
donde where
donjuanismo *m*. Don Juan
  phenomenon
dorarse to brown, become golden
dormir (ue) to sleep
droga *f*. drug
duda *f*. doubt
durante during

E

echar to throw
edad *f*. age
edificar to build
educado well-mannered; polite
efectivamente really; exactly
efectuar to carry out
ejemplar *m*. example; copy
ejemplo *m*. example
elaboración *f*. production; working out
elaborar to produce
electricista *m*. electrician
elegir (i) to choose
elenco *m*. list; cast
ello it; that
embarcación *f*. boat; embarkation
embarcar to embark
emisora *f*. radio station
emitir to emit; give off
emocionante exciting
empatar to draw (in a match)
empezar (ie) to begin
empleo *m*. work; job
empresa *f*. enterprise; company
encalmado becalmed
encantar to charm; delight, **me
  encanta** I love it
encantador charming
encanto *m*. charm; delight
encargado *m*. agent; person in charge
encargarse to take charge of
encargo *m*. assignment; post
encender (ie) to light
encierro *m*. bull-pen
encima above
encontrar (ue) to meet
encuadernación *f*. binding
enero January
enfado *m*. anger
enfermedad *f*. sickness; illness
enfermo ill
enganchar to hook
engordar to put on weight
ensalada *f*. salad
ensayar to try; rehearse
enseñanza *f*. teaching
ensogar to tie with a rope
entender (ie) to understand
enterar to inform
entero whole; total
entonces then
entorno *m*. surroundings
entrada *f*. entry
entrañable intimate; loved
entrar to enter
entre between
entremeses *m.pl*. hors d'oeuvres
entronque *m*. connection; link
enviar to send
envolver (ue) to wrap
época *f*. epoch
equipaje *m*. luggage
equipo *m*. team

equitación f. horse-riding
equivocado mistaken
erguirse to straighten up
erizo m. hedgehog, **erizo de mar** m. sea-urchin
ermita f. hermitage
escalador climber
escalar to climb
escaparate m. shop-window
escaso scarce
escena f. scene
escéptico sceptical
escoger to choose
escribir to write
escuchar to listen
escuela f. school
esfuerzo m. struggle; effort
eso that
espacio m. space
espalda f. back
España Spain
español Spanish
especializar to specialize
especie f. sort; class
espectáculo m. show; spectacle
espectador spectator
esperar to wait
espeso thick
espino m. thorn
espionaje m. espionage; spying
espolvorear to sprinkle
espontáneo spontaneous
esporádicamente sporadically
esposo husband
esquí m. ski
esquina f. corner
estación f. station
estadio m. stadium
estado m. state
estándar m. standard
estar to be
estatal state
este this
estéreo m. stereo
esterlina f. sterling
estilo m. style
estipulado stipulated
esto this
estofado stuffed
estómago stomach
estrecho narrow; tight
estrellarse to smash
estrenar to wear or do for the first time
estreno m. first night
estructura f. structure
estruendo m. noise; clamour
estudiante m. student
estudiar to study
estudio m. study
estupendo marvellous
estupor m. astonishment
etapa f. stage; phase
evangelio m. gospel

evasión f. escape
evitar to avoid
excavadora f. excavator
exigir to demand
existencias f.pl. stocks
éxito m. success
expansionar to expand
experiencia f. experience
extraño strange

F
fabada f. bean-stew
fábrica f. factory
fácil easy
facilidad f. ease
facilitar to make easy
factura f. bill
facturación f. billing
falsear to falsify
falso false
falta f. lack
faltar to lack
fama f. reputation; fame
familiar of the family
farmacia f. chemist's shop
fase f. phase
fe f. faith
febrero February
fecha f. date
felicidad f. happiness
feliz happy
fenomenal marvellous
fenómeno m. phenomenon
feo ugly
feria f. market; fair
feroz savage
ferrocarril m. railway
festejar to celebrate
fiabilidad f. trustworthiness
ficción f. fiction
ficha f. token; counter
fiebre f. fever; temperature
fijo fixed
fijar to fix
fin m. end
firma f. signature
firmar to sign
fluidez f. fluidity
fondo m. bottom
footing m. jogging
forma f. form; shape
formar to train
fracaso m. failure
francés Frenchman
franco m. franc
freír to fry
frenar to brake
freno m. brake
frente m. front, front part
fresco fresh
frigorífico m. fridge
frío cold
frito fried

frontón *m.* pelota court
fruta *f.* fruit
fuego *m.* fire, **fuegos artificiales**
  m.pl. fireworks
fuente *f.* source, fountain
fuera outside
fuerte strong
fuerza *f.* strength

G

gafas *f.pl.* glasses
gafe jinx
galleta *f.* biscuit
gama *f.* range
gana *f.* desire, **tener ganas de** to
  want to
ganar to win
garbanzo *m.* chickpea
garganta *f.* throat
gasto *m.* expenditure
gaznate *m.* gullet
gazpacho *m.* cold soup
generoso generous
gente *f.* people
gerente *m.* manager
gestión *f.* management; conduct
gesto *m.* gesture
gigante *m.* giant
gimnasia *f.* gymnastics
gimnasio *m.* gymnasium
giro *m.* phrase; idiom
globo *m.* globe, **globo ocular** eye-ball
gobierno *m.* government
gol *m.* goal
golpe *m.* blow
golpear to hit, strike
gordo fat
grabación *f.* recording
grabar to record
gracias *f.pl.* thanks
gracioso funny
grado *m.* step; degree
gráfico *m.* graph
grande big
grano *m.* spot; seed
grasa *f.* fat
grasiento fatty
gratis free
gratuitamente free, for nothing
grave serious
griego Greek
guapo pretty
guardameta *m.* goalkeeper
guardar to keep
guardia *m.* policeman
guerra *f.* war
guía *m.* guide, *f.* guidebook; handbook
guiso *m.* stew
gustar to like

H

haber to have
habitación *f.* room

habitante *m.* inhabitant
habituado accustomed to
habitualmente normally
hablar to speak
hacer to do, make
hacia towards
hada *f.* fairy
hallar to find
harto full; fed up
hasta up to; towards
hay there is, there are
helado frozen; ice-cream
herida *f.* wound
hermano *m.* brother
hervir (ie) to boil
hielo *m.* ice
hierba *f.* grass
hijo *m.* son
hispanoamericano Spanish-American
historia *f.* history; story
hogar *m.* home
hoja *f.* leaf
hojear to leaf through
hola hello
hombre *m.* man
homenaje *m.* homage
honrado honourable
hora *f.* hour
horario *m.* timetable
hormiga *f.* ant
horno *m.* oven
hotelero hotelkeeper

I

idear to think
idioma *m.* language
igual same; equal
imagen *f.* image
impedir (i) to prevent
impertinencia *f.* irrelevance; fussiness
imponer to impose
importar to be important, **no importa**
  it doesn't matter
imprescindible necessary
impresionante stunning; spectacular
inaguantable unbearable
incauto unwary; incautious
inclinarse to bow
incluir to include
incluso even; including
incrementar to increment; grow
indemnización *f.* compensation
independiente independent
independizarse to become
  independent
indicado right; suitable
infantil childish
informativos *m.pl.* news
informe *m.* report
Inglaterra England
inglés English
iniciar to begin
inicio *m.* beginning

inolvidable unforgettable
instantánea *f.* snapshot
instante *m.* moment
instituto *m.* college; state school
intentar to try
intercambio *m.* interchange
interesante interesting
intermedio intermediate
intermitente intermittent; (noun)
   flashing light, indicator
intérprete interpreter
invadir to invade
invierno *m.* winter
invitado *m.* guest
ir to go
Irlanda *f.* Ireland
isla *f.* island

J
jabón *m.* soap
jamón *m.* ham
japonés Japanese
jefe chief; boss
joven young; (noun) young man
joya *f.* jewel
jueves Thursday
jugada *f.* throw, move (in game)
jugador *m.* player
jugar (ue) to play
jugoso juicy
julio July
justificar to justify

L
labor *f.* work
laboral of work
labrar to work
lado *m.* side
ladrar to bark
lago *m.* lake
langosta *f.* lobster
lanzar to throw
largo long
lastre ballast
Latinoamérica *f.* Latin America
lavar to wash
lavadora *f.* washing machine
lechal sucking
lechazo *m.* young lamb
leche *f.* milk
lector *m.* reader
lectura *f.* reading
leer to read
lejos far; distant
lengua *f.* tongue
lenguaje *m.* language
lentamente slowly
lente *m./f.* lens
lento slow
león *m.* lion
letra *f.* letter; script
levantar (se) to get up
ley *f.* law

leyenda *f.* legend
libertad *f.* freedom
libra *f.* pound
libre free
libreta *f.* notebook; bank-book
libro *m.* book
liceo *m.* school
ligeramente lightly
limpiar to clean
limpieza *f.* cleanliness
lindo pretty
línea *f.* line
listo ready; clever
local place
loco mad
luchar to struggle

LL
llamada *f.* call
llamar to call
llegada *f.* arrival
llegar to arrive
lleno full
llevar to carry
llorar to cry
lluvioso rainy

M
machacar to crush; pound
madera *f.* wood
madre *f.* mother
madrugada *f.* early morning
maestro *m.* master
magistral masterly
maíz *m.* maize
maizena *f.* maize flour
mal badly
maleta *f.* suitcase
mallorquino Mallorcan
malo bad
mañana *f.* morning
manar run with, flow with
manchego Manchegan
mandar to send
manejar to manage; drive
mano *f.* hand
mantener (ie) to maintain
manzanilla *f.* camomile drink;
   manzanilla
mar *m./f.* sea
maravilla *f.* marvel
maravilloso marvellous
marca *f.* brand
marcha *f.* march; gear
marido *m.* husband
marinero marine
marisco *m.* shell-fish
marrón brown
martes *m.* Tuesday
más more
mastín *m.* mastiff
matanza *f.* killing
matar to kill

matriarcado *m.* matriarchy
matrícula *f.* fee
matrimonio *m.* marriage
mayo *m.* May
mayor older
mayoría *f.* majority
mayormente mainly
mayúscula *f.* capital letter
media *f.* average
mediante via
médico *m.* doctor
medida *f.* measure
medio middle
medios *m.pl.* means
medir (i) to measure
medrar to increase; improve
mejicano Mexican
Méjico *m.* Mexico
mejor better
mejorar to improve
melocotón *m.* peach
menor younger
menos less
mensual monthly
menta *f.* mint
mente *f.* mind
mentira *f.* lie
mentiroso deceitful
menudo small
mercado *m.* market
mercancía *f.* merchandise
merecer to deserve
merienda *f.* snack
merluza *f.* cod
mes *m.* month
mesa *f.* table
mezcla *f.* mixture
microordenador *m.* microcomputer
microprocesador *m.* microprocessor
miedo *m.* fear
miel *f.* honey
mientras meanwhile
mil thousand
mili *f.* military service
milla *f.* mile
mina *f.* mine
minero *m.* miner
ministro *m.* minister
minúscula *f.* lower-case letter
mirar to look
misa *f.* Mass
mismo same; very; -self
mitad *f.* half
mito *m.* myth
moda *f.* fashion
modalidad *f.* sort; type
módico reasonable
modificar to change
modo *m.* way
mojar to wet
molestar to annoy
molestia *f.* annoyance
momentáneamente momentarily

moneda *f.* coin
mono pretty
monstruo monster
montaña *f.* mountain
montañero *m.* mountaineer
monte *m.* mountain; woodland
morcilla *f.* black pudding
moreno dark
morir (ue) to die
morro *m.* snout; frront of car
mosca *f.* fly
mostrar (ue) to show
motor *m.* engine
mover (ue) to move
móvil mobile
movimiento *m.* movement
mucho much
mueble *m.* furniture
muelle *m.* quay
muerte *f.* death
mujer *f.* woman; wife
mundial of the world; worldwide
mundo *m.* world
musa *f.* muse
muy very

N
nada nothing
nadar to swim
nadie no one
naranja *f.* orange
nariz *f.* nose, **hasta las narices** 'up to the eye-balls'
nata *f.* cream
naturaleza *f.* nature
náutico nautical
navidades *f.pl.* Christmas
neblina *f.* mist
necesidad *f.* necessity
necesitar to need
negro black
nevar (ie) to snow
nevera *f.* fridge
ni neither
niebla *f.* fog
nieto *m.* grandchild
nieve *f.* snow
niñez *f.* childhood
ninguno none
niño *m.* boy
nítido clear
nivel *m.* level
noche *f.* night
nombre *n.* name
norma *f.* regulation
noroeste northwest
norte *m.* north
nota *f.* note
noticias *f.pl.* news
novia *f.* bride; girlfriend
noviembre *m.* November
novillada *f.* bullfight with young bulls
nube *f.* cloud

nuez *f.* nut
nuevo new

O
obligar to compel
obrero *m.* worker
obviamente obviously
ocio *m.* leisure
ocurrir to happen
oferta *f.* offer
oficinista *m.* office-worker
oficio *m.* job, profession
ofrecer to offer
ola *f.* wave
olfatear to sniff
olfateo *m.* sense of smell
opinar to think, to have an opinion
oriental eastern

P
padecer to suffer
padre *m.* father
padres *m.pl.* parents
pagar to pay
país *m.* country
paisaje *m.* countryside
paja *f.* straw
pájaro *m.* bird
pala *f.* shovel; spade
palabra *f.* word
palo *m.* stick
panocha *f.* corncob
pantalla *f.* screen
papel *m.* paper
paquete *m.* package
para for
parado unemployed
parar to stop
parecido similar
pared *f.* wall
parientes *m.pl.* relations
parlamento *m.* talk
paro *m.* unemployment
parrilla *f.* grill
participar to take part in
particularidad *f.* peculiarity
partícula *f.* particle
partida *f.* departure
partido *m.* match
partir to split; slice
párvulo *m.* child; infant
pasado *m.* past
pasar to pass
pasear to take a walk
paseo *m.* walk
paso *m.* step; passage
pastilla *f.* pill
pastora *f.* shepherdess
patata *f.* potato
patearse to stamp; trample
patria *f.* nation; country
patrocinar to sponsor
patrocinio *m.* sponsorship

pechuga *f.* breast
pedir (i) to ask, demand
pelar to peel
película *f.* film
peligro *m.* danger
pelo *m.* hair
pelota *f.* ball
peluquería *f.* hairdresser's
pena *f.* sorrow
pensar to think
pensión *f.* pension; boarding house
peor worse
pequeño small
perder (ie) to lose
perdiz partridge
perdido lost
perfeccionar to perfect; improve
periférico peripheral
periódico *m.* newspaper
periodista *m.* journalist
pero but
personaje *m.* character
pertenecer to belong
perturbación *f.* disturbance
pesado heavy; boring
pesar to weigh
pesca *f.* fishing
pescado *m.* fish
picado chopped up
picador *m.* face-worker
picadura *f.* sting
picante spicy
picar to sting
picores *m.pl.* itching; stinging
pico *m.* peak
piedra *f.* stone
piel *f.* skin
pierna *f.* leg
pimienta *f.* pepper
pimiento *m.* pepper (vegetable)
pinza *f.* tweezers
piscina *f.* swimming-pool
piso *m.* flat
pista *f.* track; trail
plancha *f.* iron; grill
plantado 'stood up'
plano flat
plantilla *f.* personnel; staff
playa *f.* beach
plaza *f.* square
plazo *m.* time; period
pleno full
pluma *f.* pen
poco little
poder (ue) to be able
pollo *m.* chicken
pomada *f.* cream
poner to put
poquitín little bit
por for; by; through
porque because
portal *m.* doorway
poseer to possess

posguerra *f.* post-war
postre *m.* dessert
practicar to practise
prado *m.* meadow
precio *m.* price
precioso pretty
precisar to need; require
preferir (ie) to prefer
pregón *m.* public announcement
preguntar to ask
premio *m.* prize
prensa *f.* press
preocupar to worry
prestar to lend
préstamo *m.* loan
prestigiado prestigious
presupuesto *m.* budget
primavera *f.* spring
primero first
primo *m.* cousin
principio *m.* beginning
prisa *f.* hurry, **tener prisa** to be in a hurry
privado private
probar (ue) to prove
procedente de coming from
proclamar to proclaim
procurar to try
profesor *m.* teacher
programación *f.* programming
promoción *f.* promotion; class; year
pronto soon
propiamente properly; exactly
propio own
proporcionar to give
propósito *m.* purpose, **a propósito** on purpose
proseguir (i) to continue
protagonizar to star
protegerse to protect oneself
proveedor *m.* provider
próximo next
proyectar to project
proyecto *m.* plan
prueba *f.* proof
pueblo *m.* town
puente *m.* bridge
puerta *f.* door
puerto *m.* port; pass
pues then
puesto *m.* market stall
pulpa *f.* pulp; flesh
pulsar to touch; tap
puñalada *f.* knife-wound

Q

quedar to stay
querer (ie) to wish
quesería *f.* cheese-shop
queso *m.* cheese
quien who

R

rábano *m.* radish, **no me importa un rábano** I couldn't care less
raja *f.* slice
ramo *m.* branch; section
rascar to scratch
rato *m.* moment
raza *f.* race
razón *f.* reason, **tengo razón** I am right
realidad *f.* reality
realizar to realize
realmente really
rebajas *f.pl.* reductions
rebelde *m.* rebel; rebellious
rebobinar to rewind
receta *f.* recipe
rechazar to reject
recibir to receive
recibo *m.* receipt
reciente recent
reclamación *f.* claim
reclamar to reclaim
recluta *m.* recruit
recoger to pick up; collect
recomendar to advise
reconocer to recognize
recordar (ue) to remember
recorrido *m.* tour
recorrer to tour
recubrir to recover
recuerdo *m.* souvenir
recurrir to have recourse to
recurso *m.* resort; means
red *f.* net; network
redactor *m.* writer
reembolsar to reimburse
reembolso *m.* reimbursement
referir (ie) to refer
refrán *m.* proverb
regimen *m.* diet; régime
reglazo *m.* blow with a ruler
reglamentación *f.* regulation
regresar to return
regreso *m.* return
regular all right
reina *f.* queen
rellenar to fill
remesa *f.* remittance
remojar to soak
remolacha *f.* beetroot
rendir (i) to produce; yield
renombrado well-known
reordenación *f.* reorganization
reparar to repair
repartir to distribute
repercutir to have repercussions
repetir(i) to repeat
reponer to replace
repostería *f.* confectionery; cake shop
reprimir to repress
repuestos *m.pl.* spare parts
requerir (ie) to need; request
requisitos *m.pl.* requirements

resaca *f*. undercurrent
rescate *m*. rescue
residir to reside; live
resultado result
respuesta *f*. reply
resultar to result
retener to retain
retirar to retire
retraso *m*. delay
retrato *m*. portrait
revelado revealed; exposed
revista *f*. magazine
revolver (ue) to move about; stir
rey *m*. king
rezar to pray
rico rich
riñón *m*. kidney
río *m*. river
ritmo *m*. rhythm
rito *m*. rite
robar to rob; steal
roca *f*. rock
rociar to sprinkle
rodar to wheel; drag
rogar (ue) to request
rojo red
romero *m*. rosemary
ron *m*. rum
ronda *f*. round
ropa *f*. clothes
rosario *m*. rosary
rozar to rub
ruido *m*. noise

S
sábado *m*. Saturday
saber to know
sable *m*. sabre; cutlass
sabor *m*. flavour
saborear to taste
sabroso tasty; delicious
sacar to take out
sala *f*. room
saldo *m*. payment; balance
salir to go out
salmonete *m*. red mullet
salón *m*. drawing room
salsa *f*. sauce
salud *f*. health
saludar to greet
salvamento *m*. rescue
sangre *f*. blood
sano healthy, sano y salvo safe and
   sound
Santina Our Lady
santo *m*. saint
sartén *f*. frying-pan
sazonar to season
secar to dry
sed *f*. thirst
sede *f*. seat; headquarters
seguido continued, en
   seguida immediately

seguidamente continuously
seguir (i) to follow
según according to
segundo second
seguramente surely
seguridad *f*. safety
seguro safe
seleccionar to choose
selecto choice; fine
semáforo *m*. traffic lights
semana *f*. week
semanal *m*. weekly
señalización *f*. sign-posting
sencillo simple
senda *f*. way; path
sentarse (ie) to sit down
septiembre September
sepultar to bury
ser to be
serie *f*. series
servir (i) to serve
seta *f*. mushroom
sexo *m*. sex
siderurgia *f*. iron and steel industry
siderúrgico of iron and steel
sidra *f*. cider
siempre always
sierra *f*. saw; mountain range
siglo *m*. century
significar to mean
significado *m*. meaning
siguiente following
silla *f*. seat
sillita *f*. push-chair
sin without
sindical union
sino but; except
sintonía *f*. tuning; station
sintonizar to tune
sitio *m*. place
situado situated
sobre on; above
sofocante stifling
soga *f*. rope
sol *m*. sun
solamente only
soler (ue) to be accustomed
solomillo *m*. sirloin
soltar (ue) to unleash
somier *m*. bedstead
sonar to sound
sonido *m*. sound
sopa *f*. soup
sorprendido surprised
sorpresa *f*. surprise
subida *f*. ascent
subir to climb; go up
subvencionar to subsidize
suceder to happen
suceso *m*. happening
sucursal *m*. branch
sueldo *m*. wage; salary
suerte *f*. fortune

sumamente extremely
superar to surpass
suponer to suppose
sur south

T
tabaco *m.* tobacco; cigarettes
taberna *f.* pub; bar
tachar to cross out
táctica *f.* tactics
tacto *m.* touch
tal such
talco *m.* talcum powder
taller *m.* workshop
talonario *m.* cheque book
tamaño *m.* size
también also
tampoco neither
tan so
tanteo *m.* score
tanto so much
tapizado *m.* carpeted
tarde *f.* afternoon
tardar to be late; delay
tarea *f.* task; homework
tarjeta *f.* card
taxista *m.* taxi-driver
taza *f.* cup
tazón *m.* large cup
té *m.* tea
teatro *m.* theatre
tecla *f.* key
teclado *m.* key-board
técnico *m.* technician
tela *f.* material
telediario *m.* television news
teleobjetivo telephoto lens
televisor *m.* television set
tema *m.* topic
temblar to tremble
temor *m.* fear
temporada *f.* period of time
temporal *m.* storm
temprano early
tener (ie) to have
tentación *f.* temptation
teórico theoretical
tercero third
tergiversar to distort
terminar to finish
ternera *f.* calf
terreno *m.* land
tesorero *m.* treasurer
tiempo *m.* time
tienda *f.* shop
tierno tender
tinta *f.* ink
tío *m.* uncle; guy
tipo *m.* type
tirar to pull
tiro *m.* throw
tocar to touch
tocino *m.* bacon

todavía still
todo all
tomar to take
tónica *f.* tonic; key-note
tontería *f.* silliness
toque *m.* touch
torear to bullfight
torero *m.* bullfighter
tormenta *f.* storm
toro *m.* bull
tortilla *f.* omelette
tostado toasted; brown
tóxico *m.* poison
trabajar to work
trabajo *m.* work
traducir to translate
trampa *f.* trick
tramposo *m.* trickster
tranquilo calm; quiet
tras behind; after
trasero rear; hind
traslado *m.* removal; change
tratamiento *m.* treatment
tratar to treat
travesía *f.* crossing
trayectoria *f.* trajectory
tren *m.* train
trigo *m.* wheat
trinchero *m.* sideboard
tristeza *f.* sadness
troncal main line
trucha *f.* trout
turista *m.* tourist

U
último last
único only; unique
unidad *f.* unit
unir to join
usar to use
uso *m.* use
usted you (formal)

V
vacaciones *f.pl.* holidays
vago lazy
valer to be worth
valientemente bravely
valor *m.* bravery
valla *f.* hurdle
vapor *m.* steam
vaquilla *f.* young cow
variedad *f.* variety
vasco Basque
vez *f.* time
vecino *m.* neighbour
vejez *f.* old age
vela *f.* wakefulness; candle
velada *f.* evening party; gathering
velero *m.* sailing ship
velocidad *f.* speed
vencer to beat; vanquish
vendedor *m.* seller

vender to sell
venir (i) to come
venta *f.* sale
ventaja *f.* advantage
ventana *f.* window
ver to see
veraniego of summer
verano *m.* summer
verbena *f.* fair; open-air dance
verdad *f.* truth
verdadero true; real
verde green
verduras *f.pl.* green vegetables
vestido dressed
vestir (i) to dress
vez *f.* occasion; time
vía *f.* road; track
viabilidad *f.* feasibility
viajar to travel
viaje *m.* journey
vicio *m.* vice
vida *f.* life
vídeoaficionado *m.* video fan

viejo old man
vinagre *m.* vinegar
vino *m.* wine
visitante *m.* visitor
visitar to visit
vistoso showy; lively
vitrina *f.* glass case
vivo alive; living
voluntad *f.* will
volver (ue) to return
voz *f.* voice
vuelta *f.* return

X
xerocopia *f.* photocopy

Y
ya already
yo I

Z
zapato *m.* shoe

A

above arriba
accessories aditamentos, complementos
accomplish, to cumplir
according to según
accustomed habituado
acquire, to adquirir
add, to añadir
advance antelación *f.*
advance, in con antelación
advantage ventaja *f.*
advice consejo *m.*
advise, to aconsejar
aerial antena *f.*
afternoon tarde *f.*
against contra
age edad *f.*
agent agente *m.* encargado
agree, to consentir, convenir
agreeable agradable, ameno
air aire *m.* aéreo
almost casi
also también
annoy, to molestar
annoyance molestia *f.*
anti-allergic antialérgico
anti-pollutant anticontaminante
appear, to aparecer
arrangement ordén *m.*
arrival llegada *f.*

B

baby bebé *m.*
back espalda *f.*
bacon tocino *m.*
bad malo
bad luck, to have tener mala suerte
balance-sheet balance *m.*
bald calvo
ball pelota *f.*, bola *f.*
bank balance saldo *m.*
bank-book libreta *f.*
bar barra *f.*
bark, to ladrar
barley cebada *f.*
based on basado en
basket cesta *f.*
Basque vasco
bath baño *m.*
bathe, to bañarse
battle batalla *f.*
be, to estar, ser
be able, to poder
be important, to importar
beach playa *f.*
beard barba *f.*
beat, to vencer
beautiful bello
beauty belleza *f.*
becalmed encalmado
because porque

become brown, golden, to dorarse
bed cama *f.*
beetroot remolacha *f.*
before antes
begin, to comenzar, empezar, iniciar
beginning principio *m.*, inicio *m.*
behaviour conducta *f.*
behind tras, detrás de
believe, to creer
belong, to pertenecer
below abajo
besides además
better mejor
between entre
big grande
bill factura *f.*
binding encuadernación *f.*
bird pájaro *m.*
biro bolígrafo *f.*
bomb bomba *f.*
birthday cumpleaños *m.pl.*
birthday, to have a cumplir años
biscuit galleta *f.*
black negro
black pudding morcilla *f.*
blood sangre *f.*
boarder pensionista *m.*
body cuerpo *m.*
boil, to hervir
book libro *m.*
book-keeping contabilidad *f.*
boring aburrido, pesado
bottle botella *f.*
bow, to inclinarse
bowling alley bolera *f.*
box caja *f.*
boxer boxeador *m.*
boxing boxeo *m.*
boy niño *m.*
brake, to frenar
brake freno *m.*
branch ramo *m.* (of bank, shop etc) sucursal *m.*
Brazilian brasileño *m.*
bravely valientemente
bravery valor *m.*
breast pechuga *f.*
bridge puente *m.*
bring, to aportar
bring up to date, to actualizar
brother hermano *m.*
bull toro *m.*

C

cake-shop repostería *f.*
calf ternera *f.*
call llamada *f.*
call, to llamar
calm tranquilo
camp campamento *m.*
campsite camping *m.* acampada *f.*
capable of capaz de

cape cabo *m.*
capital letter mayúscula *f.*
car coche *m.*
card tarjeta *f.*, cartoncito *m.*
career carrera *f.*
carnival time carnavales *m.pl.*
carpet alfombra *f.*
carpeting tapizado *m.*
carry, to llevar
carry out, to efectuar
cart carreta *f.*, carro *m.*
cast elenco *m.*
catch, to coger
cave cueva *f.*
celebrate, to celebrar, festejar
century siglo *m.*
chain cadena *f.*
chain of mountains sierra *f.*
championship campeonato *m.*
change, to cambiar
change cambio *m.*
channel canal *m.*
character personaje *m.* carácter *m.*
charge, to cobrar
charm encanto *m.*
charm, to encantar
cheap barato
cheese queso *m.*
cheese shop quesería *f.*
chemist's shop farmacia *f.*
cheque-book talonario *m.*
chicken pollo *m.*
chickpea garbanzo *m.*
chief jefe
child niño *m.*, párvulo *m.*
childhood niñez *f.*
childish infantil
chilly frío, álgido
choose, to elegir, escoger, seleccionar
chopped up (meat) picado
Christmas navidades *f.pl.*
cider sidra *f.*
cigarette cigarillo *m.*
cinema cine *m.*
city ciudad *f.*
claim reclamación *f.*
clean, to limpiar
clean limpio
cleanliness limpieza *f.*
clear claro, nítido
clear, it is c. that consta que
clear, to be c. from constar
clever inteligente, listo
climate clima *m.*
climb, to escalar, subir
climber escalador
close, to cerrar
close by cerquita
cloth tela *f.*
clothes ropa *f.*
cloud nube *f.*
coach carroza *f.*
coal carbón *m.*

coast costa *f.*
coat abrigo *m.*
cod merluza *f.*
coin moneda *f.*
cold frío, **it's cold** hace frío
college (private) academia *f.*
college, state school instituto *m.*
come, to venir
comfortable cómodo, confortable
coming from procedente de
commit suicide, to suicidarse
companion compañero *m.*
company compañía *f.* (firm) empresa *f.*
comparison comparación *f.*
compel, to obligar
compensation indemnización *f.*
competition concurso *m.* certamen *m.*
composed of compuesto de
computer computador *m.* ordenador *m.*
conclude, to concluir
condemned condenado
confectionery repostería *f.*
conference congreso *m.*
congress congreso *m.*
connection entronque *m.*
conquered conquistado
considerable apreciable
contain, to contener
contents contenido *m.*
continue, to continuar, proseguir
continuously seguidamente
contrary, on the c. al contrario
convenient; good idea conveniente
convertor convertidor *m.*
cook cocinero *m.*
cook, to cocinar
copier copiador *m.*
copy copia *f.* ejemplar *m.*
corncob panocha *f.*
correct acertado, correcto
correct, to corregir
cost, to costar
cost costo *m.*
costly costoso
count, to contar
country país *m.*
country patria *f.*
countryside paisaje *m.* campo *m.*
cousin primo *m.*
crave, to apetecer
cream crema *f.* nata *f.*
cream pomada *f.*
create, to crear
crime crimen *m.*
cross, to cruzar
cross cruz *f.*
cross out, to tachar
crossing travesía *f.*
crown, to coronar
crown corona *f.*
cruiser crucero *m.*
crush, to machacar
cup taza *f.*

D

dance baile *m.*
danger peligro *m.*
dark moreno
date cita *f.* (calendar) fecha *f.*
daughter hija *f.*
death muerte *f.*
deceitful mentiroso
delay retraso *m.*
delay, to tardar
delicatessen charcutería *f.*
demand, to exigir
departure partida *f.*
deserve, to merecer
desire, to querer, tener ganas de
desire gana *f.*
dessert postre *m.*
develop, to (film) revelar
develop, to desarrollar
die, to morir
diet régimen *m.*
dine, to cenar
dining room comedor *m.*
dinner cena *f.*
distant lejos
distort, to tergiversar
distress angustia *f.*
distressing angustioso
distribute, to repartir
do, to hacer
doctor médico *m.*
door puerta *f.*
doorway portal *m.*
doubt duda *f.*
down bajo
drag, to rodar
draw, to (a match) empatar
draw near, to acercar(se)
drawing room salón *m.*
dress, to vestir

E

each cada
early temprano
eastern oriental
easy fácil
eat, to comer
edge borde *m.*
end fin *m.* cabo *m.*
endure, to comportar
engine motor *m.*
England Inglaterra *f.*
enliven, to animar
enough bastante
enough, to be bastar
entrust, to confiar
entry entrada *f.*
equal igual
escape evasión *f.*
even incluso
event acontecimiento *m.*
exactly efectivamente, exactamente
example ejemplo *m.*

excavator excavadora *f.*
except excepto, salvo
exciting emocionante
expenditure gasto *m.*
expensive caro
experiment experimento *m.*,
   experiencia

F

face-worker picador *m.*
factory fábrica *f.*
failure fracaso *m.*
fair feria *f.*
fairy hada *f.*
faith fe *f.*
falsify, to falsear
fan aficionado
farmer agricultor *m.*
fashion moda *f.*
fat gordo
father padre *m.*
fatty (food) grasiento
fear miedo *m.* temor *m.*
feasibility viabilidad *f.*
February febrero
fed-up harto
fee matrícula *f.*
fertilizer abono *m.*
fever fiebre *f.*
field campo *m.*
fill, to rellenar
filled out rellenito
film película *f.*
find, to hallar
fine selecto
finish, to acabar, terminar
fire fuego *m.*
fireworks fuegos artificiales *m.pl.*
first primero
first night estreno *m.*
fish pescado *m.*
fish or meat stew caldereta *f.*
fishing pesca *f.*
fix, to fijar
flat plano *m.* (apartment) piso *m.*
flavour sabor *m.*
fluidity fluidez *f.*
fly mosca *f.*
fog niebla *f.*
follow, to seguir
following siguiente
fondness afición *f.*
food comida *f.* alimentos *m.pl.*
for por, para
foretaste anticipación *f.*
foreign currency divisas *f.pl.*
forget, to olvidar
fortune suerte *f.*
free gratis, libre
freedom libertad *f.*
freeze, to congelar
Frenchman francés *m.*
front frente *m.*

front (of car) morro *m.*
frozen helado

G
garlic ajo *m.*
garlic sauce ajillo *m.*
gear marcha *f.*
German alemán
Germany Alemania *f.*
gesture gesto *m.*
get married, to casarse
get one's bearings, to orientar (se)
get up, to levantar (se)
giant gigante *m.*
gift don *m.*
girl chica *f.*, niña *f.*
girlfriend novia *f.*
give, to dar, proporcionar
glass copa *f.*
glasses (spectacles) gafas *f.pl.*
go, to ir(se)
go down, to bajar
go out, to salir
goal gol *m.*
gospel evangelio *m.*
government gobierno *m.*
grammar gramática *f.*
grandson nieto *m.*
graph gráfico *m.*
grass hierba *f.*
Greek griego
green verde
greens verduras *f.pl.*
greet, to saludar
grill parrilla *f.* parrillada *f.*
grow, to incrementar
growing creciente
guest invitado *m.* comensal *m.*
guide (person) guía *m.*
guidebook guía *f.*
guilt culpa *f.*

H
hair pelo *m.*
hairdresser's peluquería *f.*
half mitad *f.*
ham jamón *m.*
hand mano *f.*
happen, to ocurrir, suceder
happening suceso *m.*
happy alegre, feliz
happy, to be alegrarse
hardly apenas
harvest cosecha *f.*
have, to tener
head cabeza *f.*
head (top of) coronilla *f.*
headquarters sede *f.*
health salud *f.*
healthy sano
hear, to oír
heat calor *m.*
heavens! ¡caramba!

height altura *f.*
hello ¡hola!
here aquí
hermitage ermita *f.*
high alto (of voice) agudo
hill colina *f.*
hire, to alquilar
hit, to golpear
holidays vacaciones *f.pl.*
home hogar *m.*
homemade casero
homage homenaje *m.*
honey miel *f.*
honourable honrado
hook, to enganchar
hors d'oeuvres entremeses *m.pl.*
hot caliente
house casa *f.*
housewife ama de casa *f.*
how much cuánto

I
I yo
ice hielo *m.*
if si
ill enfermo
immediately en seguida
impose, to imponer
improve, to mejorar, perfeccionar
incautious incauto
include, to incluir
incredible increíble
independent, to
  become independizarse
inform, to enterar, informar
inhabitant habitante *m.*
ink tinta *f.*
install, to instalar
interchange intercambio *m.*
interest interés *m.*
interpreter intérprete *m.*
Ireland Irlanda *f.*
iron plancha *f.*

J
January enero
Japanese japonés
job oficio *m.*
jogging footing *m.*
join, to unir
journalist periodista *m.*

K
keep, to guardar
keep quiet, to callarse
key tecla *f.* **(of door)** llave *f.*
key-board teclado *m.*
kidney riñón *m.*
kill, to matar
killing matanza *f.*
king rey *m.*
kiss, to besar
kitchen cocina *f.*

knife-wound puñalada *f.*
know, to (thing) saber, **(person)** conocer

L
lack, to faltar
lack falta *f.*
lad chaval *m.*
lagoon laguna *f.*
lake lago *m.*
land terreno *m.*
language idioma *m.* lengua *f.*
last último
last night anoche
Latin latino
Latin America Latinoamérica *f.*
law ley *f.*
lazy vago, perezoso
leader líder *m.* jefe *m.*
leaf hoja *f.*
leaf through, to hojear
lecture conferencia *f.*
leg pierna *f.*
legend leyenda *f.*
leisure ocio *m.*
lend, to prestar
length of service antigüedad *f.*
lens lente *m./f.*
less menos
letter carta *f.*
level nivel *m.*
library biblioteca *f.*
lie mentira *f.*
life vida *f.*
light, to encender
lightly ligeramente
like, to gustar, **I like** me gusta
limestone caliza *f.*
line línea *f.*
lion león *m.*
listen, to escuchar
little poco
live, to vivir, residir
lively animado
load carga *m.*
loan préstamo *m.*
lobster langosta *f.*
lodge, to alojarse
lodging alojamiento *m.*
long largo
look, to mirar
look after, to cuidar
look out! careful! ¡cuidado!
lose, to perder
loudspeaker altavoz *m.*
love, to amar, querer
love amor *m.*

M
mad loco
magazine revista *f.*
mainly mayormente
maintain, to mantener

maize maíz *m.*
maize flour maizena *f.*
majority mayoría *f.*
make, to hacer
make easy, to facilitar
Mallorcan mallorquino
man hombre *m.*
management gestión *f.*
manager gerente *m.*
market mercado *m.*
market stall puesto *m.*
marriage matrimonio *m.*
marvel maravilla *f.*
marvellous estupendo, fenomenal, maravilloso
Mass misa *f.*
master maestro *m.*
mastiff mastín *m.*
match cerilla *f.* (football, tennis etc) partido *m.*
maternal materno
May mayo *m.*
mayonnaise mayonesa *f.*
meadow prado *m.*
meal comida *f.*
mean, to significar
meaning significado *m.*
means medios *m.pl.*, recursos *m.pl.*
meanwhile mientras
measure medida *f.*
middle medio
measure, to medir
mechanic mecánico *m.*
meet, to encontrar
meeting congreso *m.*, reunión *f.*
mellow (of wine) añejo
merchandise mercancía *f.*
method método *m.*
Mexican mejicano
Mexico Méjico *m.*
microcomputer microordenador *m.*
microprocessor microprocesador *m.*
mile milla *f.*
military service servicio militar *m.*, mili *f.*
milk leche *f.*
mind mente *f.*
miner minero *m.*
mint menta *f.*
mist neblina *f.*
mistake error *m.*
mistaken equivocado
mixture mezcla *f.*
mobile móvil
mock, to burlarse
moment instante *m.* momento *m.* rato *m.*
momentarily momentáneamente
monster monstruo *m.*
month mes *m.*
monthly mensual
more más
morning mañana *f.* (early) madrugada *f.*
mother madre *f.*

mountain montaña *f.*
mountaineer montañero *m.*
moustache bigote *m.*
movement movimiento *m.*
mushroom seta *f.*

N
name nombre *n.*
narrow, tight estrecho
nation patria *f.*
nature naturaleza *f.*
nautical naútico
near cerca
necessary imprescindible, necesario
need, to necesitar, requerir
needle aguja *f.*
neighbour vecino *m.*
net red *f.*
network red *f.*
new nuevo
news noticias *f.pl.* informativos *m.pl.*
newspaper periódico *m.*
nice bonito
night noche *f.*
noise ruido *m.* estruendo *m.*
north norte *m.*
northwest noroeste
nose nariz *f.*
not recommended contraindicado
note nota *f.*
nothing nada

O
obtain, to conseguir
obviously obviamente
occasion vez *f.*
offer oferta *f.*
offer, to ofrecer
office-worker oficinista *m.*
oil aceite *m.*
old antiguo
old age vejez *f.*
old man viejo *m.* anciano *m.*
older mayor
omelette tortilla *f.*
onion cebolla *f.*
only *adv.* sólo, solamente
only *adj.* solo, único
open, to abrir
opening apertura *f.*
orange naranja *f.*
orchestra orquesta *f.*
order ordén *f.*

P
package paquete *m.*
pain dolor *m.* dolencia *f.*
paper papel *m.*
pardon perdón
parents padres *m.pl.*
partridge perdiz *f.*
pass, to pasar
pass (mountain) puerto *m.*

pass an exam, to aprobar, pasar un examen
past pasado *m.*
path camino *m.*
pay, to abonar, pagar
peach melocotón *m.*
peak cima *f.* cumbre *m.* pico *m.*
peasant campesino *m.*
peculiarity particularidad *f.*
peel, to pelar
pelota court frontón *m.*
pen pluma *f.* (animal) corral *m.*
people gente *f.*
pepper pimienta *f.* (vegetable) pimiento *m.*
performance actuation
period of time temporada *f.*
peripheral periférico
personnel plantilla *f.*
phrase frase *f.*, giro *m.*
pick up, to recoger
pig cerdo *m.*
pill pastilla *f.*
place, to poner, colocar
place local *m.* sitio *m.*
plan proyecto *m.*
play, to jugar
player jugador *m.*
pleasant ameno, agradable
please, to complacer
poet poeta *m.*
poison tóxico *m.*
policeman guardia *m.*
polite educado
politician político *m.*
pollutant contaminante
pollution contaminación *f.* polución *f.*
port puerto *m.*
portrait retrato *m.*
possess, to poseer
Post Office Correos
post-war posguerra *f.*
potato patata *f.*
pound (money) libra *f.*
pram cochecito *m.*
pray, to rezar
preceding anterior
prepared aderezado
press prensa *f.*
pressure presión *f.*
prestigious prestigiado
pretty lindo, mono, bonito
prevent, to impedir
price precio *m.*
private privado
prize premio *m.*
programming programación *f.*
project, to proyectar
prolong, to prolongarse
proof prueba *f.*
protect oneself, to protegerse
protein proteína *f.*
prove, to probar

provider proveedor *m*.
pub taberna *f*.

Q
quality calidad *f*.
quantity cantidad *f*.
quarter cuarto *m*.
quay muelle *m*.
queen reina *f*.
queue cola *f*.

R
race carrera *f*. raza *f*.
radio station emisora *f*.
railway ferrocarril *m*.
range gama *f*.
ravine canada *f*.
raw crudo
rawness crudeza *f*.
reach, to alcanzar
reach, within r. of al alcance de
react, to reaccionar
read, to leer
reader lector *m*.
reading lectura *f*.
ready listo, preparado
reality realidad *f*.
realize, to darse cuenta de
really efectivamente, realmente,
   verdaderamente
rear trasero
reason razón *f*.
reasonable (price) módico
rebel rebelde *m*.
rebellious rebelde
receipt recibo *m*.
recipe receta *f*.
reclaim, to reclamar
recognize, to reconocer
record, to grabar
recording grabación *f*.
recourse, to have r. to recurrir
recover, to recubrir
recruit recluta *m*.
red rojo, (wine) tinto
red mullet salmonete *m*.
reimburse, to reembolsar
reductions rebajas *f.pl*.
refrigerator nevera *f*., frigorífico *m*.
regulation norma *f*., reglamentación *f*.
reimbursement reembolso *m*.
reject, to rechazar
relations parientes *m.pl*.
remember, to acordarse de, recordar
remittance remesa *f*.
removal traslado *m*.
rent, to alquilar
rental alquiler *m*.
reorganization reordinación *f*.
repair reparación *f*.
repercussions, to have repercutir
replace, to reponer
reply, to contestar

reply respuesta *f*.
report informe *m*.
repress, to reprimir
reputation fama *f*.
request, to rogar
require, to precisar, requerir
requirements requisitos *m.pl*
rescue rescate *m*., salvamento *m*.
resort recurso *m*.
responsibility competencia *f*.,
   responsabilidad *f*.
rest resto *m*. descanso *m*.
result in, to resultar
retain, to retener
return regreso *m*.
return, to volver, regresar
rewind, to rebobinar
rhythm ritmo *m*.
rice arroz *m*.
rice feast arrozada *f*.
rich rico
right, on the a la derecha
right, to be tener razón
rite rito *m*.
river río *m*.
road carretera *f*.
roadworks obras *f.pl*.
rock roca *f*.
rocket cohete *m*.
room cuarto *m*., sala *f*., habitación *f*.
rope soga *f*., cuerda *f*.
rosary rosario *m*.
rosemary romero *m*.

S
sadness tristeza *f*.
safe seguro, **s. and sound** sano y salvo
safety seguridad *f*.
sailing ship velero *m*.
saint santo *m*.
salad ensalada *f*.
sale venta *f*.
same igual, mismo
sand arena *f*.
sandwich bocadillo *m*.
satisfied satisfecho
Saturday sábado *m*.
sauce salsa *f*.
savage feroz
savings ahorros *m.pl*.
scarce escaso
scene escena *f*.
sceptical escéptico
scholarship beca *f*.
scholarship-holder becario
school colegio *m*., escuela *f*., instituto
   m.
science ciencia *f*.
score tanteo *m*.
scratch, to rascar
screen pantalla *f*.
sea mar *m./f*.
sea-bream besugo *m*.

search, to buscar
search busca *f.*, búsqueda *f.*
search, in s. of en busca de
season, to sazonar
seasoned aderezado
seat silla *f.*
second segundo
see, to ver
sell, to vender
seller vendedor *m.*
send, to enviar, mandar
sense of smell olfateo *m.*
September septiembre, setiembre
series serie *f.*
serious grave
set in (novels) ambientado en
sew, to coser
shape forma *f.*
sharp agudo
shell-fish marisco *m.*
shine brillo *m.*
ship barco *m.*
shirt camisa *f.*
shop comercio *m.*, tienda *f.*
shop-window escaparate *m.*
shopping compra, **to go s.** hacer la
compra
short corto
show espectáculo *m.*
show, to mostrar
show, to (for the first time) estrenar
showy vistoso
sickness enfermedad *f.*
side lado *m.*
sideboard trinchero *m.*
sign-posting señalización *f.*
signature firma *f.*
sign, to firmar
silliness tontería *f.*
similar parecido
simple sencillo
sing, to cantar
sirloin solomillo *m.*
sister hermana *f.*
sit down, to sentarse
size tamaño *m.*
ski esquí *m.*
skin piel *f.*
sky cielo *m.*
sleep, to dormir
slice, to partir
slice raja *f.*
slow lento
small pequeño, menudo
smash, to estrellarse
smell olor *m.*
smoked ahumado
snack merienda *f.*
snap-shot instantánea *f.* foto *f.*
sniff, to olfatear
snow, to nevar
snow nieve *f.*
so much tanto

soak, to remojar
society sociedad *f.*
sold out agotado
something algo
son hijo *m.*
song canción *f.*, canto *m.*
sorrow pena *f.*
sort especie *f.*
soul ánimo *m.*
sound, to sonar
sound sonido *m.*
soup sopa *f.*
source fuente *f.*
souvenir recuerdo *m.*
space espacio *m.*
spade pala *f.*
Spain España
Spanish español *m.*
Spanish American hispanoamericano
Spanish railway network RENFE
spare part repuesto *m.*
speak, to hablar
speciality especialidad *f.*
specialize, to especializar
specifically concretamente
spectacular impresionante,
espectacular
spectator espectador *m.*
speed velocidad *f.*
speed up, to agilizar
spicy picante
spicy sausage chorizo *m.*
splendid espléndido
sponsor, to patrocinar
sponsorship patrocinio *m.*
spot grano *m.*
spread, to (gossip, news) divulgar
spring primavera *f.*
sprinkle, to espolvorear, rociar
square plaza
squid calamares *m.pl.*
stadium estadio *m.*
stage etapa *f.*
standard estándar
star, to protagonizar
state estado *m.*
state estatal
station estación *f.*
station (radio) sintonía *f.*
statistic cifra *f.*
stay, to quedar
steam vapor *m.*
steep abrupto
step grado *m.*, paso *m.*
stereo estéreo *m.*
sterling esterlina *f.*
stew cocido *m.* guiso *m.*
stick palo *m.*
stifling sofocante
still todavía
sting aguijón *m.*, picadura *f.*
sting, to picar
stipulated estipulado

stocks existencias *f.pl.*
stomach estómago *m.*
stone piedra *f.*
'stood up' plantado
stop, to parar
store almacén *m.*
storm temporal *m.*, tormenta *f.*
straighten up, to erguirse
strange extraño
straw paja *f.*
street calle *f.*
strength fuerza *f.*
strong fuerte
struggle esfuerzo *m.*
struggle, to luchar
student estudiante *m.*
study, to estudiar
study estudio *m.*
subsidize, to subvencionar
subsidy subvención *f.*
success éxito *m.*
such tal
suffer, to padecer
summer verano *m.*
sun sol *m.*
suppose, to suponer
surely seguramente
surpass, to superar

T
table mesa *f.*
tactics táctica *f.*
take, to tomar, coger
take, to t. a walk pasear(se)
take charge of, to encargarse
take notes, to anotar
take out, to sacar
take part in, to participar
take turns, to alternar
talcum powder talco *m.*
talk charla *f.*, parlamento *m.*
talk, to hablar, conversar
tape cinta *f.*
task tarea *f.*
taste, to saborear
tasty sabroso
taxi-driver taxista *m.*
tea té *m.*
teacher profesor *m.*
teaching enseñanza *f.*
team equipo *m.*
technician técnico *m.*
technique técnica *f.*
telephoto lens teleobjetivo *m.*
television news telediario *m.*
television set televisor *m.*
tender tierno
thank, to agradecer
thanks gracias *f.pl.*
theoretical teórico
there is, there are hay
thick espeso

thing cosa *f.*
think, to pensar, creer, opinar, idear
thirst sed *f.*
thorn espino *m.*
thousand mil
throat garganta *f.*
throw, to echar, lanzar
throw tiro *m.*
Thursday jueves
thus así
ticket billete *m.*
tie, to (with a rope) ensogar
till caja *f.*
time tiempo *m.*, vez *f.*
timetable horario *m.*
tire, to cansar
tired out agotado
title título *m.*
together unido, junto
token ficha *f.*
tongue lengua *f.*
top cima *f.*
topic tema *m.*
touch, to tocar
touch toque *m.*
tour recorrido *m.*
tour, to recorrer
tourist turista *m.*
towards hacia
town pueblo *m.*
town council consistoriales *m.pl.*
town-cryer pregón *m.*
track pista *f.*, vía *f.*
trade comercio *m.*
traffic lights semáforo *m.*
train tren *m.*
training formación *f.*
trample, to patearse
translate, to traducir
travel, to viajar
traveller viajero *m.*
treasurer tesorero *m.*
treat, to tratar
treatment tratamiento *m.*
tremble, to temblar
trick trampa *f.*, carambola *f.*
trickster tramposo *m.*
trolley carretilla *f.*, carrito *m.*
trout trucha *f.*
true verdadero
trustworthiness fiabilidad *f.*
truth verdad *f.*
try, to procurar

U
ugly feo
unbearable inaguantable
uncle tío *m.*
undercurrent resaca *f.*
unemployed parado *m.*
unemployment paro *m.*
unforgettable inolvidable

union sindicato *m.*
unit unidad *f.*

V

variety variedad *f.*
vary, to variar
vegetables legumbres *m.pl.*, vegetales *m.pl.*
via mediante
vice vicio *m.*
video fan vídeoaficionado *m.*
vinegar vinagre *m.*
visitor visitante *m.*

W

wage sueldo *m.*
wait, to esperar
waiter camarero *m.*
walk, to andar, caminar
walk paseo *m.*
walking ambulante
wall pared *f.*
want, to tener ganas de, querer
war guerra *f.*
warehouse almacén *m.*
warm, to calentar
wash, to lavar (se)
washing machine lavadora *f.*
water agua *f.*
wave ola *f.*
way modo *m.*
way camino *m.* senda *f.*
wedding boda *f.*
week semana *f.*
weekly semanal *m.*
weigh, to pesar
weight, to put on engordar
well-known renombrado, conocido, consabido
well-mannered educado
wet, to mojar
wheat trigo *m.*

wheel, to rodar
while mientras
whip up, to batir
white blanco
whole entero
why? ¿por qué?
widened ampliado
wide ancho
wild bravo
will voluntad *f.*
win, to ganar
window ventana *f.*
wine vino *m.*
wine-cellar bodega *f.*
wing aleta *f.*
winter invierno *m.*
wish, to querer, desear
within dentro
without sin
woman, wife mujer *f.*
wood madera *f.*
word palabra *f.*
work empleo *m.*, labor *f.*, trabajo *m.*
work, to trabajar
worker obrero *m.* trabajador *m.*
workshop taller *m.*
world mundo *m.*
worried inquieto
worry, to inquietar(se), preocupar(se)
worse peor
worth, to be valer
wrinkled arrugado
write, to escribir

Y

year año *m.*
yellow amarillo
young joven

Z

zero cero *m.*

Index

Breakthrough Language Packs

Complete self-study courses

Each Breakthrough Language pack is designed as a complete self-study course using audio cassettes and a course book. Each pack contains:

* Three 60 minute audio cassettes
* The course book

Breakthrough Language Packs available

Breakthrough French	ISBN 0-333-48191-7
Breakthrough German	ISBN 0-333-48187-9
Breakthrough Italian	ISBN 0-333-48179-8
Breakthrough Spanish	ISBN 0-333-48183-6
Breakthrough Greek	ISBN 0-333-48714-1
Breakthrough Further French	ISBN 0-333-48193-3
Breakthrough Further German	ISBN 0-333-48189-5
Breakthrough Further Spanish	ISBN 0-333-48185-2

Companion Language Grammars

Companion French Grammar
Chris Beswick,
Head of Modern Languages,
Shena Simon Sixth Form College, Manchester
0-333-48079-1   144 pages

Companion German Grammar
Isabel Willshaw, formerly lecturer in German,
Ealing College of Higher Education
0-333-48180-1   176 pages

Companion Spanish Grammar
Sandra Truscott,
Adult education tutor in Spanish
0-333-48181-X   128 pages

These basic pocket grammars, designed for easy reference by travellers and
students on non-examination courses, cover the most important rules for
speaking and understanding everyday French, German and Spanish.

Contents include:
* Clear explanations of grammatical points with examples of the use of each
  item in common situations
* 'Try it yourself' and 'learn by heart' sections with a range of activities to
  test the most important points
* A grammar glossary to familiarize the reader with terms such as pronouns,
  direct objects, auxiliary verbs etc
* Verb tables
* An index referring the user to an explanation of the particular grammatical
  point.

All these books are available at your local bookshop or newsagent, or
can be ordered direct from the publisher. Indicate the number of copies
required and fill in the form below.

Name _____
(Block letters please)

Address _____

_____

Macmillan Education Ltd, Houndmills, Basingstoke, Hants RG21 2XS